T0246551

Those of us in the workplace need frequent reminders to keep God first. Like manna that nourished God's people in the wilderness, Os Hillman's new book will feed your heart, mind, and spirit each day with timeless truth and rich perspective.

—**John D. Beckett,** author, *Mastering Monday:*
*A Guide to Integrating Faith and Work*;
CEO, Beckett Corporation

For many years now, *TGIF* has been a daily inspirational and transformational tool that God has used in my life particularly with the scriptural applications in a workplace context. We have also used *TGIF* to daily encourage the members of the Coca-Cola Christian Fellowship to apply their faith in the workplace!

—**Steve Hyland,** former director of retail merchandising,
Coca-Cola North America

Os Hillman presents a present, true word for God's ministers in the marketplace. He reveals how the kingdom of God can be implemented on earth as it is in heaven. This is a word of truth in due season for what God is seeking to accomplish on planet earth.

—**Dr. Bill Hamon,** bishop, Christian International Ministries Network;
author, *Apostles, Prophets and the Coming Move of God*

As much as we seek to honor God with our best, it's easy to get caught up in the busyness of business. *TGIF* brings inspiration to our days, fresh wisdom to our work, and clarity to our calling.

—**Larry Julian,** author, *God Is My CEO* and *God Is My Success*

My heart is blessed and challenged each morning as a pastor when I read the Christ-honoring words of Os Hillman. Read and be blessed.

—**Johnny Hunt,** senior pastor, First Baptist Church in Woodstock, Georgia

God has blessed Os Hillman with a special gift of insight into Scripture, which he applies in very practical ways to everyday challenges found in the workplace.

As a Catholic involved in an ecumenical workplace ministry, I find his reflections inspiring to all Christians, whatever their denomination.

—**Bill Dalgetty,** president, Christians in Commerce

Os Hillman is a man "touched by God" and weakened by him for service and insight. These are the kinds of men and women who change our lives, not just our opinions. *Today God Is First* will help make it so for its readers.

—**Dennis Peacocke,** president, Strategic Christian Services; author, *Doing Business God's Way*

Os Hillman's *TGIF* helps people succeed in the workplace while staying committed to Jesus Christ. With so many committed Christians caught between what they hear at church on Sunday and what they do at work Monday through Friday, Os Hillman connects the dots in this book by providing easy-to-read antidotes for daily workplace success. This book is a must-read for everyone who desires to see God's grace move in the workplace. Os has hit another home run!

—**Robert Watkins,** founder, Kings & Priests International

Os Hillman delivers yet another masterpiece! He has gone to the diamond mines of God's Word and pulled out treasure after treasure that will enrich your life beyond measure. God has spoken to me profoundly through his daily devotionals, building my faith, strengthening my resolve, and softening my heart. The marketplace is a better place because of the invaluable contribution made by Os Hillman and this book.

—**Michael Q. Pink,** author, *Selling among Wolves*

Os Hillman has compiled and written one of the best daily devotional books I have ever read. There is spiritual nutrition on every page. I guarantee a year full of nourishment.

—**Pat Williams,** cofounder, NBA's Orlando Magic; former general manager, Philadelphia 76ers; author, *The Warrior Within*

Whatever your situation may be, *TGIF* will impact your life. It did mine. Whether you are on a wave of success or on a stony path in the valley, this book will be your highlight in the early morning hours or in the evening together with your spouse in front of the fireplace. It will encourage you, comfort you, or provide you prophetic guidance.

—**Jurg Opprecht,** founder and president, Business Professional Network; owner, Lenkerhof Alpine Resort in Switzerland

What a joy to have distributed more than four hundred of *Today God Is First*, Os's most powerful and inspirational daily devotional book. These biblically based vignettes are moving moments with our Lord and have proven to warm hearts, inspire thoughts, and compel love and devotion to Jesus. The CEOs and presidents whom I have shared this book with have come closer to Jesus Christ as they have begun the day with prayer and a desire that God will be first that day. Thank you so much for writing a book from the lay perspective and a businessman's insights. Your book is a winner and so are the people who read and practice its contents. May God continue to bless your efforts and mine, too, as I continue to share *Today God Is First* with everyone I can.

—**Gil A. Stricklin,** founder, Marketplace Chaplains in Dallas, Texas

In the often-lonely environment of the marketplace, God comes near as Os Hillman invades with a word of hope from the God of hope. Os's background in business and his current calling of ministering to marketplace ministry leaders have uniquely equipped him for this task. I have been blessed over the last year by reading these meditations on a daily basis. The very concept of this book—meditations for those in the marketplace—excites me. For too long, the church system has forgotten to equip and train its members for ministry in the very place where they spend the most time—the marketplace.

Os Hillman is a leader of the growing band of those committed to bringing about change in our world through very practical means. I am confident that these meditations will bless you as they have me.

—**Rich Marshall,** host, *God@Work* TV show on GodTV

# TGIF

## FOR
## MEN

### 365 DAILY DEVOTIONS
### FOR THE WORKPLACE

## OS HILLMAN

**BroadStreet**
PUBLISHING

BroadStreet Publishing® Group, LLC
Savage, Minnesota, USA
BroadStreetPublishing.com

TGIF for Men: 365 Daily Devotions for the Workplace
Copyright © 2023 Os Hillman

9781424565214 (faux leather)
9781424565221 (ebook)

Stock or custom editions of BroadStreet Publishing titles may be purchased in bulk for educational, business, ministry, fundraising, or sales promotional use. For information, please email orders@ broadstreetpublishing.com.

Cover and interior by Garborg Design Works | garborgdesign.com

Printed in China

23 24 25 26 27 5 4 3 2 1

# Dedication

To J. Gunnar Olson, my spiritual father in the marketplace.
Thank you for your fathering and mentorship.

# Foreword

Os Hillman is a longtime leader in teaching, training, equipping, and encouraging Christian leaders in the marketplace to understand their God-given call and purpose so that they can fulfill their destiny in any sphere of influence that God has uniquely designed for them. As a result, hundreds of thousands around the world have been launched into the workplace with the understanding that they are full members of the body of Christ and that they are daily called to do their part to influence all those around them for Jesus with their gifts.

The *TGIF: Today God Is First* devotional has been a great influence and encouragement over the years. Now, *TGIF for Men* will continue that process as it is written specifically for men. I encourage every Christian man in the marketplace to read these devotionals and activate what they learn every day. This will change daily behavior and grow your influence with all those around you. When you activate what you learn and become a solution, not part of the problem, to those around you, you will have influence beyond your wildest dreams. Don't miss out on the Great Awakening taking place globally in every sphere of society right before our eyes.

Os, thank you for your obedience over all these years by continually encouraging marketplace believers that they are not "less than" any other believers because they are not in a "traditional" full-time ministry. Thank you for showing those with faith in Jesus that they are the answer to the world's problems.

I do and will continue to encourage all men to read and activate these daily devotionals in every aspect of their lives.

Ford Taylor
Founder, FSH Consulting Group
Founder, Transformational Leadership (TL)
Author, *Relactional Leadership*

# Introduction

The story behind *TGIF: Today God Is First* began in 1994 after I went through a major crisis. I lost over $500,000 from a "Bernie Madoff" type of scam. My financial advisor called me one day and said the investments he was handling for me had been taken by a scammer who fled the country. I would not recover one penny. I was also experiencing a marriage crisis at the time that would lead to a divorce. My largest client in my ad agency refused to pay a $140,000 bill. Life went from one place to a whole other place in the space of three months. This took me into a seven-year crisis.

It was during this time I sought God for answers. I met a man in 1996 who told me I had a "Joseph Calling" on my life. He said it was a marketplace calling to be a spiritual and physical provider to others. But the key was that I would have to press into Jesus with all my heart. He became my mentor that day. Everything he said has come true. I began writing *TGIF* as therapy for myself. I just happened to share some of the messages with friends. One friend owned a website. He asked if I would put the messages on his website. The rest is history. I began to get emails from people around the world. The common messages were, "You read my mind today" and "You spoke right into my situation. Thank you!" *TGIF* is now read in 105 countries, and hundreds of thousands of readers subscribed to receive its messages daily. I pray this devotional book will be a blessing and encouragement to you.

God turned my Valley of Achor ("trouble"; see Hosea 2:15) into a door of hope for many through my crisis. He restored my finances after seven years (just like Joseph), I married Pamela many years later, and I have traveled to twenty-six countries and have written twenty-four books as a result of the process God took me through.

He can do the same for you!

Os Hillman

# Failure That Leads to Godliness

*All those who were in distress or in debt or discontented gathered around him, and he became their commander.*

1 SAMUEL 22:2 NIV

God uses broken things to accomplish his greatest work. When David was anointed to be the next king, he was just a boy. Little did he know that he would flee from Saul's sword for the next several years or that Saul's failures would turn into obsessions as a leader who had fallen from God's anointing. Perhaps David thought, *Why am I living a life as a fugitive? I am the next king of Israel.* Yet, his life was filled with adversity before he ever fulfilled the ultimate calling God had for him. But it was his failures that attracted others to him. It was "those who were in distress or in debt or discontented" who would be part of his army—and what an army it was!

God often uses failure to make us useful. When Jesus called the disciples, he did not go out and find the most qualified or the most successful. He found the most willing, often among everyday people.

## Question
Do you sometimes confuse what success is in the kingdom of God?

*Father, help me to understand that failing does not make me a failure. Help me to fail forward in my life.*

# Full-Time Christian Work

*Whatever you do in word or deed,*
*do all in the name of the Lord Jesus,*
*giving thanks to God the Father through Him.*
COLOSSIANS 3:17 NKJV

Jonathon was a twenty-five-year-old son of a pastor who was working in his local Christian bookstore. He started seminary but was unable to finish because of a lack of finances. He was fine with working in the store but felt it was second best. In fact, sometimes he felt he had "missed his calling."

Then one day a young woman wandered into the store. She was distressed. She was not a believer. Her husband had just left her, and she did not know where to turn. While she was walking through the mall, she noticed the store, so she decided to walk in, not knowing why.

"Hello, may I help you?" said Jonathon.

"Well…I don't know. I saw your sign and just came in." Right then, she began to cry. She told Jonathon about her plight though Jonathon didn't know why she would share such personal details with a perfect stranger. Jonathon listened and began to talk with her. Before the conversation was over, Jonathon had prayed with the woman and led her to faith in Christ.

That night Jonathon felt a new sense of purpose behind what he thought was simply a job to put food on the table until he could get to his *real* ministry. He confessed to the Lord his wrong view of his work. For the first time, he realized it was ministry too.

## Question

Have you elevated the role of the Christian vocational worker to be more holy and committed than the person who is serving in other arenas?

*God, demonstrate your power through my life so that others might experience you through me today.*

# Called by Name

*These were the chiefs among Esau's descendants:*
*The sons of Eliphaz the firstborn of Esau: Chiefs Teman, Omar, Zepho, Kenaz.*
GENESIS 36:15 NIV

Years ago, I discovered that God gave me a name that had something to do with my future call from him. I was forty-four years old and had just gone through two of the most difficult years of my life. During that time, God brought a man into my life who discipled me in areas where I had never been trained. As a result, I came to identify with the struggles of Esau and Joseph in their desire to understand their own birthrights. I'd been writing about these discoveries to help believers understand their own callings through their work. One morning my friend looked at me and said, "Do you know the meaning of *Omar*?"

Omar is my first name. My full name is Omar Smallwood Hillman III. Dr. Smallwood had delivered my grandfather. No one, not even my mother, knew the origin of the name *Omar*. They put the *O* and the *S* together to call me "Os."

"You need to know the meaning of *Omar*. It has something to do with your future," said my friend.

Startled by his assertion, that night I looked up the name *Omar*. Here is what I found: Arabic: "flourishing" and "long-lived" and Hebrew: "speaker." Rooted in the Middle East. Omar was the grandson of Esau.[1]

I was shocked. I'd just completed three hundred pages of material on the relationship of Christian businessmen to the life of Esau. My friend quickly concluded that God had called me to free Christian businessmen and women from the "Esau life." And he had allowed me to receive a name that related to the person of Esau.

## Question
Is there a meaning behind your name that you need to know?

*Father, thank you for knowing the very hairs on my head.*

# The Blame Game

*Sarai, Abram's wife, had borne him no children. And she had an Egyptian maidservant whose name was Hagar. So Sarai said to Abram, "See now, the LORD has restrained me from bearing children. Please, go in to my maid; perhaps I shall obtain children by her."*

GENESIS 16:1–2 NKJV

Marriage can be difficult at times. If you are married, you already know this. Sometimes we can do what our wife asked us to do, and if the outcome is bad, we get blamed for it even if it was our spouse's idea. Such was the case with Abram when Sarai concluded that the best way to have a son was to have it through their maidservant, Hagar.

A few verses later we see Sarai blame Abram for her actions: "Then Sarai said to Abram, 'My wrong be upon you! I gave my maid into your embrace; and when she saw that she had conceived, I became despised in her eyes. The LORD judge between you and me'" (v. 5).

The interesting thing we see in this passage is what Abram did not say in response. Most of us would have said, "Well, *you* told me to do that, you know." Instead, Abram did not bring it up. He simply advised his wife to handle it as she saw fit.

Sometimes we as husbands simply need to absorb wrongs committed and be Christ to our wives, forgiving and moving forward.

## Question

Is there a wrong committed against you by someone you need to forgive?

*Father, let me forgive my wife when she accuses me of a wrong I never committed.*

# Why God Blesses

*David knew that the LORD had established him as king over Israel,*
*for his kingdom was highly exalted for the sake of His people Israel.*

1 CHRONICLES 14:2 NKJV

King David learned an important lesson every leader must learn if he is to ensure God's continual blessing. He knew why God blessed him. It wasn't because he deserved it, though he was a man who sought God with his whole heart. It wasn't because of his great skill, though he was a great military strategist. It wasn't because he was perfect, for he committed some horrible sins during his reign as king. No, it was for none of these reasons. God blessed David "for the sake of His people Israel." God never blesses an individual just for that person's exclusive benefit. God calls each of us to be a blessing to others. So often we forget this last part.

R. G. LeTourneau, a businessman who built heavy construction equipment, came to realize this only after God took him through many trials. Once the Lord had all of him, LeTourneau came to realize that the question wasn't whether he should give 10 percent of what the Lord gave him. Rather, the question was, "What amount does he want me to keep?" LeTourneau was known for giving 90 percent of his income toward the end of his career and was a great supporter of world missions. But the Lord doesn't bless workplace believers just for the ability to give financially.[2]

## Question

What is happening with the spiritual fruit of God's blessing on your life? Is it clogged, or is it freely flowing to others?

*Lord, free me to be a blessing to those in my circle of influence.*

# Called to Craftsmanship

*The LORD said to Moses, "See, I have chosen Bezalel son of Uri, the son of Hur, of the tribe of Judah, and I have filled him with the Spirit of God, with wisdom, with understanding, with knowledge and with all kinds of skills—to make artistic designs for work in gold, silver and bronze, to cut and set stones, to work in wood, and to engage in all kinds of crafts."*

EXODUS 31:1–5 NIV

Bezalel was called by God to perform a most important work for him. I am sure that Bezalel believed that he was naturally gifted with his hands to make fine crafts with gold, silver, and bronze. He probably did not associate it with God's work. But the Scripture tells us that God chose him and filled him with God's Spirit.

Does God call men and women into their vocations to fulfill his purposes? Have you ever thought about how the balance of interest among each human throughout the world happened? Was it by chance that we have only so many doctors, only so many accountants, only so many geologists?

Your interest in your vocation is not born of your own making. So many workplace believers and even pastors have made the mistake of encouraging those of us who have a deep desire to walk with Christ in the workplace to pursue vocational ministry. To remove us from the workplace where the greatest harvest is yet to occur would be to remove us from where God called us. Do not take the bait. Serve the Lord in the workplace where he has gifted you and called you.

## Question
Do you see your work as a ministry?

*Father, use me in the area of my calling to manifest your presence and power.*

# Discovering the Source of Problems

*After that, God answered prayer in behalf of the land.*
2 SAMUEL 21:14 NIV

During the reign of David, there was a famine in the land for three years. So David sought the Lord regarding this famine, asking him why there was famine on this land. The Lord answered David, "It is on account of Saul and his blood-stained house; it is because he put the Gibeonites to death" (v. 1).

Years earlier, Joshua made a peace treaty with the Gibeonites (see Joshua 9). This, too, was an act of disobedience. When God called Israel to come into the promised land, they were to destroy all the enemies of God. Joshua failed to see through the ruse of deception when the Gibeonites portrayed themselves as travelers. The Israelites signed a peace treaty only to later discover who the Gibeonites truly were. Still, they had to honor the treaty. However, this led to intermarriages and much sorrow for Israel. Years later, Saul made a decision to kill the Gibeonites in violation of the treaty.

The nation was now receiving the punishment through a famine for their sin of disobedience. David knew that famines could have a spiritual source, so he inquired of God, and God answered. The source of the sin was Saul's murder of the Gibeonites. Once David knew the source of the problem, he took action. He repented on behalf of the nation and made restitution. God then lifted the famine.

## Question
Do you have a problem that seems to be a continually unresolved issue?

*God, tell me the reason for this continual problem. If it has a spiritual root that is unresolved with you, show me that root so I may repent.*

# The Pitfall of Being Entrepreneurial

*When they came to the threshing floor of Kidon, Uzzah reached out his hand to steady the ark, because the oxen stumbled. The LORD's anger burned against Uzzah, and he struck him down because he had put his hand on the ark.*

1 CHRONICLES 13:9–10 NIV

The most difficult challenge a Christian believer in the workplace will face is knowing which things to be involved in and which to avoid. Many workplace believers have a great ability to see opportunity. What appears to be a "slam dunk" may come back to haunt us if God has not ordained for us to enter that arena. Still, we can be involved with many good things.

Uzzah was a good man in David's sight. The setting of today's verse was a time of celebration, and David and the people were transporting the ark of God. However, the ark hit a bump, and Uzzah reached for the ark to hold it steady. Upon touching the ark, he immediately died. David became very upset with God about this situation; he questioned whether he could serve God (see vv. 11–12).

God's ways are not our ways. The most important quality God desires to develop in us is our dependence on him and him alone. When we begin to make decisions based on reason and analysis instead of the leading and prompting of the Holy Spirit, we get into trouble with God. David later learned the importance of this principle in his own life. He ran the nation successfully, but he, like each of us, had to learn the difference between "good things" and "God things."

## Question
Are you involved in anything in which God has not directed you to be involved?

*God, show me how to walk with you in all things.*

# The False Self

*There is a way that seems right to a man,*
*but its end is the way of death.*
PROVERBS 16:25 NKJV

Whenever we are wounded, we seek to hide from our true self because our shame says we will not be acceptable to others as we are. We are driven to hide behind our fig leaf (living as our false self), which keeps us from our true self. This all happens on a subconscious basis as a built-in protection mechanism. The story of your life is a long and destructive assault on your heart by Satan, who knows what you could become and fears it. Satan wants your true heart to remain hidden behind your wounds. The marketplace encourages us to live behind our fig leaf in order to succeed at all costs.

There is a passage in Isaiah 50, described in the *Amplified Bible*, that expresses this issue better than any Scripture I know:

> Who is among you who fears the LORD, who obeys the voice of His Servant, yet who walks in darkness and has no light? Let him trust and be confident in the name of the Lord and let him rely on his God.
>
> Listen carefully, all you who kindle your own fire [devising your own man-made plan of salvation], who surround yourselves with torches, walk by the light of your [self-made] fire and among the torches that you have set ablaze. But this you will have from My hand: You will lie down in [a place of] torment. (vv. 10–11)

The false self is a self-made fire that prevents us from seeing our own splendor in our heart. It masquerades a false heart that only causes torment.

## Question
Do you ever find yourself portraying yourself as someone you are not?

*Father, help me to be true to who I am, inside and out.*

# Seeing Situations Clearly

*"I have reserved seven thousand in Israel, all whose knees have not bowed to Baal, and every mouth that has not kissed him."*

1 Kings 19:18 NKJV

One of the great acts of the prophet Elijah took place at Mount Carmel, where he called down fire upon the altar of Baal and slaughtered four hundred prophets of Baal. Once the miracle took place, Elijah was forced to flee because Jezebel swore to take his life for what he did. He did what he felt God wanted him to do, but now he was faced with the consequences of his actions. He felt alone and was now fearful of what might happen.

Elijah went into depression after this event. He fled to the desert and sat under a broom tree and asked God to let him die (see v. 4). He was so discouraged because he felt he was the only prophet left in Israel. This is often what happens after God does a significant work through us. Satan comes along and wants to steal what God has done and bring the servant of God down. Satan makes us believe a lie about our situation. This was the case for Elijah.

Elijah wasn't seeing the situation clearly from God's perspective. He thought he was the last of the prophets. He could not see what God was doing. God informed Elijah that there were seven thousand of his prophets in the land who had not bowed down to Baal. Now give some thought to that statement. Elijah thought he was the only one left. God says there are seven thousand left! What a discrepancy between what he thought versus reality.

Be careful not to draw conclusions about your situation that may not be based in truth. God always has a plan for his servants that we may not know about. Our only role is to obey.

## Question

Is there any situation you might be seeing incorrectly?

*God, give me your eyes to see my situation as you do.*

# Your Irrevocable Calling

*When God chooses someone and graciously imparts gifts to him,*
*they are never rescinded.*
ROMANS 11:29 TPT

It is dangerous to align your calling and your vocation so that they are dependent on each other. God calls us into relationship with him. That is our foremost calling. It is from this relationship that our "physical" calling results. A change in vocation never changes his call on our lives. When we define our work life exclusively as our calling, we fall into the trap of locking up our identity in our vocation. This promotes aspiration because of a need to gain greater self-worth through what we do.

Os Guinness, author of *The Call*, describes the great artist Picasso, who fell into this trap.

"When a man knows how to do something," Pablo Picasso told a friend, "he ceases being a man when he stops doing it." The result was drivenness. Picasso's gift, once idolized, held him in thrall. Every empty canvass was an affront to his creativity. Like an addict, he made work his source of satisfaction only to find himself dissatisfied. "I have only one thought: work," Picasso said toward the end of his life, when neither his family nor his friends could help him to relax.[3]

Calling involves different stages and experiences in life. Disruptions in your work are an important training ground for God to fulfill all aspects of his calling on your life. Trust in your God who says your calling is irrevocable.

## Question

What happens if you lose your job? Do you lose your calling? Do you lose your identity? Do you lose your sense of well-being? No.

*God, help me to see that my identity is in Christ alone.*

# God's Messengers

*Surely the Sovereign Lord does nothing*
*without revealing his plan to his servants the prophets.*
AMOS 3:7 NIV

Y ou are called to free workplace believers from the Esau life." Those were the words spoken to me years ago by someone God sent into my life. I had been in the midst of trying to understand some catastrophic events that shook my world. Years later, I was able to see that God gave this person supernatural insight that revealed God's calling on my life.

God still uses his prophets today to reveal his plans. I have seen this Scripture proven over and over in the lives of people. It is as though God sends out his "scouts" to inform his servants of what is ahead for them. Sometimes he does this because he knows the event will require significant changes in that person's life, so he wants to assure them of his love. I have experienced the Lord using me in this way in the life of other individuals. God did this in the life of Moses. He came to Moses at the burning bush to reveal his purposes for the people of Israel and his call on Moses to free them.

Elisha had a servant who could not see or hear with spiritual eyes and ears until Elisha prayed that they would be opened. Then the servant could see the great army of God protecting them (see 2 Kings 6:17).

## Question

Has God placed individuals in your life to speak his plans for you?
Are your eyes and ears spiritually sensitive so that you will know who are messengers of God?

*Lord, allow me to see and hear with the Spirit should you reveal your plans for me through another.*

# A Shoe Salesman

*Jesus looked at them and said, "With man this is impossible,*
*but with God all things are possible."*
MATTHEW 19:26 NIV

Dwight L. Moody was a poorly educated, unordained shoe salesman who felt God's call to preach the gospel. Early one morning, his friend Henry Varley said, "The world has yet to see what God can do with and for and through and in a man who is fully and wholly consecrated to him." Moody was deeply moved by these words. He later went to a meeting where Charles Spurgeon was speaking. Moody recalled the words spoken by his friend, "The world had yet to see!…with and for and through and in!…A man!" Varley meant any man! Varley didn't say he had to be educated, brilliant, or anything else. Just a man![4]

Well, by the Holy Spirit in him, Moody would be one of those men. Then suddenly he saw something he'd never realized before. It was not Mr. Spurgeon, after all, who was doing that work; it was God. And if God could use Mr. Spurgeon, why should we not all just lay ourselves at the Master's feet and say to him, "Send me! Use me!"

D. L. Moody was an ordinary man who became fully committed to Christ. God did extraordinary things through this man. He became one of the great evangelists of modern times. He founded a Bible college, Moody Bible Institute in Chicago, which sends out men and women trained in service for God.

## Question

Are you an ordinary man through whom God wants to do extraordinary things? God desires that for every child of his.

*God, do extraordinary things in my life. Strengthen my trust in you as you accomplish great things for your kingdom through me.*

# Visions and Dreams

*"This is what I will do in the last days—I will pour out my Spirit on everybody and cause your sons and daughters to prophesy, and your young men will see visions, and your old men will experience dreams from God."*

ACTS 2:17 TPT

I need to meet with you," said a man from England to me during a break at a conference overseas. We walked outside to have a coffee break and sat down. "God wants you to know that he removed your finances in order to reserve his reward for you in heaven. He has done you a great service."

I was shocked. I'd never met this gentleman before. How would he have known I had lost a half-million dollars in the previous few years, virtually all of my financial net worth, to some unusual calamities? We shared for the next several minutes.

When it came time for the gentleman and me to conclude our coffee break, we bowed in prayer. As we prayed, the man began to describe a picture he was seeing in his mind.

"I see a picture of a large orange tree. The tree is full of large, ripened oranges. They are beginning to fall to the ground. You are the tree!"

Again, I looked at the man with shock and amazement and now tears in my eyes. "You are the third person in three years who has had a similar vision during a prayer time like this," I told him. "The first two people were also strangers to me."

I went back into the meeting, rejoicing that God could be so personal in my life.

## Question
Has God ever used others to confirm the direction he is leading you?

*Father, thank you for using the body of Christ to encourage one another.*

# The Booster Rocket

*After the death of Moses the servant of the LORD, the LORD said to Joshua son of Nun, Moses' aide: "Moses my servant is dead. Now then, you and all these people, get ready to cross the Jordan River into the land I am about to give to them—to the Israelites."*
### JOSHUA 1:1–2 NIV

A rocket launch is truly an amazing phenomenon to me. Tons of weight is stacked vertically to the sky with thousands of gallons of fuel exploding in a matter of moments. Soon the rocket drops its take-off boosters and uses additional boosters to move the rocket to the next stage of the mission. The first engines have a unique purpose…to get the rocket to the next stage.

Joshua was known for almost forty years as "Joshua, servant of Moses." God's preparation for him required years of selfless service, training in the desert, and tests of faith. Those preparation years were booster rockets designed to move Joshua into each new stage of his development and his ultimate calling.

God allows each of us preparation times to lay a foundation that he plans to build on. Some of those foundation times appear to be laborious and meaningless, yet these varied experiences are what God is using to frame your life for the message he plans to speak through you. Without these foundational experiences, the Jordan River can never be crossed, and we cannot enter our promised land.

Embrace these times of seeming inactivity from God. They, too, are a rocket booster to the next stage of your walk with God.

## Question
Do you feel you are experiencing delays in fulfilling your mission?

*Father, give me grace to accept your timetable for fulfilling your purposes in me.*

# Changing Our Paradigm of Experience

*Moses thought, "I will go over and see this strange sight—
why the bush does not burn up."*

Exodus 3:3 NIV

Have you ever heard someone say, "God doesn't work that way. He would never do that"? Well, God chooses at times to confound the foolish in order to change our paradigm of experience. Moses had never seen a bush that burned but did not incinerate. It got his attention, and it drew him to God.

When Jesus appeared on the water in the middle of the night during a storm, the disciples exclaimed, "It's a ghost!" They had never seen a man walk on water. This led to a great miracle—Peter walked on the water too. When Jesus asked Peter to catch a fish and get the coin from its mouth to pay their taxes, you can imagine what Peter must have thought about those instructions. When Moses got to the Red Sea with the Egyptian army closing in, he ran out of options. God had an unexpected solution to the Israelites' problem. He parted the Red Sea.

Each of these new paradigms was a stepping-stone of an encounter with God so that the individual would experience God in a new way. God used these times to enforce the principle that his ways are not our ways. Whenever we try to predict that God will act in a certain way, he changes the paradigm to keep us from becoming our own little gods.

## Question

Have you ever been guilty of judging someone for an experience they've had that you've never had? Did you dismiss it as extreme or something not of God?

*Father, allow me to be open to your activity when it is outside the box of my experience.*

# The Goal of Life

*"For I know the plans I have for you," declares the LORD,*
*"plans to prosper you and not to harm you,*
*plans to give you hope and a future."*
JEREMIAH 29:11 NIV

For many people in the world, real meaning in life depends on the next vacation, career success, or step up the income ladder. It is a life based on pleasurable experiences. Many a human being has toiled his whole life to gain a pleasurable lifestyle only to end up with a life that is empty and meaningless. You only have to watch television for one evening to discover that advertisers want us to believe this is the goal of life. The work-to-play theme is consistent with most advertising messages.

Solomon was a man who withheld nothing from his own appetite. He was a great builder, a great businessman, and a great lover of women. Every imaginable pleasure was his. Nevertheless, he was to discover that these things alone could not satisfy the human soul.

A recent trip to a beautiful island left me grateful that God had allowed me to understand the futile trap of the work-to-play lifestyle. It is great to experience times of refreshing and visit beautiful places as long as we don't fall into the trap of thinking that these experiences equal a meaningful life.

Knowing Christ brings the only real meaning and purpose to the human soul. Spend time today getting to know the Lord in a more intimate way. Then you will discover real meaning and purpose in life.

## Question
Where are you finding meaning and purpose in life?

*Father, protect me from seeking a life of pleasure instead of building your kingdom.*

# The Need to Control

*"You have done a foolish thing," Samuel said.*
1 SAMUEL 13:13 NIV

Through the Lord's direction, the prophet Samuel had anointed Saul the first king of Israel. Saul was now thirty years old and was leading the nation in battle against the Philistines. The Philistines had gathered at Micmash to come against Saul and his army. Samuel instructed Saul to go ahead of him to Micmash, and he would follow in seven days. He would then make a burnt offering on behalf of the people of Israel.

The pressure began to build as the Philistines gathered around Micmash preparing for battle. The people of Israel grew fearful and began to scatter throughout the countryside. Saul was also afraid. Samuel did not show up on the morning of the seventh day. Finally, Saul, fearing the impending attack, took it upon himself to offer the burnt offering. After he had done this, Samuel showed up.

Saul believed he needed to take control of the situation. Whenever we try to take control of a situation out of God's will, we demonstrate that fear leads us. Many a boss is so driven by fear that he attempts to manage by overcontrolling his people. This results in codependent relationships in which the employees are fearful of making the wrong decisions and are driven to please the manager at all costs. This results in a loss of respect for the manager.

## Question
Do you see any signs of overcontrol in how you relate to others?
Can you allow others the freedom to fail?

*God, allow me to walk in the freedom of trusting in you and those around me.*

# Redeeming the Time

*When they came up out of the water, Philip was suddenly snatched up by the Spirit of the Lord and instantly carried away to the city of Ashdod, where he reappeared, preaching the gospel in that city.*

ACTS 8:39–40 TPT

Many times, I've heard men or women say they cannot participate in an event, a service, or activity for God because of the time it will take away from their jobs. God has called each of us to be good stewards of our time and our resources.

Philip was in the city of Samaria preaching when many miracles began to take place, and the crowds came to see what was happening. Then, in the midst of this great move of God, the angel of God spoke to Philip and told him to leave Samaria and go to a desert road that led from Jerusalem to Gaza. Imagine how Philip must have questioned the logic of this decision when he was seeing such results in Samaria. But Philip was obedient to the angel. Along the road, he met an Ethiopian eunuch who wanted to have the Scriptures explained to him. Philip explained the Scriptures to the Ethiopian—who was the treasurer of Ethiopia under Queen Candace—led him to the Lord and then baptized him in a nearby lake. A few moments later, Philip was supernaturally transported many miles northwest of his location to Azotus (Ashdod), where he preached Christ along the way toward his final destination of Caesarea.

God desires that we respond as Philip did in order to be used by him in the life of another person.

## Question
Is your time available to God 24/7?

*Father, help me to live moment by moment, always led by your Spirit.*

# Mount Horeb

*He got up and ate and drank. Strengthened by that food, he traveled forty days and forty nights until he reached Horeb, the mountain of God.*

1 KINGS 19:8 NIV

Elijah and Moses were men of great zeal. They were passionate about their causes. Moses sought to free the Hebrews from the tyranny of slavery by killing an Egyptian with his own hand. Elijah, after calling down fire on the evil prophets of Baal, found himself spent physically and emotionally to the point where he asked God to take his life.

After these two events, five hundred years apart from one another, both men were led to the same Mount Horeb, the mountain of God. In Hebrew, *Horeb* means "desolation." This barren environment mirrored the condition of Moses and Elijah. For Moses, it was forty years of barrenness. For Elijah, it was forty days without food. Elijah became tired of standing alone for God.

As workplace believers, we often become so focused on the goal that we forget to meet God at our own Mount Horeb. This was the place God met both Moses and Elijah. It was a place of renewal, a place of new beginnings, a place of personal encounter with the living God.

To remain balanced, we must reign in and harness our zeal through strategic encounters with the living God. We otherwise become frustrated with people and discouraged with delays. Many of us become so consumed with our battles that we are no longer aware of the presence of Jesus.

## Question

Do you have zeal for God? Make sure you spend time in his presence.

*Jesus, teach me that intimacy with you is the greatest measure of success. Lord, guide me to the mountain of your presence.*

# The Place of Obedience

*Saul got up from the ground,*
*but when he opened his eyes he could see nothing.*
ACTS 9:8 NIV

A place of obedience exists for all of us. For Paul, it was being struck blind on the Damascus road. God literally knocked him down with a blinding light. Jesus' voice from heaven asked Paul, "Why do you persecute me?" (v. 4). When Paul arose, he could not see. Jesus told him to go to Damascus and meet a man named Ananias. There, Jesus restored Paul's sight through Ananias.

For some, our obedience requires only a nudge of pressure to gently lead us toward God. For others of us, a lightning bolt is necessary to get our undivided attention. Many who are hard-hearted rebel against the living God. Yet God's love for these individuals is so great that he takes extreme measures to gain their attention—and their hearts. When you encounter people like this, do not fear their arrogance. It is a sign to begin praying for them.

We've all heard the saying, "The bigger they are, the harder they fall." In many cases this is true. God has called many hard cases into his kingdom through miraculous circumstances to save their souls from the pit of hell and transform their lives. Do not let the hard exterior fool you. These are needy people who are crying out for help in their own way.

## Question

Has God placed such an individual in your path? Perhaps God desires to use you to be an "Ananias" in the life of one of his wayward children.

*Heavenly Father, make me willing to come alongside the one who needs my help, whether that person be but a neighbor or the next apostle Paul.*

# When Insecurity Turns Evil

*Rejoice with those who rejoice;*
*mourn with those who mourn.*
ROMANS 12:15 NIV

Saul was the king of Israel. David was in Saul's army and beginning to build a reputation as a great warrior. One day when David came back from a battle, the women danced and sang: "Saul has slain his thousands, and David his tens of thousands" (1 Samuel 18:7).

Saul became angry, thinking, "They have credited David with tens of thousands…but me with only thousands. What more can he get but the kingdom?" (v. 8).

This statement caused something to snap in King Saul. From this point on, Saul was never the leader God intended him to be. He allowed pride and insecurity to drive his every decision. Insecurity leads to the need to control people and circumstances. The need to control leads to anger once we realize we are unable to control the circumstance. King Saul could not accept David's success, much less rejoice over it. David's life would never be the same because Saul sought to kill David every chance he had. Saul had a choice; he could have seen David as an up-and-coming general in his army who could have become an important part of his team and made the kingdom of Israel even stronger. Instead, Saul looked at David as a threat. If you find yourself comparing your life's circumstances to others and don't feel you measure up, recognize that this is one of Satan's greatest ploys to destroy you.

## Question
When you hear good news about fellow workers or associates,
do you rejoice with them?

*Thank you, Father, for equipping me for every good work. My confidence is in you.*

# Being Left Out

*He asked Jesse, "Are these all the sons you have?"*
*"There is still the youngest," Jesse answered.*
*"He is tending the sheep." Samuel said,*
*"Send for him; we will not sit down until he arrives."*
1 SAMUEL 16:11 NIV

Have you ever been left out when there was a big opportunity available? Perhaps your boss introduced a new program and was looking for someone to run it, but you were not considered. Perhaps you were not included in a company function for some reason. Discrimination can take place in many ways in our society.

When the prophet Samuel was told by God that the next king of Israel would come from the sons of Jesse, he was surprised when God did not indicate that one of the sons Jesse presented to him was the anointed one. So, he inquired of Jesse if these were all of his sons.

We don't know why Jesse did not include David as a choice, but it's possible that Jesse saw David differently than he saw his other sons. In Psalm 51, David says, "I was brought forth in iniquity" (v. 5 ESV). What does that mean? Was he an illegitimate son born out of wedlock? It isn't clear, but it could be one reason why David was not included as an option for Samuel.

God is the great equalizer in our lives if we are willing to trust him. He knows when there are injustices. Trust him with every detail of your life.

## Question
Are you struggling with any injustice in your life?

*Father, I trust you to make any injustice toward me right.*

# God's Double-Talk

*The LORD said to Moses, "When you return to Egypt, see that you perform before Pharaoh all the wonders I have given you the power to do. But I will harden his heart so that he will not let the people go."*
EXODUS 4:21 NIV

Have you ever had a boss tell you to do something only to have him sabotage your ability to complete the task? Nothing is more frustrating than to begin to carry out a task and have your superior thwart your effort. Moses must have felt this way after God told him to go tell Pharaoh to release the people of Israel. God told Moses that he would give Moses the power to perform miracles in front of Moses. Yet at the same time, God told Moses that Pharaoh would not release the Israelites because God was going to put a hard heart in Pharaoh. How do we reconcile this?

In the case of Moses and Israel, God wanted to demonstrate his power in such a way that generations would be able to hear the story of their deliverance from their ancestors. God wanted greater glory from the situation. God also wanted to deal with Egypt by sending specific plagues. Finally, the very process built character in Moses and tested Moses to see if he would stay the course.

## Question

Do you ever question why God has not opened a door or provided what you need when you thought you needed it?

*Father, help me trust you with the timetable for breakthrough and provision in my life.*

# Are You God's Next Deliverer?

*When they cried out to the Lord, he raised up for them a deliverer,
Othniel son of Kenaz, Caleb's younger brother, who saved them.*

JUDGES 3:9 NIV

Have you ever heard of a man named Othniel? Probably not. He was Caleb's nephew. When the people of Israel went into the promised land, they were victorious through the courageous efforts of Joshua and Caleb. As this generation grew older, a new generation began to emerge. Israel again fell into sin by worshiping idols. The anger of the Lord burned against Israel, and he allowed their enemies to enslave them once more. However, the people again cried out to the Lord, and God heard them.

Whenever God's people cry out to the Lord, he hears them. When they are truly repentant, he responds. He responds by raising up those whom he has prepared for such a time. Every soldier looks forward to the day when he can use the training he has received. God had been preparing Caleb's nephew for such a time as this. He had the same spirit as his uncle, Caleb.

"The Spirit of the Lord came on him, so that he became Israel's judge and went to war. The Lord gave Cushan-Rishathaim king of Aram into the hands of Othniel, who overpowered him. So the land had peace for forty years, until Othniel son of Kenaz died" (vv. 10–11).

## Question

Has God been preparing you for a time when you will be called upon to deliver God's people? Has he placed you in this moment to be a deliverer?

*Lord, give me the same spirit as Joshua, Caleb, and Othniel.*

# How and Where God Speaks

*The hand of the LORD was on me there, and he said to me,*
*"Get up and go out to the plain, and there I will speak to you."*
 EZEKIEL 3:22 NIV

God speaks in many different ways to his children. He spoke through a bush to Moses. He spoke through a donkey to Balaam. He spoke through prophets to his kings. He speaks through other believers. He speaks directly to us through the invisible Holy Spirit. And he speaks even through circumstances.

When God wants to speak a very important word directly to us without interruption from the noise of our busy lives, he will take us "out to the plain." The plain is a place of no distractions and no other people. It is a place of silence. It can be a place of great need as it often fails to have the normal provisions we are accustomed to. It can be a place we go to voluntarily to seek his face, or we can be moved there without choice by his supernatural ability. More often, it is the latter method that brings us into the plain. In modern times, going out to the plain often means a separation from our normal activities, such as jobs or families.

Each day God calls us to our own mini-plain in order to speak to us and for us to hear. If we neglect this time of open communication, we may be invited to his plain in order to hear without distraction.

## Question
Do you need to hear God's voice today? Is your life so crowded that you cannot even hear his voice?

*Lord, help me to make time with you a priority so I will hear your voice.*

# Seeing What Others Cannot See

*It was by faith that Abraham obeyed when God called him to leave home and go to another land that God would give him as his inheritance. He went without knowing where he was going.*

HEBREWS 11:8 NLT

Several years ago, a movie was made called *Field of Dreams*. The story is about a man who had a vision to build a baseball field in the middle of a cornfield on his rural farm. He did not know why; he just knew he was to do it. To the chagrin of his neighbors, he built the baseball diamond in the farm community. One night some players showed up. The man realized these were no ordinary players but the great players from the past. When the skeptical neighbors came to view this phenomenon, they were unable to see what the farm owner could see. This made it even worse for him. Now he was really a lunatic in their eyes.[5]

This fictitious story has a spiritual application for us. First, if God tells us to "build a ball field," we should do it. It is not for us to determine the reason we are instructed to do it. Once we are obedient, God will allow us to see what others cannot see. It is the rite of passage for those who are willing to risk all for God's purposes. God increases the spiritual senses to levels we never knew before. Those around us will observe this.

## Question

Do you want to see what others cannot see? If so, it will require a level of obedience that will go beyond human reason.

*Father, give me spiritual eyes to see what I need to see.*

# Sold Out

*All of the accomplishments that I once took credit for,*
*I've now forsaken them and I regard it all as nothing*
*compared to the delight of experiencing Jesus Christ as my Lord!*
PHILIPPIANS 3:7 TPT

George Mueller was a man known for building orphanages by faith in the mid-1800s. He raised literally millions of dollars for his orphanages, yet he died with little in his own bank account. When asked about his conversion experience, he commented,

> I was converted in November of 1825, but I only came into the full surrender of the heart four years later, in July 1829. The love of money was gone, the love of place was gone, the love of position was gone, the love of worldly pleasures and engagements was gone. God, God, God alone became my portion. I found my all in Him; I wanted nothing else. And by the grace of God this has remained, and has made me a happy man, an exceedingly happy man, and it led me to care only about the things of God. I ask affectionately, my beloved brethren, have you fully surrendered the heart to God, or is there this thing or that thing with which you have taken up irrespective of God? I read a little of the Scriptures before, but preferred other books, but since that time the revelation He has made of Himself has become unspeakably blessed to me, and I can say from my heart, God is an infinitely lovely Being.[6]

## Question
What will it take for you to fully surrender?

*Father, I fully surrender to you today to fulfill your purposes in and through me.*

# Real Customer Service

*While they were leaving, some people brought before Jesus
a demonized man who couldn't speak.*
MATTHEW 9:32 TPT

Many years ago, it was not uncommon to have your milk delivered to your home. Doctors made house calls. And when you made a call to a company to discuss a problem, you actually spoke to a human being. Those days of personal service are gone, and if we are not careful, we will follow the same trend in how we share the gospel.

So often we are encouraged to bring people to church. Yet, we see no examples of where Jesus brought people into the synagogue to get them saved or healed. The miracles happened more often in the workplace because that was where Jesus could be found. Jesus had less response and found more resistance in the synagogue than in the workplace. He took the gospel to the marketplace. That is where the power of God was manifested. This is not to say we should not bring people to church, only that our priority should be to bring the church into the marketplace, not bring the marketplace into the church.

Paul understood this when he said, "My message and my preaching were not with wise and persuasive words, but with a demonstration of the Spirit's power, so that your faith might not rest on human wisdom, but on God's power" (1 Corinthians 2:4–5 NIV).

Paul understood that it wasn't words that impacted people; it was the power of God manifested through him.

## Question

When was the last time someone saw something happen through your life that had no explanation other than God working in your life?

*Father, demonstrate your power through me to touch others and build your kingdom.*

# The Ultimate Franchise

*Jesus said to them, "Why would you need to search for me? Didn't you know that it was necessary for me to be here in my Father's house, consumed with him?"*
LUKE 2:49 TPT

Earth is God's business. He has set up many franchises (churches) designed to send his representatives (body of Christ) into the world to make known the best product ever given to mankind (Jesus). His branch managers (pastors) have been given the responsibility to teach and support those in the field. God's goal is to establish a franchise in every nation, state, and city. It is the ultimate business because when you introduce someone to his product (Jesus), you receive a reward from the home office (heaven). God has promised that his representatives will have all the tools and customer support needed to accomplish their strategic plans.

Jesus knew that he was to be about his Father's business. He knew he was sent to earth not to enjoy the pleasures of man but to accomplish a task only he could undertake. When he had accomplished his goal, he was to entrust this mission to other representatives into whom he poured his life for three years. This field training allowed Jesus to mentor, model, befriend, and demonstrate firsthand the model for a successful business to be launched and sustained.

God wants every human being to partake of his franchise; however, even God knows that not everyone will. Nevertheless, this does not thwart his efforts in seeking to make his kingdom known among his audience.

## Question
You have been called to be part of the ultimate franchise. How many new recruits have you brought into the franchise lately?

*Father, make me a fisher of men and a disciple of others.*

# Product Testing

*"Commending his servant, the master replied, 'You have done well, and proven yourself to be my loyal and trustworthy servant. Because you have been a faithful steward to manage a small sum, now I will put you in charge of much, much more.'"*
MATTHEW 25:21 TPT

Testing allows one to discover how well a product is made when placed under extreme stress. Increasing the pulling pressure between two objects reveals the amount of tension that a chain link can withstand. Eventually, the "choking" point occurs. For example, at what point will the athlete lose concentration and collapse under the pressure?

In my younger days, I played sports. I came to observe that we fail under pressure usually because we reach a point where our ability to focus on execution yields to concern about the outcome.

In life, we see giving in to pressure in the form of compulsive behavior, withdrawal, anger, moral failure, and dishonesty, to name just a few manifestations.

Jesus never yielded to pressure. He never made decisions based on outcome. He always made the right decision. He always performed the same no matter the circumstance. He lived a life based on absolutes, not circumstances. He never gave in to "situational ethics."

As God entrusts us with more and more responsibility, he brings more and more pressures into our lives to "test the product," to make sure that he can give even more responsibility to us. This process helps us see where we are in our maturity and determines our level of future responsibility.

## Question
Are you someone who can withstand the product test? Will you perform as the maker designed no matter what outside pressures come?

*Father, help me to pass the test so I will be a valued player in your kingdom.*

# Discerning the Work of God

*Remember Tobiah and Sanballat, my God, because of what they have done;*
*remember also the prophet Noadiah and how she and the rest of the prophets*
*have been trying to intimidate me.*

NEHEMIAH 6:14 NIV

Nehemiah set out to rebuild the wall at Jerusalem that had been destroyed. Nehemiah held a position in the Persian empire that would be comparable to chief of staff in our government. Nehemiah wept over the destruction of the city wall and repented for the sins of his generation and the generations before him that had led to the fall of Jerusalem. Nehemiah asked his superior if he could take time off to rebuild the wall. The religious and political leaders of his day opposed him.

Whenever God does a new work, it is often met with resistance by those in the established religious community and sometimes among those from whom we would expect support. Jesus met the same resistance when he began his public ministry. When God begins a new work that we cannot easily explain based upon our prior experiences, we might make the mistake of assuming the work is not from God. The very people who should embrace and encourage the work often oppose it.

Before you are tempted to criticize or oppose something that looks different from your experience, ask God for wisdom and discernment. Examine why you might be tempted to oppose it. The Lord delights in doing things in ways that may not fit our former paradigms.

## Question

Are you open to new moves of God that may not look familiar to you?

*Father, help me to recognize where you are moving and to embrace your activity.*

# Fulfilling Vows

*When you make a vow to God, do not delay to fulfill it.*
*He has no pleasure in fools; fulfill your vow.*

ECCLESIASTES 5:4 NIV

Have you ever had a business relationship with someone who made a commitment but later said, "Well, things changed, so I cannot honor our original agreement"? Sometimes this may be the case, but often, it is simply an opportunity to avoid fulfilling an agreement. God is big on fulfilling vows. God's nature is righteousness and truth. You will always see God honor his word. He expects the same of his people.

God says there are consequences when we do not fulfill our vows. Subsequent verses from Ecclesiastes reveal the following:

> Do not let your mouth cause your flesh to sin, nor say before the messenger of God that it was an error. Why should God be angry at your excuse and destroy the work of your hands? For in the multitude of dreams and many words there is also vanity. But fear God. (vv. 6–7 NKJV)

God tells us that he will destroy the work of our hands for failure to fulfill vows. That's pretty strong language. It gives us an indication of how important to God fulfilling vows is. He will not prosper our work if there are unfulfilled vows in our lives.

## Question
Are there any unfulfilled vows in your life
that may be hindering your projects?

*Lord, make me a faithful steward of all you entrust to me. Make me a man of my word.*

# A Romans 8:14 Christian

*"My servant Caleb, because he has a different spirit in him and has followed Me fully, I will bring into the land where he went, and his descendants shall inherit it."*
NUMBERS 14:24 NKJV

Scripture describes Joshua and Caleb as men who had a different spirit. They were two of the twelve spies sent into the promised land to determine if it could be taken, as God had promised it to them. Joshua and Caleb assured the people that the land was exceedingly good and that they should not doubt that God was with them. The other ten gave a bad report that instilled fear in the people, which ultimately caused a rebellion. As a result, an entire generation died in the desert. Joshua and Caleb were the only two led by the Spirit of God versus the spirit of fear. They were the only ones from their generation to enter the promised land.

"For as many as are led by the Spirit of God, these are sons of God" (Romans 8:14). Many of us have failed to enter into our own promised land because we have failed to be led by the Spirit rather than by fear. The Spirit must lead you to enter. You cannot be led by fear, reason and analysis, or even skill.

Commit yourself to being a Romans 8:14 man. Then you will enter into the land God has promised for you.

## Question
Are you a person led by the Spirit?

*Father, make me a Romans 8:14 man.*

# Humble Circumstances

*Believers in humble circumstances*
*ought to take pride in their high position.*

JAMES 1:9 NIV

Do you find yourself in humble circumstances? If so, James tells us that we are to take pride in this "high" position. These two things would seem to be an oxymoron. Most of us would not consider humble circumstances a high position.

J. C. Penney is a name synonymous with department stores. James C. Penney first launched his Golden Rule Store in 1902. In 1910, his first wife died. Three years later, he incorporated as the J. C. Penney Company. In 1923, his second wife died giving birth to his son. In 1929, the stock market crashed, and he lost $40 million. By 1932, Penney had little money.

> Crushed in spirit from his loss and his health suddenly failing, Penney wound up in a Battle Creek, Michigan, sanitarium. One morning he heard the distant singing of employees who gathered to start the day with God: "Be not dismayed, whate'er betide, God will take care of you…" Penney followed the music to its source and slipped into a back row. He left a short time later a changed man, his health and spirit renewed, and ready to start the long climb back at age fifty-six.[7]

By 1951, every state had a JCPenney store, and sales surpassed $1 billion a year. The success of J. C. Penney can be traced to God's mercy in his life to bring him out of his humble circumstance.

## Question
Do you find yourself in a humble circumstance?

*Father, help me to trust you to bring me through my adversity today.*

# Validation from God

*"Whoever wants to save his life will lose it."*
LUKE 9:24 NASB

Recently I went through a season where every source of validation and everything I could control was removed from me. Some of these things I removed myself. Others were removed without my say in the matter. Some of these actions were a result of my own stubbornness to see facts due to my childhood woundedness that set up boundaries of defense against truth.

I can tell you that when all of these things are removed from your life, there is a shock to your system. You cannot survive unless Christ alone is your all, and even then, you will face an enormous loss of value, a wavering sense of belonging, and feelings of abandonment.

God allows us to recognize and revisit our wounds so we can be healed and live from our true self. Unfortunately, most men refuse to recognize or acknowledge their wounds because of fear and pride. Our false self is often strengthened even more when we feel threatened. Sometimes it takes a total crash before some men are willing to examine the root of their problems.

When there are unresolved wounds, we cling to our natural gifts that God wants to put a sword through in order to reveal his life through them, instead of hiding behind them. Once we recognize our false-self masks, we must voluntarily begin to dismantle them in order to reveal our true self.

The false self prevents us from having intimacy with God and others in our lives. God's love of his sons drives him to destroy the false self in us so each of us realize true intimacy. True validation comes only from God.

## Question
What false self does God need to destroy to allow your true self to come forward?

*Father, reveal my true self in you.*

# A Question of Ownership

*"Those who cling to their lives will give up true life. But those who let go of their lives for my sake and surrender it all to me will discover true life!"*
MATTHEW 10:39 TPT

Otto Koning was a missionary in New Guinea. He worked among a native tribe that had known only their village ways, which sometimes included stealing from others.

The only fruit Otto could grow on the island was pineapples. Otto loved pineapples, and he took pride in the pineapples he was able to grow. However, whenever the pineapples began to ripen, the natives would steal them.

Otto attended a conference on personal rights where he discovered that he was frustrated over this situation because he had taken personal ownership of his pineapple garden. God convicted him to give his garden to God. Soon after the natives discovered that Otto gave his garden to his God, they realized this was the reason for recent problems in the village: not catching fish, sickness in their tribe, and other calamities. The natives saw a correlation between stealing God's pineapples and the calamities in their own lives. Otto no longer got angry when his pineapples went missing.

A native said, "You have become a Christian, haven't you…You don't get angry anymore…We'd hoped we'd meet [a Christian] someday." They had never associated Otto with being a Christian until that point. Otto was broken over being such a failure.

Seven years passed before he got his first conversion, and many began coming to Christ once he fully gave his garden to God. Otto realized, "To gain your life you must lose it, along with your possessions."[8]

## Question
Do you have some possessions that you need to give up to God today?

*Father, I yield all my possessions to you today.*

# Standing in the Gap

*"I looked for someone among them who would build up the wall and stand before me in the gap on behalf of the land so I would not have to destroy it, but I found no one."*
EZEKIEL 22:30 NIV

The people of Israel fell into sin when they worshiped the golden calf. It would not be the last time God's people would fall into idol worship. They had forgotten the great things God had done for them. This angered God so much that he was going to destroy the whole nation. Only one thing changed God's mind in the matter—Moses. Psalm 106:23 says God would have carried out his plan "had not Moses, his chosen one, stood in the breach before him to keep his wrath from destroying them." Moses was a man willing to stand in the gap, sacrificially, for those who were not deserving of such sacrifice.

This sacrificial love by Moses is called for among his people today. Just as Christ did, we are to be those who will stand in the gap on behalf of others who are not aware of their own vulnerable condition. It is a proactive sacrificial position. In Ezekiel 22:30, God asks if there is not someone willing to stand in the gap to intercede so that he does not have to destroy that nation. You are and I are called to stand in the gap and bring heaven on earth in every area of life, work, and even our nation.

## Question

Whom has God called you to stand in the gap for? Perhaps your wife, children, or work associates. Perhaps it is a wayward child who is fighting an addiction.

*Father, I commit to stand in the gap for those you call me to stand for.*

# God's Recruitment Strategy

*You need the strength of endurance to reveal the poetry of God's will and then you receive the promise in full. For soon and very soon, "The One who is appearing will come without delay!"*

HEBREWS 10:36–37 TPT

When God calls one of his servants into service, there is often much travail. There are many examples where God makes his presence known through circumstances that tax the individual to his very soul.

Consider Paul, who was stricken blind on the Damascus road.

Consider Peter, who was in total despair after he denied Jesus after the crucifixion.

Consider Shadrach, Meshach, and Abednego, who were thrown into the fiery furnace.

Consider Daniel, who was thrown into the lions' den.

Consider David, who was forced to flee his former employer for many years and lived as a fugitive.

It may seem strange to us that God uses such incredible adversity to prepare his servants for greater service, but this is God's way. God knows that the human heart is incapable of voluntarily stepping into situations that take us beyond our comfort zone. He intentionally brings us into hard places to prove us and to drive us deeper into the soil of his grace.

Friend, God may take you through times when you will question his love for you. In such times, you must cling to his coattail so that you see his purposes in the events around you. Do not throw away your confidence; it will be richly rewarded.

## Question

Do you find yourself in a place that challenges your faith?

*God, give me grace to trust in this time.*

# Learning to Receive

*It is vain for you to rise up early, to sit up late, to eat the bread of sorrows;
for so He gives His beloved sleep.*
PSALM 127:2 NKJV

One of the paradigm shifts every believer must learn once he makes Jesus Lord of his life is how to move from receiving by sweating and toiling to receiving by trusting and obeying. In the Scripture, Egypt represents sweat and toil and bondage. The promised land represents a land of milk and honey received by trust and obedience based upon Joshua 24:13.

I learned this principle when God began to transition me from owning and operating an advertising agency to a vocational marketplace ministry. Many times I could not see how I would receive provision to do my work because it was not based on a traditional contract-for-services model. But God was faithful to provide during this transition. I was then invited to speak to a small group of people on a Caribbean island. I knew it would require three days of my time, and I'd receive very little compensation. The Lord instructed me to go anyway. Just as I thought, I did not receive what I expected was a commensurate income for the time invested for the three days.

However, a businessman received some of the books I left behind at the meeting. He called me one day and invited me to speak at a conference for twenty-two Caribbean islands later that year. One man was touched by my teaching in one of the breakout sessions. A few months later I received a check for $5,000 from this man. It was because of my obedience to the small things that God was able to give me a land on which I did not toil.

## Question
Are you being faithful to the small things?

*Father, help me walk in obedience in every area of my life.*

# Worldly Planning

*When I revised my itinerary, was I vacillating? Or do I make my plans with unprincipled motives, ready to flip-flop with a "yes" and a "no" in the same breath? Of course not!*

2 CORINTHIANS 1:17 TPT

The apostle Paul was discussing his plans to come to the church at Corinth. He was acknowledging the serious nature of his trip and informing the Corinthians that he did not flippantly come to this decision to visit them. It was a matter that he had given serious prayer, not one he made on the spur of the moment.

Planning from God's view is a process. It requires our entering into the mind of Christ together to determine which course to take. In the Old Testament, the priests wore breastplates with the Urim and Thummim in a pouch, which the priests were required to use to know which direction they were to take on a matter. It was the ultimate release of all decisions into God's hand. God did not want the priests to rely on their own intellects for final decisions. Today we rely on the Holy Spirit's direction in our lives.

God desires that we seek him to know his plans for us. Sometimes this requires more time given to the process in order to hear his voice. Sometimes it may even require fasting and prayer. Sometimes it may require input from other godly friends.

## Question

Are you a man who makes decisions based on God's purposes for your life? Do you take every major decision and put it before the throne to determine God's mind on the matter?

*Father, help me to discern every decision through your guiding hand.*

# Life Is Fragile

*You can rationalize it all you want and justify the path of error you have chosen, but you'll find out in the end that you took the road to destruction.*
PROVERBS 14:12 TPT

In 2006, a man named Jim had a friend from Atlanta who forwarded him a daily devotional called *TGIF: Today God Is First*, which talked about work being a spiritual calling. Reading *TGIF* started transforming his perspective on work and calling. He was always taught that there was the pastor and then there were the workplace guys, and the workplace guys were supposed to support the pastor.

It was 2008 during the financial crash in America. The company Jim worked at had lost a lot of money. Jim had four bosses at the time, and he began sharing the *TGIF* messages with them. He had a business trip with one of the bosses, and after landing, they rented a car and almost got in a major car accident. He turned to the boss and said, "You know. We could have been killed in that car wreck. I would have been okay with it because I know where I would have gone. But I don't think you could confidently say you would have gone to heaven." Jim shared how the *TGIF* devotional helped him understand the spiritual nature of his work and life. He told his coworker that life is fragile and that we never know when our lives may be taken.

Jim kept sharing the devotionals with his bosses. Over time, every one of his bosses' lives was transformed by reading the devotional. The boss who was almost in a car accident with Jim accepted Jesus into her life.

Jim went on to say that the *TGIF* devotional inspired him to start *iWork4Him* radio show.

## Question
Are you sharing the love of Christ with a coworker?

*God, give me the opportunities to share with a coworker who needs Christ.*

# Face-to-Face

*Although I have many more subjects I'd like to discuss with you, I'd rather not include them in this letter. But I look forward to coming to visit and speaking with you face-to-face—for being together will complete our joy!*

2 JOHN 1:12 TPT

It is easy to fire off a letter to someone in this age because of the expediency of electronic communication. However, there are times when only a face-to-face meeting is the appropriate means of communication. We know that verbal skills are a very small portion of communication. Body language, voice tone, and our facial expressions make up the majority of overall communication. This cannot be experienced through a letter or electronic medium.

For John, it meant some major trouble to get from one place to another. It wasn't as simple as getting into a car or hopping on an airplane. John's desire and determination to visit and talk face-to-face reinforces the importance of one-on-one personal communication.

I once had to confront a businessman about some problems we were having in a business deal. He lived in another town. The negotiations had stalled to some degree. I realized the serious nature of the issues required a face-to-face meeting, so I drove two hours to his office and met with him. My actions demonstrated to my business friend that I was serious enough about solving the problem to take a day to come see him. It also showed that I valued him and that he was worth the effort. This resulted in him giving greater emphasis to the issue.

## Question
Do you have an issue that needs to be resolved?
Consider a face-to-face meeting.

*Father, give me wisdom to work through conflicts by honoring the relationship with my time.*

# For Your Bride

*To the husbands, you are to demonstrate love for your wives with the same tender devotion that Christ demonstrated to us, his bride. For he died for us, sacrificing himself to make us holy and pure, cleansing us through the showering of the pure water of the Word of God.*

EPHESIANS 5:25–26 TPT

Husbands are to be a physical representation of what Christ has done for each of us for our wives. As we do this, we experience the love of the Father. In turn, wives will experience the love of the Father. It is the very laying down of our lives that allows us to connect to the Father just as Jesus did.

If husbands willingly lay down their lives for their wives, they will not feel something is being taken. It is when husbands defend, negotiate, and withdraw from the needs of a woman that they hinder this process of connection. We must realize that we are the initiators called to lay down our lives for our wives. Women respond to this sacrificial act by giving their heart and physical love to their husbands. Both husband and wife experience the love of the Father when this happens. Consider where you might lay down your life for the sake of your wife today. You will be modeling what Christ did for you and me.

## Question

If you are married, are you laying down your life for your bride daily?

*Father, give me the grace to love my wife unconditionally and to lay my life down for her.*

# Divine Setups

*"Peter, my dear friend, listen to what I'm about to tell you. Satan has obtained permission to come and sift you all like wheat and test your faith."*
LUKE 22:31 TPT

Have you ever perceived yourself to be at one place spiritually only to discover that you were far from this place? Peter perceived himself to be so spiritually strong that he was prepared to suffer greatly for his master. Yet Jesus knew where Peter really was in his own pilgrimage. He knew that Peter's enthusiasm did not match his reality. So, how did Jesus help Peter match his perception to his reality? Peter was the object of a divine setup.

First, notice that Satan asked permission to sift Peter as wheat. Jesus determined that Satan would be used to bring Peter to the maturity level both Jesus and Peter really desired. And Jesus was praying that Peter would pass the test. Jesus told Peter that he would deny him three times that very day. Peter could not believe what Jesus was saying.

Sometimes the lessons we must learn are very painful. This experience was necessary in Peter's life. It was necessary to purge Peter from his sin of self-righteousness. This very lesson would allow Peter to come face-to-face with his own misperception of where he was in his relationship and devotion to Jesus. When he was forced to confront this, it nearly broke him apart. He wept bitterly once he realized he had done just as Jesus had predicted.

This confrontation with reality is necessary at times in our lives. Do not be surprised if Jesus allows you to experience some painful circumstance.

## Question
Where do you perceive yourself in your loyalty and obedience to Jesus?

*Father, help me be a faithful follower.*

# The Skillful Worker

*Do you see a person skilled in his work?*
*He will stand before kings;*
*he will not stand before obscure people.*
PROVERBS 22:29 NASB

The Lord has called each of us to be excellent in what we do. Those whom God used in the Bible as workplace ministers were skilled and exemplified excellence in their field. Not only were these men skilled, but they were also filled with God's Spirit.

Consider Huram, the master craftsman of bronze in whom Solomon entrusted much of the temple designs. He was a true master craftsman (see 1 Kings 7:14). Consider Joseph, whose skill as an administrator was known throughout Egypt and the world. Consider Daniel, who served his king with great skill and integrity. The list could go on—David, Nehemiah, Aquila, and Priscilla.

I recall the first issue of an international publication we began. It was common to hear the comment, "It doesn't even look like a Christian magazine." They were saying the quality and excellence exceeded what they equated to Christian work. What a shame. Has inferior quality become synonymous with Christian work?

May we strive for excellence in all that we do for the Master of the universe.

"Whatever you do, work at it with all your heart, as working for the Lord, not for human masters, since you know that you will receive an inheritance from the Lord as a reward. It is the Lord Christ you are serving" (Colossians 3:23–24 NIV).

## Question
Do you see your work as a holy calling from God?

*Father, help me to see my work as a holy calling from you.*

# Blessing Those Who Curse You

*"Leave him alone; let him curse, for the LORD has told him to.
It may be that the LORD will look upon my misery
and restore to me his covenant blessing instead of his curse today."*

2 SAMUEL 16:11–12 NIV

As David's enemies were increasing and he was fleeing the city from his son Absalom, who was seeking to take his throne, a man named Shimei began heaving rocks and cursing David as he passed by.

What does God desire to accomplish with those who wrong us? Has he brought this affront to find out what is in your heart today? Will you seek revenge? Or will you find the grace to allow God to carry out vengeance in his time if it is needed?

A. W. Tozer tells us, "It is doubtful whether God can bless a man greatly until He has hurt him deeply."[9] God allows storms of conflict in relationships at times in order to accomplish a deeper work in our character. Are you willing to enter this school? He brings us through these tests as preparation for greater use in the kingdom. God uses adversity to make spiritual deposits in our lives so we can have greater authority to be his witness.

## Question
Is there someone in your life you need to forgive today?

*Father, I choose to forgive _____ today. Give me the grace today to love them as you would love them.*

# The Value of Hard Places

*Death is at work in us but it releases life in you.*
2 CORINTHIANS 4:12 TPT

Being forced into hard places gives us a whole new perspective on life. Things we once held dear no longer hold the same value. Small things become big things, and what we once thought big no longer carries such importance.

These hard places allow us to identify with the sufferings of others. They keep us from having a shallow view of the hardships of others and allow us to truly identify with them. Those who speak of such trials from no experience often judge others who have had such hardship.

Those who have walked in hard places immediately have a kinship with others who have walked there also. They do not need to explain; they merely look at one another with mutual respect and admiration for their common experience. They know that death has worked a special thing in them. This death leads to life in others because of the hard places God has taken them through.

It is impossible to appreciate any valley experience while you are in it. However, once you have reached the top of the mountain, you are able to appreciate what terrain you have passed through. You are able to appreciate the beauty of the experience and lay aside the sorrow and pain it may have produced.

Death works in you for a greater purpose. If you are there today, be assured that God is producing something of much greater value than you will ever know.

## Question

Do you need special grace for the season in which you find yourself?

*Father, thank you that your grace is sufficient for every trial I may encounter.*

# God's Tests

*"What have I done? What is my crime?*
*How have I wronged your father, that he is trying to kill me?"*
1 Samuel 20:1 NIV

The cost of being one of God's anointed can be great. Those whom God has anointed for service and influence in his kingdom go through a special preparation. David was anointed to be the next king over Israel. Shortly after this, while still a young boy, he was brought into King Saul's service to play music in Saul's court. While there, the opportunity to stand up against Goliath elevated David for his next stage of development as future king. As his popularity grew so did Saul's jealousy. David would become a fugitive because of Saul's jealousy. However, even Saul's jealousy was God's instrument for molding and shaping David.

When God anoints us, it often is accompanied by some severe tests. These tests are designed to prepare us for the calling God has on our life. Should we fail these tests, God cannot elevate us to the next level.

## Question
What if God has chosen you for a specific purpose in his kingdom? Are you passing the tests he is bringing about in your life?

*Father, I thank you for every test you bring my way to see what is in my heart and how I will respond.*

# Hindrances to Christ's Rule

*The weapons of our warfare are not carnal but mighty in God*
*for pulling down strongholds.*
2 CORINTHIANS 10:4 NKJV

The Bible says when Christ comes to live in your heart, old things pass away, all things become new (see 2 Corinthians 5:17). The Lord has put a new spirit in us. Previously, I could not understand why so many of us who proclaimed Christ had such little impact on the kingdom of darkness. It seemed to me that our culture should be affected much more if his children walked in the light as Jesus did.

Then God took me through a time of testing that led to a discovery of influences that affected the way I viewed people and circumstances subconsciously. I discovered this was a stronghold that had been implanted many generations earlier. Because the stronghold operated on a subconscious level, I did not easily recognize it. Strongholds keep us from being free to reflect Christ in and through our lives because they require allegiance until they are dealt with. A stronghold of fear, control, rebellion, insecurity, idolatry, pride, or bitterness may be hidden until it is revealed through circumstances.

All strongholds are built in our lives as a result of seeking to meet one or more of the basic needs God has created in us. Once we believe a lie that God cannot meet a need without our effort, we open our spirit to a stronghold.

## Question

Are you ineffective in your Christian experience? Are there besetting sins that seem to recur in your life?

*God, show me the strongholds affecting my life today and help me to repent of their influence. Father, deliver me from their influence.*

# God's Word and God's Work

*O Lord our God, let your sweet beauty rest upon us. Come work with us,*
*and then our works will endure; you will give us success in all we do.*
PSALM 90:17 TPT

Martin Luther brought the *Word* of God back to the people. Today, God is bringing the *work* of God back to the people. God never intended the clergy to be the primary distribution channel of his gospel. You and I in the workplace are that distribution channel.

The local church is simply where his army is equipped and released into the world to affect every aspect of society. Today, God is establishing mini battalions in the form of prayer groups and Bible studies in the workplace. He is igniting the silent remnant of workplace believers who have not realized until now that their work really is their ministry. It is a holy calling on par with vocational ministry.

Our local churches should be viewed as mini battleships designed to raise an army of qualified warriors who can pray, create, and influence their workplaces and industries with a biblical worldview. We must be reminded of God's perfect plan found in Ephesians 4:11–13 (NKJV):

> He Himself gave some to be apostles, some prophets, some evangelists, and some pastors and teachers, for the equipping of the saints for the work of ministry, for the edifying of the body of Christ, till we all come to the unity of the faith and of the knowledge of the Son of God, to a perfect man, to the measure of the stature of the fullness of Christ.

## Question
Do you see yourself as the primary distribution tool of the gospel for God?

*Father, thank you that the work of God is just as important as the Word of God.*

# Attack on Identities

*For this reason God gave them over to their own disgraceful and vile passions. Enflamed with lust for one another, men and women ignored the natural order and exchanged normal sexual relations for homosexuality. Women engaged in lesbian conduct, and men committed shameful acts with men, receiving in themselves the due penalty for their deviation.*

ROMANS 1:26–27 TPT

We're living in a time throughout the world where human identity is being attacked like never before. One of the meanings of Satan's name is "deceiver." The Bible warns, "The evil men and sorcerers will progress from bad to worse, deceived and deceiving, as they lead people further from the truth" (2 Timothy 3:13).

The Bible teaches us that there are only two genders—male and female. "But from the beginning God created male and female" (Mark 10:6). Any effort to claim anything different is rooted in deception. The devil is seeking to deceive many in an effort to destroy lives and bring confusion to people's identity.

Those who are struggling with their sexual identities are seeking love and acceptance in a distorted reality. Satan is attacking them at the core of their identities—how God created them in his image. It is the saddest of all conditions. Those caught up in this lie need our prayers and our love, but we must not retreat from the truth of God's Word in this battle. We must not succumb to the world's deceptive ploys to require God's people to compromise God's Word in this area. Sin is sin, and no one sin is greater than another.

## Question
Do you know someone caught in an identity crisis?

*Pray for anyone God shows you who may be caught in this identity deception.*

# In the Zone

*"Be strong and very courageous. Be careful to obey all the law my servant Moses gave you; do not turn from it to the right or to the left, that you may be successful wherever you go."*

JOSHUA 1:7 NIV

In sports, there is a term known as "in the zone." It is a description of a person executing his skills so well that total concentration is taking place, and the athlete is performing flawlessly.

I grew up playing competitive golf. I turned pro out of college for a few years, but later God led me away from playing professionally. When I played competitively, I knew when I was in the zone and when I wasn't. A few years ago, I played in my club championship. It was the opening round, and I was in the zone. I could visualize the swing so well; it was like a movie picture in my mind. I knew that if I could make the right swing, the outcome would take care of itself. That day I shot 4-under-par 68. I went on to win the golf tournament.

Obedience in the Christian life is being in the zone. When we live a life of obedience, we begin to experience the reality of God like never before. Wisdom grows in our life. Meaning and purpose are accelerated. In the early church, the Hebrews gained wisdom through obedience. Later, the Greeks were characterized as gaining wisdom through reason and analysis. Today, we live in a very Greek-influenced church. Many Christians determine if they will obey based on whether the outcome will be beneficial to them. Imagine if the early followers of God had adopted this philosophy. No walls would have fallen down at Jericho. No Red Sea would have parted. No one would have been healed. Trust and obey. Leave the outcome to God.

## Question
### Are you abiding in Christ daily?

*Father, help me to abide in the vine of your presence all day long.*

# Discovering Your Purpose

*You know me inside and out, you know every bone in my body; you know exactly how I was made, bit by bit, how I was sculpted from nothing into something.*
PSALM 139:13–16 MSG

If you are going to discover how God wants to use your life and work, you must know why you were created. If you don't, you will inevitably use the things you do as the basis for fulfillment in your life, which will only lead to frustration and disappointment.

First and foremost, God created you to know him and to have an intimate relationship with him. In fact, God says that if a man is going to boast about anything in life, "boast about this: that they have the understanding to know me" (Jeremiah 9:24 NIV). Mankind's relationship with God was lost in the garden when Adam and Eve sinned. Jesus' death on the cross, however, allows us to restore this relationship with God and to have an intimate fellowship with him. The apostle Paul came to understand this when he said, "I gave up all that inferior stuff so I could know Christ personally, experience his resurrection power, be a partner in his suffering, and go all the way with him to death itself" (Philippians 3:10–11 MSG).

As you develop your relationship with God, he will begin to reveal his purpose for your life. "'For I know the plans I have for you,' declares the LORD" (Jeremiah 29:11 NIV).

## Question
How can you grow in your intimate relationship with God?

*Father, thank you for allowing me to have an intimate relationship with you and for giving me a unique purpose.*

# Sacred versus Secular

*The LORD God took the man
and put him in the garden of Eden
to tend and keep it.*
GENESIS 2:15 NKJV

Imagine for a moment that Jesus has just completed his three years of training with the disciples. He has been crucified and is now commissioning the Twelve to go into the world and disciple the nations.

Now imagine him also making this statement to them: "Dear brothers, it is now time for you to share what you have learned from me. However, as you share with others, be sure that you keep what I taught you separate from your work life. The principles I have shared with you only apply in situations outside your office, workshop, or store. Do not make them fit into this context. The miracles you saw in me can only be done in certain situations outside work life. Keep this in mind when thinking about praying for the sick or the lost. These truths will not work in the marketplace."

These are the thoughts expressed so much in our day and time although they are not expressed in such direct terms. Jesus came as a carpenter. He was a man given to work with his hands and to provide an honest service to his fellow man. He did not come as a priest although he was both a King and a priest (Revelation 1:6). When it came time to recruit those for whom the church would be founded, he chose twelve men from the workplace—a fisherman, a tax collector, a doctor, and so on.

## Question
Are you embracing your work life as a holy calling?

*Father, thank you that my work is a holy calling from you.*

# Jesus Was a Workplace Minister

*"Isn't this the carpenter? Isn't this Mary's son and the brother of James, Joseph, Judas and Simon?"...And they took offense at him.*

MARK 6:3 NIV

Jesus was a carpenter until age thirty. We can imagine Jesus making a table in his carpentry shop with his mother standing by, playfully observing. Isn't it amazing that God allowed his son to work as a carpenter until age thirty before he began his public ministry? What does that say about the importance of daily work and how our Father in heaven sees work as a holy calling? Do not despise your daily work. Instead, see it as a holy calling and a place to manifest his glory in how you do your work. The words *work* and *worship* come from the same Hebrew word, *avodah*.

Work, in its different forms, is mentioned more than eight hundred times in the Bible—more than all the words used to express worship, music, praise, and singing combined. God created work, and he is a worker. "My father is always at his work to this very day, and I too am working" (John 5:17).

God has called you and me to reflect his glory in our work.

## Question
How can you worship God through your work?

*Father, thank you for giving me work through which I can glorify you.*

# Sails without Wind

*God stilled the storm, calmed the waves, and he hushed the hurricane winds
to only a whisper. We were so relieved, so glad as he guided us safely to harbor
in a quiet haven.*
PSALM 107:29–30 TPT

Imagine for a moment you began an exciting sailing adventure. You've been trained to navigate and sail on the ocean and be ready should trouble arise. However, midway through the journey, your resources have dried up. It almost seems as if God has intentionally destroyed all the skills you had gained to deal with the weather and the obstacles, and your sails are now damaged. Even your engine has broken down. And your oars were lost overboard. You're stuck in the middle of the ocean, and there is no wind. You are, as they say, "up the creek without a paddle."

All of this leads you to the end of yourself, and you say, *Lord, I don't know why you brought me out here only to die.* The silence is deafening.

Finally, the Lord speaks, *Yes, you are right. I did bring you out here. I did destroy your sails. I did break your engine. And yes, I do want you dead—not in a physical sense but in a spiritual sense. In order that you may truly live. You see, my child, you cannot do anything without my grace and power in your life.*

You quietly yield. Suddenly, a gentle wave lifts the front of the boat. An easterly wind blows through the broken sail, and you realize God is moving your boat! Your role now is to steer it.

## Question

Do your sails no longer have wind to move you?

*Father, show me how to let you fill my sails with your wind.*

# Secret Places

*"I will give you the treasures of darkness and hidden riches of secret places, that you may know that I, the L*ord*, who call you by your name, am the God of Israel."*

Isaiah 45:3 nkjv

When God takes you to a depth of soul experience, be alert to new truths and new perspectives. During these times God often leads us to amazing new discoveries.

Bible teacher F. B. Meyer once observed:

Whenever you get into a prison of circumstances, be on the watch. Prisons are rare places for seeing things. It was in prison that Bunyan saw his wondrous allegory, and St. Paul met the Lord, and St. John looked through heaven's open door, and Joseph saw God's mercy. God has no chance to show his mercy to some of us except when we are in some sore sorrow.[10]

I began writing *TGIF: Today God Is First* daily devotionals in the middle of a seven-year period of darkness. Today hundreds of thousands of people around the world in 105 countries read the devotionals each day. God revealed to me secret things that have benefited countless others. Writing has become a central focus of God's work in me. If I had not gone through that dark time, I wouldn't be an author today.

When you go through a trial of adversity, you need to understand that God is performing radical surgery on your life designed to give you a new heart. He will reveal treasures from these secret places if you are willing to walk through the process patiently.

## Question
Has God placed you in a season of isolation?

*Father, I pray you reveals secret things in hidden places so I may know you better.*

# Two by Two

*Two are better than one,*
*because they have a good return for their labor.*

ECCLESIASTES 4:9 NIV

God made us to need others. We may not discover this until we fail—fail in a business, a marriage, a close friendship, or in a client relationship. We are incomplete without the ongoing input from others into our lives. An independent spirit is one of the most detestable sins from God's viewpoint. It is the highest form of pride. "Where there is strife, there is pride, but wisdom is found in those who take advice" (Proverbs 13:10).

David had Jonathan. Paul had Silas. John Wesley had George Whitefield. Martin Luther had Philip Melanchthon, who was fourteen years younger. Martin Luther learned that he needed someone in his life to complete the work God called him to do. Luther had the greatest respect for this friend who helped him reform the church of that time and the church as we know it at present. Luther learned a great deal from Melanchthon, who was a great scholar at a young age. He could speak several languages, and he became a professor of Greek at the new University of Wittenberg at twenty-one years of age. This was ten months after Luther posted his famous theses on the church door in Wittenberg. Melanchthon helped shape the protestant movement of the sixteenth century through his research, writings, moral purpose, and religious conscience. Luther and Melanchthon became inseparable, and when they died, they were buried next to each other.[11]

## Question

Who has God placed in your life to complete you? Perhaps it is a mate. Perhaps it is a close friend. Perhaps it is a business partner.

*Father, thank you for putting people in my life to complete me.*

# When a Problem Becomes a Calling

*"As for the donkeys you lost three days ago, do not worry about them;*
*they have been found. And to whom is all the desire of Israel turned,*
*if not to you and your whole family line?"*

1 SAMUEL 9:20 NIV

Saul and his servant were out seeking his father's lost donkeys. This was symbolic of the waywardness of the nation of Israel. The people of Israel had just asked the prophet Samuel to have a king rule over them. This saddened God greatly, yet God granted their request.

Saul and his servant heard of a man of God named Samuel. "Perhaps this man of God can tell us where to find our donkeys," said the servant (author paraphrase). Isn't that just like us? We seek God to solve the issues related to material life. Saul was about to be crowned as king of Israel. His life would never be the same. What was he concerned about? His donkeys. We don't have to be worried about the material things of life if we are about the things God has called us to do.

God sent a messenger to Saul to inform him of his new career. The messenger also had to ease his mind about his donkeys, saying, "You don't need to worry about your business if you respond to the call of God on your life. All the material things will take care of themselves" (author paraphrase).

When God calls us, it often involves making major adjustments in our lives. Saul went from one kind of business to another. He went from working for his father to being a king.

## Question
What changes is God calling you to make today to join him in his work?

*Father, help me be an obedient son.*

# A Cause Greater than Yourself

*"Defend the defenseless, the fatherless and the forgotten, the disenfranchised and the destitute. Your duty is to deliver the poor and the powerless; liberate them from the grasp of the wicked."*

PSALM 82:3–4 TPT

God raises up leaders to take on causes that are much greater than themselves. However, these causes are often first birthed as a result of a personal crisis or conviction.

Martin Luther King Jr. had a personal conviction that racial discrimination was wrong. He sought to change this through preaching and nonviolent demonstrations. It wasn't long before this became the conviction of others, and it became a movement larger than any one person.

William Wilberforce was a political statesman in England. He came to Christ when he was twenty-eight years old. He began to have personal convictions about slavery in England, and he committed his life to the goal of destroying slavery. He finally achieved his goal after thirty years of work. His work also resulted in sixty-four world-changing initiatives before he died.

William Wallace was burdened about the persecution his country received from the wicked English king named Edward Longshanks. Born in 1272, Wallace grew up under the persecution from the wicked king. When he was older, he led a rebellion against England that resulted in the freedom for the nation of Scotland. The popular movie *Braveheart* was based on the story of William Wallace.

My own ministry to those in the workplace first began as a personal crisis. This developed later into a call to serve believers in the marketplace.

## Question
Has God allowed a crisis in your life?

*Father, I pray you use my crisis events to bring me into my larger story.*

# The New Employee

*We are like common clay jars that carry this glorious treasure within,
so that this immeasurable power will be seen as God's, not ours.*

2 CORINTHIANS 4:7 TPT

What would happen if Jesus took your place for a year in your workplace? Let's consider some hypothetical things that he might do.

He would do his work with excellence. He would be known around the office for the great work he did (Proverbs 22:29).

He would develop new ideas for doing things better (Ephesians 3:20).

He would hang out with sinners to develop a relationship with them and speak to them about the Father (Matthew 9:10).

He would strategically pray for each worker about their concerns and their needs. He would even pray for those who disliked him (Matthew 5:44).

He would rally the office to support a needy family during Christmas (Jeremiah 22:16).

He would offer to pray for those who were sick in the office and see them get healed (Matthew 14:14).

He would honor the boss and respect him or her (Titus 2:9).

He would consider the boss as his authority in his workplace (Romans 13:1).

He would be truthful in all his dealings and never exaggerate for the sake of advancement (Psalm 15:2).

He would be concerned about his city (Luke 19:41).

He would always have a motive to help others become successful, even at his own expense (Proverbs 16:2).

Hmm. Sounds like some good ideas we could each model.

## Question
How many of these things are you doing?

*Father, help me manifest your presence and power in my workplace.*

# Knowing Our Limits

*Those who work their land will have abundant food,*
*but those who chase fantasies will have their fill of poverty.*
PROVERBS 28:19 NIV

King David often demonstrated an entrepreneurial spirit. He grew up as a shepherd boy and later became Israel's greatest warrior. He responded to opportunities, like the time when no one would fight Goliath. He asked what would be done for the man who defeated Goliath and learned that the victor would not have to pay taxes and he'd get Saul's daughter in marriage.

David learned an important lesson somewhere along the way that each of us should learn. As an entrepreneur, the greatest danger is engaging ourselves in activities in which God never intended us to be involved. This is poor stewardship of what God has entrusted to us.

When the Philistines attacked David, he always inquired of God as to whether he was to counterattack. When he was attacked a second time on one occasion, David asked God whether he was to attack yet. This time God said, "Yes, but wait until you hear the sound of marching in the mulberry trees" (2 Samuel 5:24, author paraphrase). This story tells us that David had learned an important lesson about staying vertical in his relationship with God at all times. He was an opportunist but only through the filter of the Holy Spirit in his life.

## Question
How do you approach opportunities? Do you consider the merits of the opportunity only? Or do you inquire of God as to whether he desires you to pursue?

*Holy Spirit, direct me as I seek to use the skills you have given me.*

# It's Time for a Funeral

*I have been crucified with Christ and I no longer live,*
*but Christ lives in me.*
GALATIANS 2:20 NIV

There's nothing wrong with you that a good funeral won't solve," I said to the man. "I'll even send you flowers!" He smiled in response. I was speaking figuratively to the man who was feeling pressured about an issue in his life.

His problem was the same problem most of us have—too much of "us" and not enough of Jesus and the cross. Many of our daily problems in life can be solved by coming to an end of ourselves so Jesus can take over. The psalmist said, "Precious in the sight of the LORD is the death of His saints" (Psalm 116:15 NKJV).

The apostle Paul recognized the need for a funeral, too, when he penned these words:

> What shall we say then? Shall we continue in sin that grace may abound? Certainly not! How shall we who died to sin live any longer in it? Or do you not know that as many of us as were baptized into Christ Jesus were baptized into His death? Therefore we were buried with Him through baptism into death, that just as Christ was raised from the dead by the glory of the Father, even so we also should walk in newness of life. (Romans 6:1–4 NKJV)

Whenever we stress over a matter, get angry over a daily circumstance, or seek to have our own way, it is a sign there is still life in the grave.

## Question
Do you need to have a good funeral? Send yourself some flowers today.

*Father, help me to die to self so only Christ lives through me.*

# The Works of the Flesh

*You may say to yourself, "My power and the strength of my hands have produced this wealth for me."*
DEUTERONOMY 8:17 NIV

We've all heard someone say, "He's a self-made man." What are they saying in this statement? Are they saying that this individual achieved success by his hard work and sweat? Many a person has achieved success through honest, hard work. There is a danger for any of us who may have achieved significance through our work. That danger is the belief that we achieved it through our own efforts apart from God's grace and mercy. When we live in this belief, we assert that we are entitled to certain rights and privileges because of the position we have earned and feel we deserve.

The prodigal son's brother who refused to celebrate the wayward son's return was a man who felt he was entitled to certain rights. He saw himself as one who had been faithful to his responsibilities and deserving of more attention. He could not appreciate his brother's failure and the pain of falling into a sinful life because, in his mind, he had never failed. This pride kept him from experiencing God's real grace. This is how legalism develops in believers. It grows into a cold heart and an insensitive attitude toward others who may have stumbled in their lives. This same brother did not truly understand the love of his father apart from works, for he felt he gained acceptance only by doing his job.

## Question

Do you feel accepted by God regardless of what you do? Have you wrongfully viewed your successes as something you alone have achieved?

*God, allow me to see life's successes and failures through your eyes.*

# His Work, His Way

*"Therefore I also have made you contemptible and base before all the people, because you have not kept My ways but have shown partiality in the law."*
MALACHI 2:9 NKJV

We can fulfill our calling on earth in four ways:

1. My work, my way: When you and I live in this world without Christ, we live a life just as Esau lived his life. Esau despised his birthright and failed to enter into a relationship with God that allowed him to fulfill his destiny. In essence, Esau fulfilled his work his way. His life represented the carnal life of the flesh.

2. His work, my way: When you and I become born again by the Spirit of God, we begin to focus our attention on living for Christ. We realize it is his work we are doing, but it takes time before we learn what it means to do his work his way.

3. My work, his way: As the Holy Spirit does his work in us, we learn to walk with God. We discover what it means to see our work as his work, and we desire to do it his way.

4. His work, his way: When we begin to walk with God, we realize that all we do is his work and he calls us to do it his way. When we begin to walk with God in this manner, we begin to see the kingdom of God manifested in our working lives. We begin to experience his power and learn what it means to do his work his way.

## Question
### Which best describes your life today?

*Lord, help me to learn to do your work your way.*

# The Power of a Mentor

*"Let us go with you, for we have heard that God is with you."*
ZECHARIAH 8:23 NKJV

Few men of God have become extraordinary people of faith without the influence of mentors. A mentor is one who takes responsibility for the spiritual and sometimes physical care of another. It requires a commitment from the teacher and the student.

Elijah mentored Elisha. Elisha became one of the greatest prophets in the entire Bible. One of the primary reasons for this was Elisha's hunger. Elisha wanted a double portion of Elijah's spirit. It was this hunger that drove Elisha to be sold out to God's purposes for his life.

I have been privileged to have had many mentors throughout my spiritual life. In each stage of my maturity, God brought new mentors who had unique gifts that the previous mentor did not have. God has given me the hunger for a double portion of those positive attributes of my mentors. This desire is sorely missing among many today. I fail to see the hunger among many who could be used greatly in the kingdom. Instead, the cares of this world distract them. It is an attitude of à la carte versus an attitude of pressing in to the full measure of what God might have for them.

God may have brought mentors into your life to prepare you to be a man of God with great anointing. However, there is a time of training and waiting to prove out your own faith.

## Question

Who are the people of God whom he has placed in your life? Are you learning from them? Are you seeking a double portion of their anointing? What prevents you from gaining from their wisdom and experience?

*Father, guide me to the perfect mentor I can learn from.*

# Masquerading as a Dentist

*Yes, feast on all the treasures of the heavenly realm and fill your thoughts with heavenly realities, and not with the distractions of the natural realm.*

COLOSSIANS 3:2 TPT

Hello, my name is Dr. Bengel. I am a Christian, masquerading as a dentist. What is your name?" I laughed as I met this man for the very first time. He was boldly proclaiming that he wanted to be known by who he was in Christ instead of who he was in his occupation.

If Christ is Lord over all of your life, then he must be Lord over your work too. Our identity must be wrapped up in who we are, not just what we do. Whatever we do for work, we should do it in the name of the Lord Jesus (see Colossians 3:17) with a concern for his approval and in a manner that honors him.

The Spirit empowers us to live and work with Christlikeness. Christ gives the Holy Spirit to help us live in a way that pleases him, which has enormous implications for how we do our jobs.

God values our work even when the product has no spiritual value. A common measure of the significance of a job is its perceived value from the eternal perspective. Will the work "last"? Will it "really count" for eternity? The assumption is that God values work for eternity but not work for the here and now. This is not a biblical truth but heresy.

Your work does matter to God. You are called to first to be a Christian but masquerading as a doctor, lawyer, construction worker, secretary, or whatever.

## Question
Do you see your vocation from an eternal perspective?

*Father, help me to see my work as a calling and a ministry unto you.*

# Called to Someone versus Something

*The Lord Yahweh answered him, "Arise and go! I have chosen this man to be my special messenger. He will be brought before kings, before many nations, and before the Jewish people to give them the revelation of who I am."*

ACTS 9:15 TPT

Sometimes we can place the idea of God's calling on our lives too much on the thing we do versus the one we are called to serve. Paul said that he was "called to be an apostle." Some feel that if we each do not have a "special call," then we are second-class citizens.

Paul saw his calling like any other believer's call to salvation and obedience. Paul had a dramatic encounter with the Lord that had broad significance to the rest of the body of Christ. And there are some assignments that are going to impact the body of Christ more than others. However, this is not the case for every believer, and we should not feel slighted.

Every believer shares the same basic calling with Paul, "And you also are among those Gentiles who are called to belong to Jesus Christ," as he says in Romans 1:6 (NIV). Paul was saying to the Roman Christians that their call was the same as his. They were not all apostles, but they were all "called to belong to Jesus Christ."

For most of us, God will work out his calling upon our lives in many different and varied ways. Like Paul and the rest of the New Testament Christians, we are all called with the same glorious calling and thus stand as equals before God.

## Question

Do you ever feel you are "less than" because others seem more spiritual than you?

*Father, thank you for calling me to this ministry in my workplace.*

# Greek versus Hebraic

*"I have bent Judah, My bow, fitted the bow with Ephraim,
and raised up your sons, O Zion, against your sons, O Greece,
and made you like the sword of a mighty man."*
ZECHARIAH 9:13 NKJV

In the early church there was an emphasis on developing a heart toward God. This was the Hebraic way. The Scriptures were not accessible to them like they are for us. So the relationship with God was the key focus. God related to his people on a personal and intimate level. And obedience was the key to a healthy relationship with God. Decisions were not made based on reason and analysis but by obedience. "The fear of the LORD is the beginning of wisdom" (Psalm 111:10).

This is why many of the miracles performed in the Bible went against natural reason (e.g., feeding five thousand, crossing the Red Sea, retrieving a coin from a fish's mouth, walking around Jericho to win a battle, etc.). God constantly wanted to check the leader's obedience, not his knowledge. Knowledge and reason came into the early church with the Greek scholars in subsequent centuries. Gradually the focus on knowledge and reason became more accepted in the church and replaced intimacy with Jesus.

Loss of intimacy with God has been the fallout of the influence of the Greek spirit. The primary focus has been teaching and discipleship instead of the development of a personal and intimate relationship with God. This has resulted in a form of religion but one without power.

## Question
Is your focus on gaining more knowledge or growing in intimacy and power with Jesus?

*Father, help me to know you intimately.*

# Out of Your Comfort Zone

*Yes, God is more than ready to overwhelm you with every form of grace,
so that you…overflow with abundance in every good thing you do.*
2 CORINTHIANS 9:8 TPT

I made a career change in my early twenties that required me to find a new job. I decided to apply for a job selling advertising on golf score cards. Usually this meant going into small towns and making sales calls to small retail businesses in that community. Not an easy job for a rookie in his first sales job.

The two business owners that interviewed me were non-Christian owners who refused to hire me because my answers to their questions led me to discussing my faith in Christ. They felt I should be in the ministry, not sales. However, they reluctantly decided to take a chance on me and sent me to small towns in Kentucky to sell golf scorecards in the middle of winter. I didn't know that they were trying to set me up for failure and certainly didn't think I had any chance of success.

I got into my Volkswagen bus and headed for the hills of Kentucky. I told the Lord I was not qualified for this, and he would have to help me be successful. After a week of selling and sleeping in my car at night, I returned with a full inventory of sales from several cities. The owners looked at me with shock. They couldn't believe I had been successful. I would go on to work two years at this company, become an executive, and lead one of the partners to Christ. God delights in showing his children his power so you can abound in your good work.

## Question
Do you have a major challenge in your work life?

*God, help me be successful in my assignment.*

# Forgiving Ourselves

*If we freely admit our sins when his light uncovers them, he will be faithful to forgive us every time. God is just to forgive us our sins because of Christ, and he will continue to cleanse us from all unrighteousness.*

1 John 1:9 tpt

The criminal was condemned to life in prison. Then one day something amazing happened. The guard came and opened the jail cell. "You are free to go. Someone else is taking your place," said the guard.

"How can this be? I am still guilty!" said the prisoner.

"Your debt has been paid. You are free to leave," said the guard once more.

The prisoner decided not to leave. "I cannot allow another to pay my debt," said the prisoner. Because of his pride he chose to remain in bondage.

The hardest person to forgive sometimes is ourselves. It is especially hard for high achievers to forgive themselves. We think we are above such failure. However, the Bible says we all sin, and it is impossible to remedy that sin by ourselves.

"If we boast that we have no sin, we're only fooling ourselves and are strangers to the truth" (1 John 1:8). The question is not whether we will sin; the question is what we will do when we sin

When you come to Jesus with your sin, there is nothing more you can do besides confess and renounce your sin. Sometimes it may require restitution to others. However, once you confess your sin and ask forgiveness, it is no longer on God's ledger of debts.

## Question
Do you have difficulty forgiving yourself?

*Father, I accept your forgiveness because of your death on the cross.*

# Why Work?

*Even when we were with you, we commanded you this: If anyone will not work, neither shall he eat. For we hear that there are some who walk among you in a disorderly manner, not working at all, but are busybodies.*

2 THESSALONIANS 3:10–12 NKJV

Jesus probably spent most of his life working in his family's carpentry business. We know almost nothing of his youth from adolescence until he began his public ministry at about age thirty. But we know that his father was a carpenter (Matthew 13:55) and that Jesus also practiced the trade (Mark 6:3).

Jesus may have continued his occupation even after he began to teach and travel. Rabbis (or teachers) of the day commonly spent anywhere from one-third to one-half of their time working (most likely with their hands) to provide for themselves. Jesus' opponents attacked him on numerous grounds, but they never accused him of laziness or freeloading. Indeed, he was known to them as a carpenter.

Paul tells the Thessalonians that anyone who has an ability to work should do so. Our work allows us to demonstrate integrity and provide for our families and others in need. Our vocations often allow us to connect with nonbelievers and encourage us to live out our calling upon our lives while giving us the opportunity to experience his power in the midst of daily challenges. Our work can be a place of worship when we do it with a motive to glorify him.

Today, view your work the way God views your work. It is your primary call.

## Question

Do you ever see work as a curse instead of a place of worship?

*Father, thank you for allowing me to work and express your life through my work.*

# Greater Works Shall You Do

*"Jesus of Nazareth, a Man attested by God to you by miracles, wonders, and signs which God did through Him in your midst, as you yourselves also know."*
ACTS 2:22 NKJV

The Gospels are full of miracles Jesus did while in human form. Let that sink in. It changes everything.

This does not deny the deity of Jesus incarnate. Still, Jesus lived on earth with self-imposed restriction to live as a man so he could show us what our lives can look like. This truth can often be missed if we forget that while Jesus was 100 percent God, he was also 100 percent man.

Jesus said of himself: "I tell you the truth, the Son can do nothing by himself. He does only what he sees the Father doing. Whatever the Father does, the Son also does" (John 5:19 NLT). The word *nothing* in Greek means what it does in English—"nothing."[12] Jesus acted in perfect unity with the Father. He also had a close relationship with the Holy Spirit. Scripture tells us the Holy Spirit was present during his conception (Matthew 1:20), his baptism (Luke 3:22), his temptation in the wilderness (Luke 4:1), his public ministry (Acts 10:38), his miracles (Matthew 12:28), his death (Hebrews 9:14), and his resurrection (Romans 8:11).

Jesus promised the disciples that, with his departure, the Holy Spirit would come to guide and give power to believers: "I tell you this timeless truth: The person who follows me in faith, believing in me, will do the same mighty miracles that I do—even greater miracles than these because I go to be with my Father!" (John 14:12 TPT).

## Question

How dependent on and obedient to the Holy Spirit are you so you can experience this same power?

*Father, thank you for allowing me to receive your power through your Holy Spirit.*

# God's Economy

*"To console those who mourn in Zion, to give them beauty for ashes, the oil of joy for mourning, the garment of praise for the spirit of heaviness; that they may be called trees of righteousness, the planting of the LORD, that He may be glorified."*

ISAIAH 61:3 NKJV

The world has its own economy that includes buying and selling, methods for getting ahead, and ways to advance a cause. It often includes distorting truth and manipulating people to get the desired outcome.

God has an economy in which we are called to operate that is very different from the world's economy. He says go low to get high, serve others instead of being served, give to receive, praise when you have heaviness, die to live, and forgive instead of getting even.

Living in God's economy is not always easy. However, when you live under this economy, your life will be blessed. You will experience supernatural living. You will receive from God things you never thought you'd receive or deserve to receive. We find a key truth of God's economy found in Joshua 24:13: "I have given you a land for which you did not labor, and cities which you did not build, and you dwell in them; you eat of the vineyards and olive groves which you did not plant."

What does this verse mean? It means sometimes your obedience may get you less than what you think you should get, but other times, you may get more. Obedience is the key to opening the windows of heaven in your life. God will open doors based on your obedience versus your skill and abilities.

## Question

Are you living in God's economy? If not, what adjustments do you need to make?

*Father, help me to live in your economy.*

# Creating a Memory

*The greatest among you will be your servant.*
MATTHEW 23:11 NIV

A business consultant was training more than three thousand employees of a grocery chain to approach their jobs with a goal of creating a memory for their customers. She stated that creating special experiences will distinguish one store from all others.

Johnny, a nineteen-year-old bagger with Down syndrome, went home and shared with his mother what the consultant said. They pondered how he could create a memory for his customers. Johnny often collected and meditated on inspirational thoughts. He decided to print and share these sayings, placing one in each of the bags of his customers. He said, "When I finish bagging someone's groceries, I put my thought of the day in their bag and say, 'Thanks for shopping with us.'"

One day the store manager noticed that all the customers were lined up at only one cashier station when there were other stations open. He began to panic, thinking the other stations were broken. After further investigation, he found this was not the case. Actually, customers wanted to come through Johnny's line in order to get his saying of the day.

One woman came up to the manager and said, "I used to come to the store once a week, but now I come in every day every time I go by." Johnny's example spread to other departments in the store. The florist began giving a flower to each florist customer. This one act by a bagger changed the entire climate of the store.[13]

## Question
How can you create a memory for someone in your workplace today?

*Father, help me create a memory for someone in my workplace today.*

# Manifesting God's Power

*The LORD spoke to Moses, saying, "Take the rod; you and your brother Aaron gather the congregation together. Speak to the rock before their eyes, and it will yield its water."*
NUMBERS 20:7–8 NKJV

The Bible says that Moses had a unique walk with God. He said Moses was the humblest man on earth and that he spoke with him face-to-face.

When Moses met God at the burning bush, God said, "Moses, I'm going to perform miracles through your staff." And he did. God turned Moses' staff into a snake. He brought plagues upon the nation and even parted the Red Sea with Moses' staff. Moses even struck the rock with his staff to bring forth water.

But later, God called Moses to operate on a new level. God called Moses to manifest his power through his words. "Speak to the rock, Moses!" But Moses, frustrated by the stiff-necked people, struck the rock out of anger instead. Amazingly, in spite of his disobedience, God still allowed Moses to get water out of the rock. God will often work through your anointing, just for the sake of others, even when you do it in your flesh. But it will be at a great cost. Like Moses, you will not enter your promised land.

God is calling us to manifest breakthroughs by operating at times as God did—by speaking to the problem. Be available to the Holy Spirit at times when God calls you to use your authority to manifest his power in a situation that needs a breakthrough.

## Question

Is God calling you to manifest his kingdom through a higher level of relationship with him. Are you willing?

*Father, I pray you manifest your power through me today.*

# Deep Things

*He uncovers deep things out of darkness,*
*and brings the shadow of death to light.*
JOB 12:22 NKJV

God uses the dark times in our lives to reveal greater depths of understanding of his ways. The only way we can receive these deeper things is to be driven to the depths of darkness. It is here that we discover important truths that he plans to use in our lives and the lives of others.

The first phase involves a depth of soul experience that often causes great pain in our lives. We seek God for deliverance from the incredible emotional pain this causes. Our primary motivation for seeking God is to get out of our pain.

During this time, God meets us in the depths of darkness. We discover that he never left us but is in the midst of the darkness. We develop a new relationship with God. Gradually our motivation turns from removal of pain to love and intimacy with God.

God will make spiritual deposits into your life during this season. Others will be blessed through your life as you serve them through your work-life calling. God reveals deep things in darkness that will be revealed in the light.

If you find yourself in great distress, know that God will bring your deep shadows into the light. The key to your deliverance is becoming satisfied in God. He becomes your life. You will know your deliverance is near when your circumstances simply don't matter to you anymore.

Love the Lord your God with all your soul and see what things he will show you in the deep things of darkness.

## Question
Do you find yourself in a place of despair?

*Father, I cast all my cares upon you today. Thank you for your grace that sustains me.*

# God's Proving Ground for Faith

*This was only so that the generations of the children of Israel might be taught to know war, at least those who had not formerly known it.*

JUDGES 3:2 NKJV

God brought the nation of Israel into the promised land of Canaan through Joshua. After Joshua, there came an entire generation who had very little experience in fighting battles like the ones fought by Joshua. Training and testing God's people is one of God's important strategies that enable his children to succeed in spiritual warfare. This is why we do not live a life free of trials. These trials are sent specifically to see if our faith is real or simply empty words.

God allows circumstances to provide opportunity to prove your faith. It is only when we are tested in battle that we become skilled warriors. You can be confident God will allow trials to come your way through situations like an unreasonable boss, a vendor who refuses to pay, a false assault on your character, a lawsuit, or a difficult relationship that requires unconditional love. These battles are sent your way to test what you know in the mind so that they might become part of your heart.

You will discover whether you have passed the tests or if you need more battles that will give you the opportunity to learn the art of spiritual warfare. Do not fear these battles. God has already given you the victory if you choose complete dependence and obedience to him. Then you will become one of God's greatest warriors, skilled in spiritual warfare.

## Question
Do you find yourself in the middle of a battle?

*Father, thank you that your grace is sufficient in all things.*

# How God Makes Fishermen

*He said to them, "Follow Me,*
*and I will make you fishers of men."*
MATTHEW 4:19 NKJV

Our calling has three distinct stages on the way to becoming mature fishers of men who greatly impact God's kingdom. First, there is the gestation period. It may involve years of normal work experiences. Paul spent years in religious and political training, persecuting believers most of his early life. Moses spent years in the court of Pharaoh and forty years tending flocks in the desert. However, all these years were part of their preparation.

Next is the crisis stage. Sooner or later, God calls you into relationship with him. For many, like Paul, it comes through dramatic encounters like being blinded and spoken to personally by God. Some people are more difficult than others to reach and so require this level of crisis. This is a time when God requires us to undergo major changes before we can follow him fully. Paul's earthly experiences would be used in his calling to the religious and political leaders of his day. For Moses, the burning bush experience would begin his journey in which he would discover his ultimate calling after years of preparation.

Last is the fruit-bearing stage. God's power is manifested in your life. God takes all your experiences and uses them to build his kingdom in and through your life. Your obedience to this final call results in fruitfulness you could never imagine without the long preparation process.

## Question

What does God want to achieve in the stage of life you're in right now?

*Father, I pray your power is manifested in my life and I bear fruit for your kingdom, fulfilling my complete destiny through whatever is required.*

# Receiving Only from God

*"I will take nothing, from a thread to a sandal strap, and that I will not take anything that is yours, lest you should say, 'I have made Abram rich.'"*
GENESIS 14:23 NKJV

Abraham's nephew was a man named Lot. Lot was part of Abraham's household until the land on which they fed their flocks could no longer support both of their growing families and herds. Abraham allowed Lot to choose the land where he wanted to live. Lot chose the land of Sodom.

Afterward, four kings invaded Sodom, and Lot's family and goods were taken into captivity. When Abraham learned of this, he immediately gathered his best fighting men and pursued the armies to free Lot and his family. He was successful in freeing Lot's family and the families of Sodom. The king of Sodom was grateful to Abraham for what he did and wanted him to keep the goods he recovered. Abraham had made a decision before the battle that he would only keep what he recovered for his nephew Lot and a portion of the goods to give as payment to the men who fought.

Abraham understood the principle of receiving from God. He was a man with great integrity in God. He did not want to be known as someone who became wealthy because of the kindness of a wicked king.

As workplace believers, there are situations that allow us to manipulate, sweat, and toil our way to profit. There is also profit as a result of hard work done in obedience to our calling to the workplace. Knowing the difference in these two concepts is a sign of integrity before God.

## Question
Are you receiving the fruit of your labor in God?

*Father, show me how to receive by living a life of obedience.*

# Unwholesome Talk

*Never let ugly or hateful words come from your mouth,*
*but instead let your words become beautiful gifts that encourage others;*
*do this by speaking words of grace to help them.*
EPHESIANS 4:29 TPT

The way you interact with fellow employees at work can often determine whether you will be the leaven for Christ in your workplace or be viewed as one of the multitudes. Two defining situations in the workplace involve joke telling and discussions about employees and bosses.

If we laugh at off-color jokes, we give permission to the person telling the joke that it is fine to continue this activity in your presence. If we fail to laugh, we discourage this behavior. When someone is about to tell a joke in my presence, I stop them and ask, "Is this a clean joke? If not, I don't want to hear it." This will define future situations with that person, and it will get communicated to others in the office because of your response. You might become known as the religious person in your office, but that is okay.

Another situation is how you talk about management in front of other employees. In a workplace it can easily become a "we" versus "them" culture. If this happens, you violate Paul's command to honor those who employ you. "Exhort bondservants to be obedient to their own masters, to be well pleasing in all things, not answering back, not pilfering, but showing all good fidelity, that they may adorn the doctrine of God our Savior in all things" (Titus 2:9–10 NKJV).

Remember, you are always a witness at work, whether you use words or not.

## Question
What kind of witness are you at work?

*Father, help me be a good witness to those I work with daily.*

# Created for His Good Pleasure

*Even before we were born, God planned in advance our destiny
and the good works we would do to fulfill it!*
EPHESIANS 2:10 TPT

Eric Liddell was an Olympic runner from Britain who won a gold medal in the 1924 Paris Olympics. He was a man who had a deep commitment to the Lord and had plans of being a missionary. In the meantime, he knew God had given him a special gift to run, and he often said, "I feel God's pleasure when I run."

He spent years training and qualified for the Olympics. Finally, the day came for him to run in the games that were held in Paris. There was only one problem. One of his running events was held on Sunday. Liddell refused to run on Sunday, believing it dishonored the Lord's Sabbath. He held to his convictions and brought great persecution on himself. He made the decision that, even if it meant losing his opportunity to compete, he would not run. To Eric, God's laws were greater than man's applause. Just when the circumstances seemed hopeless, another situation arose that allowed Liddell to run on a different day.

God often tests our hearts to see if we will remain faithful to him at the cost of something important to us. Once he knows where our loyalty lies, he opens a new door that meets the desires of our hearts. Liddell won a gold medal and went on to serve God on the mission field.[14]

## Question

Does your life work bring pleasure to the Lord? Do you understand that God instilled certain gifts and talents in you so that he might find pleasure in his creation of you?

*Father, use my gifts and talents for your glory.*

# Treasures in Darkness

*I will give you hidden treasures, riches stored in secret places,*
*so that you may know that I am the LORD, the God of Israel,*
*who summons you by name.*
ISAIAH 45:3 NIV

I have never been in this place before. It is new ground for me, and I find I am way out of my comfort zone. I am scared to death to trust him at this level. I had to confess to the Lord I have not been able to accept or believe his love for me in this area." Those were the words I expressed to a friend when I was in a difficult place in my life. That day when I confessed those words, God led me to this passage of Scripture.

What we perceive as dark periods in our lives are designed to be treasures from God. They are actually riches stored in secret places. We cannot see those times in this light because of the often-accompanying pain or fear that prevents us from accepting these times as treasures. They have a particular purpose from God's viewpoint: "So that you may know that I am the LORD…who summons you by name."

You see, unless we are cast into times in which we are completely at God's mercy for breakthroughs in our lives, we will never experience God's faithfulness in those areas. We will never know how personal he is or that he can be trusted to meet the deepest needs in our lives. God wants each of us to know that we are "summoned by name." Every hair of our head is numbered. He knows every activity we are involved in. His love for you and me knows no bounds, and he will take every opportunity to demonstrate this to us.

## Question

Has God brought you into a place of darkness? Trust him today to reveal that hidden treasure that can be found in this darkness. Let him summon you by name.

*Father, I trust you for the place you have me today.*

# Prosperity in Afflictions

*The name of the second he called Ephraim:*
*"For God has caused me to be fruitful in the land of my affliction."*
GENESIS 41:52 NKJV

When Joseph was elevated to rule over the Egyptian kingdom, he revealed some profound truths gained from the experiences of his years of adversity. He named his first son Manasseh, for he said, "God has made me forget all my trouble and all my father's household" (Genesis 41:51 NIV). His second son was named Ephraim because, "God has made me fruitful in the land of my suffering" (v. 52 NIV).

Whenever God takes us through the land of affliction, he will do two things through that affliction: (1) He will bring such healing that we will be able to forget the pain, and (2) he will make us fruitful from the painful experiences.

God does not waste our afflictions if we allow him the freedom to complete the work in us. His desire is to create virtue that remains during the times of testing so that he can bring us into the place of fruitfulness in the very area of our testing. He has never promised to keep us from entering the valleys of testing, but he has promised to make us fruitful in them. He is the God who turns the Valley of Achor (meaning "trouble") into a door of hope (see Hosea 2:15).

## Question
Are you in the valley of affliction?

*God, I pray you will heal my memories and bring fruit from this very time.*

# Enlarging Your Territory

*"Oh, that You would bless me indeed,
and enlarge my territory."*
1 CHRONICLES 4:10 NKJV

He is mentioned only once in a brief description in the Old Testament, yet what he says and what his life conveys could fill volumes. He was a man whom God saw as worthy of a request that had significant consequences for him and his family. His name was Jabez. Here is how the Scripture describes him:

> Jabez was more honorable than his brothers. His mother had named him Jabez, saying, "I gave birth to him in pain." Jabez cried out to the God of Israel, "Oh, that you would bless me and enlarge my territory! Let your hand be with me, and keep me from harm so that I will be free from pain." And God granted his request. (1 Chronicles 4:9–10 NIV)

The only reason God will enlarge a person's territory is that he knows that person will use it responsibly. He will steward what is given in light of God's kingdom. God truly wants to increase our territory so we will have greater influence in the world around us. That territory can mean personal influence or physical territories.

It is nearly impossible to have a life without pain. Pain is often necessary to mold us and shape us. This is the only exception I have seen in Scripture. Jabez must have been quite a man with incredible integrity and purity of heart.

## Question

Are you this kind of person? Can God enlarge your territory and entrust you to use it for his purposes?

*Father, enlarge my territory and make me the kind of man worthy of such trust.*

# The Silver Coin

*For example: The Spirit gives to one the gift of the word of wisdom.*
*To another, the same Spirit gives the gift of the word of revelation knowledge.*
1 CORINTHIANS 12:8 TPT

Michael owned a home décor company, and his main supplier was in India. He had to make periodic trips to India to meet his suppliers. When his mentor learned of a planned trip to India, he said, "I believe you are to buy a silver coin to take with you on this trip, but I do not know the reason. God will show you how you are to use it." It was a strange word from his mentor, but after praying about it, Michael felt it was an instruction from the Lord; however, instead of one silver coin, he felt led to buy three silver coins.

He purchased the three coins and traveled to India. One evening he and the CEO of the supplier company were walking through the plant having a casual conversation. The Holy Spirit spoke to Michael and said, *Give the coin to this man.* Michael responded by telling the man he had a gift for him. The man was excited.

Upon receiving the silver coin, the man responded, "Oh, my. I am a collector of silver coins, and the one coin I have been missing is a US silver coin for my collection. This will complete my collection. How did you know?"

"I felt God wanted me to give this to you." The man shared how his uncle was also a silver coin collector. Michael pulled out a second coin and said, "I believe this coin is for your uncle."

Michael believed the third coin was for him to hold on to as a remembrance of this testimony of God speaking through his mentor.

## Question
Are you available to the Holy Spirit's promptings in your life?

*Father, help me to listen to your voice through others.*

# Adversity for Greater Use

*Though we experience every kind of pressure, we're not crushed. At times we don't know what to do, but quitting is not an option. We are persecuted by others, but God has not forsaken us. We may be knocked down, but not out. We continually share in the death of Jesus in our own bodies so that the resurrection life of Jesus will be revealed through our humanity.*

2 CORINTHIANS 4:8–10 TPT

The Bible is clear that all believers will experience some level of adversity in our lives. John Bunyan (1628–1688), the author of *The Pilgrim's Progress*, grew up in poverty and taught himself to read. Growing up, he struggled with feelings of not being forgiven by God and was tortured by visions of eternal punishment. His devout wife helped him to overcome his fear, but then, while still in her twenties, she died of a sudden illness. In his grief, Bunyan devoted himself to preaching. The English government, however, repeatedly imprisoned him for preaching without a license.

On one occasion, Bunyan was sentenced to three months in prison, but when he told the officials he intended to go on preaching, his sentence was extended to twelve years. John Bunyan experienced God's presence in a special way while he was in prison. In fact, it was in his cell that he penned his enduring classic, *The Pilgrim's Progress*. It's a book that could only have been written by a soul that was refined by the fires of adversity.

## Question
Are you in a place of extreme adversity?

*God, give me your grace to walk through this time with you.*

# "Not a Chance!"

*"Nothing is impossible with God!"*
LUKE 1:37 TPT

I walked into the doctor's office for my pre-op visit. The doctor came in and told me all about my procedure of arthroscopic knee surgery.

"So, doc. I have been told this is pretty routine. I have a golf outing I am responsible for that is four days after the surgery. Is there any chance I would be able to play golf that soon?" I asked.

"Not a chance," the doctor responded. I resigned myself to the fact that I'd have to host my friend's surprise fiftieth birthday celebration as a spectator. I prayed anyway that God would let me play.

My day of surgery came, and when I awoke, I was given my crutches and greeted in the recovery room by my wife. "How are you doing?" she asked.

"I feel groggy, but pretty good," I replied.

By that afternoon, I put away the crutches and began walking unaided. The doctor called to inquire about my progress. "Am I supposed to have soreness and pain from this procedure?" I said.

"Oh, yes. You should be pretty sore and experience some pain," said the doctor.

"Well," I said, "I have no pain and no soreness. I'm walking like I never had surgery!"

"That is hard to believe," said the doctor. "In fact, that is incredible!"

The next day, I could go up and down steps with full weight on my right knee. Only four days after surgery, I played 18 holes of golf for my friend's birthday. The day after the golf outing, I awoke with no soreness and no pain.

## Question
Do you need something special from God?

*Father, may I experience your miracles today.*

# Your Ministry to the Poor

*"Is it not to share your bread with the hungry, and that you bring to your house the poor who are cast out; when you see the naked, that you cover him, and not hide yourself from your own flesh?"*
ISAIAH 58:7 NKJV

For many years, I have read this passage without responding to it personally. I read it and moved on to the rest of my Bible reading without any action steps. It was just another verse of Scripture. Then one day the Holy Spirit asked me, *Os, how are you ministering to the poor in my name?* It was a very convicting question.

I realized I had no specific focus on the poor. Sure, I give to my local church that often gives to the poor. However, I was not directly involved in any specific activity that served the poor. I believed God was challenging me to change this.

Soon after that, God connected me with a Christian leader in the nation of Uganda. I had never been to a third-world nation. I had not seen poverty up close and personal. I decided this was God's answer to my prayer. Paying all my own expenses, I traveled to Uganda. I visited the camps where thousands of people have come to live—having abandoned their lands because of a twenty-year rebel war and the brutal treatment by a man named Joseph Kony, who killed and maimed many children. During my stay, I experienced limited basic needs we take for granted in the West. It is a stark contrast to how so many of us live.

This trip began my long-term relationship with the nation of Uganda.

## Question
What do you have in your hand that you can offer?

*Father, show me how I can be a blessing to the poor.*

# Withholding Your Natural Gifting

*God intended that your faith not be established on man's wisdom
but by trusting in his almighty power.*

1 CORINTHIANS 2:5 TPT

In the work world, we are trained to press through obstacles, no matter the cost. However, perseverance that is not directed by the Holy Spirit is only sweat and toil. We must learn to walk the fine line between these two concepts. On this subject of relying on our human strength, Watchman Nee wrote in his book *Latent Power of the Soul*:

> I feel that many people are too rich and too strong; there is no room for God to work in them. I often consider two words to be most precious: "utter helplessness." We can say to God, "All that I have is Yours; I have nothing besides You. Apart from You, I am utterly helpless." We will then have an attitude of total trust in God; we will feel as if we cannot breathe without Him. We will see that our holiness is from Him and our power is from Him. Whatever we need is from Him. It is God's desire that we come to Him in utter helplessness. A brother once asked me what the conditions are for the Holy Spirit to work. I said that the Holy Spirit never needs any help from the power of the soul. The Holy Spirit must first bring us to a place where we can do nothing by ourselves.[15]

The apostle Paul understood that it was not his ability to deliver eloquent sermons that changed people. It was the power of God working through him. If God's power comes through our work, that brings glory to the Father.

## Question
Do you ever feel you are striving to make things happen?

*Father, help me to allow your Holy Spirit's power to work through me to fulfill my purpose.*

# Who Are You?

*Oh, continue Your lovingkindness to those who know You,*
*and Your righteousness to the upright in heart.*
PSALM 36:10 NKJV

Someone once said, "Success is when those who know you the best are those who love you the most."

Years ago, a man named Jahari developed a self-assessment tool, the Jahari Window, that helps us understand how we relate to others. See if you can identify what category you might fall in among these four:

1. Transparent Life: The transparent life is the life we should desire. I know who I am, and others know me. There is nothing hidden.
2. Bull-in-the-China Shop: This person is blinded to the things that others recognize about him. The solution to becoming a transparent person is to get feedback from those around us about the blind spots in our personality.
3. Aloof/Hidden Secrets: This person lives in a secret world. He knows himself but is fearful of letting others know. Those around him do not truly know him.
4. Hidden Potential: This is a combination of Bull-in-the-China Shop and Aloof/Hidden Secrets. It is the saddest of all conditions. These people don't know themselves, and others don't know them either.[16]

## Question

How about you? How can you take a step to find out who you really are in the eyes of others?

*Father, help me to know my true self.*

# Always Watching and Listening

*Paul and Silas, undaunted, prayed in the middle of the night and sang songs of praise to God, while all the other prisoners listened to their worship.*
ACTS 16:25 TPT

It didn't take long for nonbelievers to realize I was different. I didn't participate in the jokes, the dirty language, or criticism of management. I didn't judge them for their behavior. I viewed them as prisoners awaiting their salvation and that I might be the instrument to lead them to my Savior.

I would often be known as the "religious guy." It wasn't because I was particularly vocal or because I tried to separate myself. The Christ in me naturally made me stand out. Jesus called us to be the "salt and light" (see Matthew 5:13–16).

When Paul and Silas were in prison, their lifestyle of worship and prayer in the midst of the horrible conditions of a dirty prison stood out in stark contrast to their circumstances. They didn't pray and sing to impress their cellmates; they simply did what was natural to them. Still, the other prisoners were watching and listening.

No matter where you are, others are watching you to determine if your faith is real or if you're an imposter. The world is looking to discredit your faith. You are a witness always, whether you choose to be or not.

When you begin to reflect the love and power of Christ in your life, you won't have to have an evangelism program to win others into the kingdom. The "fish" will actually jump into the boat!

Beware how you conduct your life today because the prisoners are watching and listening.

## Question

Are you living an authentic life with Christ so that others can see?

*Father, use my life to bring others into relationship with you.*

# Microsoft Mary

*Trust in the Lord completely, and do not rely on your own opinions. With all your heart rely on him to guide you, and he will lead you in every decision you make.*
PROVERBS 3:5 TPT

I travel a lot. One of the greatest modern-day inventions I've appreciated most is the GPS. I remember a time when I used one of these when I was traveling in Germany and Switzerland. I was able to program the GPS in English. I began my drive to my destination when a pleasant voice told me: "Turn left in two hundred yards." I called my invisible road counselor Microsoft Mary.

Jesus sent the Holy Spirit to help you and me navigate through life. "When the truth-giving Spirit comes, he will unveil the reality of every truth within you. He won't speak on his own, but only what he hears from the Father, and he will reveal prophetically to you what is to come" (John 16:13).

A story is told about the Chinese underground church having to rely on the Holy Spirit to tell them when and where they were to meet. It was too dangerous to announce public meetings. So, each member had to ask the Holy Spirit the time and place. Miraculously, they would all arrive at the same place at the same time. God was giving the believers their own form of GPS among themselves.

## Question

Is the Holy Spirit active in your work life? Are you asking for his direction to succeed in your work?

*Holy Spirit, please guide me today to the place I need to be.*

# Obedience-Based Decisions

*"We are witnesses of these things, and so is the Holy Spirit, whom God freely gives to all who believe in him."*

ACTS 5:32 TPT

I recall planning a conference one time. Registration numbers were not where I felt they needed to be a few weeks before the date of the event. I was concerned. My friend encouraged me: "If God called us to put on this conference, then the outcome is up to him if we have done our part."

He then shared a story. He and a friend were led to host a Bible study group. His friend was to speak. It was nine o'clock, and they were the only two people there. His friend was discouraged and ready to leave.

"No, we have done what the Holy Spirit directed," said the man leading the study. He then stood up, faced the empty room, and began to welcome people as though there were many even though there was no one else in the room. He introduced his friend to the imaginary crowd, and the two men began the meeting. A few minutes later, people began to straggle in. By the time the meeting was over, ten had shown up.

Being led by the Spirit often means we must not use the world's standard for success as our measuring stick. You never know what an act of obedience will yield at the time. We must leave the results to God. Our role is to obey. His role is to bring results from our obedience.

## Question

Do you make decisions based on the potential outcome or by the direction of the Holy Spirit in your life? Do you overly evaluate the pros and cons without considering what the Holy Spirit might be saying deep inside?

*Father, give me the willingness and ability to hear the Holy Spirit and to obey your promptings.*

# Walk as Jesus Did

*He who says he abides in Him ought himself also to walk just as He walked.*
1 JOHN 2:6 NKJV

Jesus says that if we are truly living in him, we must walk as he did. How did Jesus walk? He healed the sick. He perceived the needs and situations of others supernaturally. He spoke boldly to the hearts of the unsaved. He solved problems in the lives of people. He met the needs of people by leading them to the kingdom of God. Jesus says we must walk as he did. So, I can only conclude from the above verse that if we are each called to live this way, he will also equip us to live this way.

In Philippians, Paul explains that Jesus is our perfect example for living a humble, selfless life. Jesus was "in the form of God," yet "being found in human form, he humbled himself by becoming obedient to the point of death, even death on a cross" (Philippians 2:6, 8 ESV). Jesus lived an obedient, sinless life and died to take our place. He lived a human life without sin, which is why he can exhort us to live like he did. This is what John means when he calls us to "walk as he walked." We are to exercise obedience and faith just as Jesus did.

Jesus modeled a way of reaching the lost. He did not use reasoning to convince a person to follow him. He often operated in the supernatural revelation about a need in that person's life. Such was the case of the Samaritan woman (see John 4).

## Question
How can you walk as Jesus walked?

*Father, help me to see the needs of others and know how I can meet those needs.*

# Fulfilling Your Purpose

*The Lord will fulfill his purpose for me; your steadfast love, O Lord, endures forever.
Do not forsake the work of your hands.*

PSALM 138:8 ESV

Your purpose in life is chosen by God. It is not negotiable. It is like calling water wet. There is no changing that fact, and there's no changing God's purpose for your life. While you may not fulfill the purpose for which you were made, you still have a purpose that God intends for you to fulfill. This is your blueprint from God. In the same way that he had a specific purpose in mind for Jesus when he sent him to the earth, he has a specific purpose in mind for your life. To fulfill your purpose, you must offer your involvement and obedience.

This doesn't mean, however, that there is one highly specific niche for you to fill and that if you miss it, too bad. It is my belief that you can achieve your purpose in many different and creative ways. This should take the pressure off. You won't throw your entire life off course by choosing the wrong college, job, or mate. God is much bigger than any miscalculation or disobedience on your part. Isn't that comforting to know?

Defining your purpose will help you to determine the activities that you should be involved in. Like Jesus, you should not involve yourself in activities that contradict God's purpose for your existence. Jesus' purpose was to do the will of the Father and become the salvation for mankind and destroy the works of the devil.

## Question
Are you seeking to fulfill your purpose?

*Father, help me to fulfill my complete purpose in my life.*

# When Satan Attacks Your Destiny

*Now when the Philistines heard that they had anointed David king over Israel,*
*all the Philistines went up to search for David. And David heard of it*
*and went down to the stronghold.*

2 SAMUEL 5:17 NKJV

When you are about to enter your destiny, there is always opposition from Satan designed to prevent you from fulfilling your destiny.

When Jesus was born, Herod tried to kill him. When Jesus was baptized and fasted forty days in the desert, Satan came to tempt him in an effort to derail his destiny. When David had been anointed king over Israel, God's destiny had been revealed for all to see—even Satan. So, Satan raised up the Philistines to try to kill David's destiny.

However, in response, we see David do two things. First, he retreats to his stronghold. It is a place of protection. It is a quiet place. Second, he inquires of God the strategy to defeat his enemy. God reveals it to him, and he goes on to defeat the Philistines. In fact, David never lost a battle because he learned to inquire of God for the strategy to defeat his enemies. Beware of Satan's strategy to attack you in the place of your destiny. His desire is to take you off this divine path.

## Question
How can you respond like David when Satan attacks your destiny?

*Father, help me to fulfill my destiny despite Satan's attacks.*

# Stepping-Stones

*Yahweh, you alone are my inheritance. You are my prize, my pleasure, and my portion. You hold my destiny and its timing in your hands. Your pleasant path leads me to pleasant places. I'm overwhelmed by the privileges that come with following you!*
PSALM 16:5–6 TPT

Most of us will have many jobs over our lifetime. As I look back over my past, I've had quite a varied history of jobs that include being a waiter, retail clerk, golf pro, advertising sales executive, ad agency executive, and ad agency owner. Today, I am an online marketer, business coach, and writer, and I lead an international workplace ministry. All of these jobs were important because they gave me a level of experience from which I now express God's ministry.

God is building something in us. Oswald Chambers says, "In the beginning we do not train for God, we train for work, for our own aims, but as we go on with God we lose all our own aims and are trained into God's purpose. Unless practical work is appointed by God, it will prove a curse."[17]

Jesus was prepared for his ultimate calling by working with his father in his carpentry shop until he was thirty years old. Most of Jesus' teaching arose out of issues in daily life experience. Moses was prepared to lead a nation out of slavery by serving in Pharoah's house and later working forty years as a shepherd.

## Question

Have you ever despised the small jobs in life? Realize they are stepping-stones to a greater purpose in God's plan for your life.

*Father, may you accomplish the intended outcome you desire to work through me today.*

# Opening Our Spiritual Eyes

*Elisha prayed, "Open his eyes, LORD, so that he may see."*
*Then the LORD opened the servant's eyes, and he looked*
*and saw the hills full of horses and chariots of fire all around Elisha.*

2 KINGS 6:17 NIV

Elisha was counseling the nation of Israel against the impending attack of the king of Aram. The Lord supernaturally gave Elisha the plans that the king was implementing, and in turn, Elisha warned Israel of each intended attack. The king could not understand why his plans were continually foiled. It seemed there was a secret informer in his midst. He was furious when he was told it was the God of Israel who was to blame. The king decided the only way to resolve the situation was to get rid of the problem—kill Elisha.

The king's forces arrived and surrounded Elisha and his servant. Elisha's servant became upset and fearful when Elisha was not upset. Elisha immediately prayed that his servant's eyes might be opened to see that there was no need to be afraid because the angels were protecting them.

And Elisha prayed, "Open his eyes, LORD, so that he may see." Then the LORD opened the servant's eyes, and he looked and saw the hills full of horses and chariots of fire all around Elisha. As the enemy came down toward him, Elisha prayed to the LORD, "Strike this army with blindness." So he struck them with blindness, as Elisha had asked. (2 Kings 6:17–18)

It is often difficult for us to see what God is really doing because we are so consumed by the circumstances of the moment.

## Question

Who is the Elisha in your life? Do you have a mentor friend who can see the activity of God in your life when you cannot see it?

*Father, open my spiritual eyes that I might see you in my circumstances.*

# Her First Car

*Now Samuel did not yet know the L*ORD*:*
*the word of the L*ORD *had not yet been revealed to him.*

1 SAMUEL 3:7 NIV

Charis, my daughter, had reached driving age. She had saved her hard-earned money to match her father's contribution to buy her first car. I told her that we needed to pray for God to lead us to that perfect car.

We prayed we would find the right car, even in the silver color and model that she wanted. Finally, after several weeks, she got discouraged and began to tear up, "We will never find a car for this price." I told her the car was out there, but it was not God's time yet. This didn't go over well with a teenager.

Finally, one day I came upon a car on the internet that seemed like it fit our criteria. I called the owner. The parents of the boy who owned it answered the call and gave me more information. I liked the parents right away. They had a nice "spirit" about them.

We drove over to the house, and there in the front yard was a silver sports car—the model she had been looking for, complete with a fantastic stereo and speaker system. We noticed a small fish symbol on the back bumper. "These people may be believers!" I said.

The price was a little higher than our budget. We asked if they could meet our price. They did. My daughter had her new car with a personal imprint from God to show my daughter that he was the source of the new car.

One of the most important roles you and I have as parents is to transfer our faith to our children.

## Question
Do your children live their faith in daily life?

*Father, help me to live my faith so my children will live it too.*

# God Requests Your Donkey

*"As soon as you enter the village, you will find a donkey tethered along with her young colt. Untie them both and bring them to me."*

MATTHEW 21:2 TPT

In Bible times, donkeys were a primary means for distributing goods and services. They represented commerce in the Scriptures. Jesus told the disciples he had need of someone's donkey to ride into Jerusalem. It would become known as Jesus' triumphal entry.

I am sure the disciples must have been uneasy with their master's request to untie a perfect stranger's donkey and take it. He was asking them to take what was the equivalent to a man's "truck." And men love their trucks! Jesus wanted to use that which represented their work to bring glory to the Father.

I was attending a Christian business conference in Singapore. It was the night before I was to speak a second time when I was prompted to add a teaching segment on the above passage of Scripture.

The next morning, we were eating, and a lady named Maggie joined us. Maggie was from Malaysia and was an intercessor for the conference. She fasted forty days in preparation for the event. "So, Maggie, has the Lord spoken to you about this conference?" I asked.

"Oh yes," she said, very excitedly. "On September 17, the Lord said that the Singapore businesspeople needed to give their donkeys to the Lord." I looked at Maggie in amazement. God was confirming his word to me from the night before.

That day the focus of our conference became the need for the Singapore businesspeople to "give their donkeys" to the Lord.

## Question
Have you ever dedicated your work life to the Lord?

*Lord, today, I commit my "donkey" to you to bring glory to you.*

# Turning the Daughter's Heart

*"He will turn the hearts of the fathers to the children, and the hearts of the children to their fathers, lest I come and strike the earth with a curse."*

MALACHI 4:6 NKJV

I came home to my bedroom one night and began to cry after having dinner with my eighteen-year-old daughter that evening. I had listened to how fearful she was of the future. I was concluding a commitment to a seven-year child support and alimony obligation from a divorce that had taken place many years earlier, but my daughter was fearful of what lay in store for her. The divorce was something I had fought against but lost. I was angry and broken. The heartache and uncertainty of where she would live all came to the surface for my daughter and me that night.

A few months later, I was speaking at a conference in Minneapolis. A dear friend said, "Os, we want to pray for you downstairs."

"Okay, I will be right down," I replied.

He and his friend began to pray for me. His friend began to speak about my life in very specific terms. "You have a daughter…the Lord says she has a gift in writing…poetry…and she has creative gifts. The Lord says she has been in a difficult place for many years of her life, but he is about to bring her out. He is turning the daughter's heart to the father's and is bringing her home. Oh, he says he has seen the tears you have shed for her in your bedroom."

By this time, I was on the floor weeping. I went home with this profound experience in my heart. Within a year, my daughter came to Christ and even came to live at my home for a year.

## Question

Do you have a son or daughter who is not walking with God right now?

*Father, thank you that you are our faithful deliverer.*

# Confirmed by Others

*Samuel grew, and the LORD was with him and let none of his words fall to the ground. And all Israel from Dan to Beersheba knew that Samuel had been established as a prophet of the LORD.*

1 SAMUEL 3:19–20 NKJV

When I was fourteen, I was an exceptional junior golfer. I had already broken 70 several times and had three holes in one. I competed in the US Junior Amateur and eventually turned pro after attending college on a four-year golf scholarship. Those who knew me affirmed the gift and calling that appeared to be on my life. I turned professional for three years, but God later redirected my life into business and vocational ministry. All of these experiences combined over many years to contribute to the calling I am living out today.

God uses our parents, teachers, uncles, coaches, and pastors to affirm the gifts and callings that are on our lives. At the time, it often seems like these people are trying to get in the way of what we want to do. However, God uses authority figures to provide key direction during the early teen and twenty-something years.

When we are young, we are often more impressionable than at any other time in our lives. The young person who can allow wisdom to rule over immaturity and impatience is a rare individual.

A. B. Simpson said, "God is continually preparing his heroes; and when the opportunity comes, He can fit them into their place in a moment, and the world will wonder where they came from."[18]

## Question

What gifts and callings are people affirming in your life? Are you letting God do the foundation work so that he can advance you to the ultimate destiny he has for your life?

*Father, use the people in my life to direct my path.*

# The Trinity's Teamwork

*Now, O LORD, You are our Father; we are the clay, and You our potter;*
*and all we are the work of Your hand.*

ISAIAH 64:8 NKJV

The Father, Son, and Holy Spirit make up three distinct aspects of the Godhead. Each of these persons form the Trinity and contribute to the overall work of God. The Trinity reveals God's belief in teamwork. Even God brought a team together to accomplish his purposes. *The Leadership Bible* gives us further insight into the distinct roles the Trinity plays.

> The three Persons of the Godhead are never independent but always work together in concert…Paul first spoke of the work of the Father in accomplishing our salvation in Ephesians 1:3–6. The Father chose us before the creation of the world and sent his Son into the world so that through him we could be adopted into his family. Second, the apostle focused on the work of the Son in verses 7–12. Christ's blood sacrifice on our behalf paid the penalty for our sins so that we could enjoy forgiveness and lay hold of God's purpose for our lives. Third, the work of the Holy Spirit, identified in verses 13–14, seals and guarantees our spiritual inheritance. Thus, the Father initiated our salvation, The Son accomplished it and the Holy Spirit made it real in our lives.[19]

May the Father, Son, and Holy Spirit take your feet of clay and build a solid foundation for the praise of his Son.

## Question
Are you giving the Trinity its rightful place in your life?

*Thank you, Father, Son, and Holy Spirit, for the role you play in my life.*

# John the Baptist Was the Greatest

*"Assuredly, I say to you, among those born of women there has not risen one greater than John the Baptist; but he who is least in the kingdom of heaven is greater than he."*

MATTHEW 11:11 NKJV

Elijah performed miracle after miracle. Daniel interpreted dreams for kings, and he and his friends influenced an entire nation. Jeremiah and Isaiah were two of Israel's greatest prophetic voices. Jesus built his church through the twelve disciples. John the Baptist did no miracles. But Jesus made a profound declaration about this man who performed no miracles: "He is the greatest among all the prophets."

Why did Jesus make such a claim? Because John the Baptist did one very important thing—he fulfilled his purpose on earth in every way.

The disciples asked John the Baptist if he was the one they had been waiting for?

John responded quickly, "No." Then he made a profound statement: "A man can receive nothing unless it has been given to him from heaven" (John 3:27 NKJV). He had a complete understanding of why he was placed on earth.

The angel Gabriel described John's purpose to his father: "He will go on before the Lord, in the spirit and power of Elijah, to turn the hearts of the parents to their children and the disobedient to the wisdom of the righteous—to make ready a people prepared for the Lord" (Luke 1:17 NIV).

Understanding your work-life purpose is key to receiving your inheritance.

## Question

Do you know why God made you? Are you fulfilling the destiny he has planned for you since the foundation of the earth?

*Father, help me know my purpose and to fulfill that purpose while I am on earth.*

# But Master...

*"Master," Peter replied, "we've just come back from fishing all night
and didn't catch a thing. But if you insist, we'll go out again
and let down our nets because of your word."*

LUKE 5:5 TPT

Have you ever questioned God's instruction to you, such as whether it had merit and whether his instruction will make a difference in anything?

Peter's fishing business was in a slump. They had just fished all night and caught nothing. Nevertheless, Peter made his boat available to Jesus to use as he wished. Jesus used it to preach to the multitudes. After Jesus used Peter's boat for his purposes, Jesus did something interesting for Peter. He blessed his business. However, Peter almost missed the blessing because he began to argue with Jesus. Peter was looking at the market conditions instead of the instruction of Jesus. Something inside of him made him reconsider Jesus' instruction. Jesus rewarded his obedience. "When they pulled up their nets, they were shocked to see a huge catch of fish, and their nets were ready to burst! They waved to their business partners in the other boat for help. They ended up completely filling both boats with fish until they began to sink!" (Luke 5:6–7).

We see in this story a number of kingdom principles we can apply in our work lives. (1) We must be willing to let God use our work life for his purposes. (2) We must not look at circumstances and argue with Jesus when his instruction seems to contradict what we have seen or experienced already. (3) We must obey the Lord.

## Question
Have you ever questioned God's instruction of you?

*Father, help me never question your instructions to me.*

# Going against Public Opinion

*When the baby was eight days old, according to their custom, all the family and friends came together for the circumcision ceremony. Everyone assumed that the parents would name the baby Zechariah, after his father, but Elizabeth spoke up and said, "No, his name is John!" "What?" they exclaimed. "No one in your family line has that name!"*

LUKE 1:59–61 TPT

Have you ever had to go against public opinion or advice from family members or peers? Elizabeth gave birth to John the Baptist. It was time to name the child. Tradition said the name would be in honor of a family member. The family members were insistent that Elizabeth and Zechariah follow this tradition. When Elizabeth didn't agree with them, they appealed to Zechariah, who supported Elizabeth.

Zechariah and Elizabeth were told by the angel Gabriel the child's name was to be "John." They were being obedient to the Lord's command, which went against tradition and public opinion.

We live in a day when leaders are often driven more by public opinion than by what is right. We are each called to live a life of obedience-based decisions, not decisions swayed by public opinion. Living a life of obedience will often go against the tide of public opinion. Jesus lived a life based on a purity of purpose and mission. The Pharisees wanted him to conform to the rules of religious tradition. The result was that he died because he lived to obey an audience of One, not public opinion.

## Question
Are you challenged to live a life of conviction versus pleasing others?

*Father, help me be true to what you have called me to do no matter the cost.*

# Filled with the Holy Spirit

*"Saul, my brother, the Lord Jesus, who appeared to you on the road,
has sent me to pray for you so that you might see again
and be filled to overflowing with the Holy Spirit."*

ACTS 9:17 TPT

Billy Graham once shared a personal story about the role of the Holy Spirit in his lifelong ministry.

> In my own life there have been times when I have also had the sense of being filled with the Spirit…We sailed for England in 1954 for a crusade that was to last for three months. While on the ship, I experienced a definite sense of oppression…Not only was I oppressed, I was overtaken by a sense of depression, accompanied by a frightening feeling of inadequacy for the task that lay ahead. Almost night and day I prayed… Then one day in a prayer meeting…a break came. As I wept before the Lord, I was filled with deep assurance that power belonged to God and He was faithful. I had been baptized by the Spirit into the body of Christ when I was saved, but I believe God gave me a special anointing on the way to England. From that moment on, I was confident that God the Holy Spirit was in control for the task of the 1954 Crusade in London. That proved true.[20]

God has provided the Holy Spirit for you and me so that we can experience the power to live the gospel.

## Question

Are you filled and baptized in the Holy Spirit? If not, invite the Holy Spirit to fill your life to overflowing so that you can be a witness in your workplace, family, city, and nation.

*Father, I pray you fill me and baptize me with your Holy Spirit.*

# The Judas Test

*It wasn't an enemy who taunted me. If it was my enemy, filled with pride and hatred, then I could have endured it. I would have just run away. But it was you, my intimate friend—one like a brother to me.*

PSALM 55:12–13 TPT

Betrayal is one of the most difficult tests that we will ever face because it involves being wounded by someone we trust. It's hard not to become bitter when a friend or family member wounds us. It takes a lot of Christlike grace to forgive a traitor.

You have probably faced the Judas Test yourself. Every day you and I work in a marketplace that is rife with betrayal, deception, duplicity, and treachery. Perhaps you have been betrayed by your boss or a coworker. Or perhaps somebody betrayed a confidence or stabbed you in the back. It may even have been someone you've gone to church with or prayed with— someone you trusted as a brother in Christ.

Almost every leader I know has experienced that sting at one time or another. Yet God is watching to see how we respond to the Judas Test. If we pass, he can take us to the next level, the next test. If we fail, we'll probably have to repeat the test until we learn to forgive.

The Judas Test is God's graduate level course in faith, designed to reveal the truth about ourselves.

## Question

Are you willing to trust him enough to forgive the Judases in your life? The book of Hebrews warns, "See to it that no one falls short of the grace of God and that no bitter root grows up to cause trouble and defile many" (Hebrews 12:15 NIV).

*Father, I choose to forgive those who have betrayed me today in obedience to you.*

# Square Peg in a Round Hole

*God composed the body, having given greater honor to that part which lacks it, that there should be no schism in the body, but that the members should have the same care for one another.*

1 Corinthians 12:24–25 NKJV

I feel like I've been attempting to fit a thousand pegs into the relationship hole but not one satisfies you with the words you are looking for me to say." Those were the words I said to my wife in complete frustration.

We were at an impasse in our relationship for days—yes, days! No matter what I said or how I said it, nothing seemed to matter. She was viewing the situation through her grid; I was viewing it through mine. It was like trying to fit a round peg into a square hole, which simply wouldn't work no matter how hard I tried.

Then I said these words: "I'm sorry I could not see your perspective and implied that you had a hurtful motive behind your actions. I know you've never done that in the past." Bingo! Something happened! This peg actually fit! She jumped out of her chair and rushed over to kiss me. Our relationship completely turned around in six seconds. *How did that happen?* I pondered what had just taken place, feeling totally perplexed but relieved over the fact a resolution came forth.

Men and women often view situations from two differing vantage points. Men often see things from a more compartmentalized view. Women can view things from the impact it may have on their relationships.

## Question
Do you ever struggle with your spouse because you view situations from the wrong lens?

*Father, help me to speaks words of love and empathy to my spouse.*

# Learning the Art of Forgiveness

*"Forgive us our sins, for we also forgive everyone who is indebted to us.*
*And do not lead us into temptation, but deliver us from the evil one."*

LUKE 11:4 NKJV

Jesus modeled this forgiveness in the Lord's Prayer: "Forgive us our sins, for we also forgive everyone who sins against us" (Luke 11:4 NIV). When I owned my advertising agency, I once filed a lawsuit against a client who refused to pay a $140,000 bill. However, the Lord instructed me that because I had also sinned in the situation, I was to drop the suit. My next move was to talk to my former client. I tried phoning him, but he wouldn't return my calls. Finally, I reached his secretary and said, "I want you to take this message down and give it to your boss, word for word—no changes: 'I have sinned against you. I know that I don't deserve your forgiveness, but I ask your forgiveness for filing the lawsuit against you. You are no longer obligated to pay the balance you owe me if you don't feel you owe it.'"

I could hear the secretary begin to cry on the other end of the line. She couldn't believe what she was hearing. About an hour later, my former client called. We hadn't spoken for six months. We reconciled the relationship.

The next few years were incredibly difficult because of the financial setback I suffered, but God provided for my needs. Looking back, I realize that this was my Judas Test. I passed the test when I let go of my resentment and asked to be forgiven, and God was glorified in the situation.

## Question
Do you need to ask forgiveness from someone?

*Father, help me to forgive those who wrong me.*

# Exceeding Expectations

*I did not believe the words until I came and saw with my own eyes; and indeed the half was not told me. Your wisdom and prosperity exceed the fame of which I heard.*

1 KINGS 10:7 NKJV

I'm shocked," said the woman on the phone. "I've just seen your picture. I was expecting a grey-haired, old man. You are too young to have the wisdom that I read in your messages."

When people meet you or experience your work-life skills, would they say that you far exceeded their expectations? Do you undersell and overproduce or oversell and underproduce? Solomon's wisdom far exceeded any man's wisdom, and it was evident to others. When people come in contact with you, do they come away with a sense of greater appreciation of you after meeting you?

"Do you see a man who excels in his work? He will stand before kings; he will not stand before unknown men" (Proverbs 22:29). Whenever we exceed the expectations of man, we bring glory to our heavenly Father, and he often elevates us among men.

If there were a kingdom project to be done, would God recommend you for the job? God calls us to live our lives and do our work with excellence.

## Question

Do you exceed expectations when people engage with you?

*Father, help me to be excellent in all I do so I bring glory to your name.*

# The University of Adversity

*Beloved friends, if life gets extremely difficult, with many tests, don't be bewildered as though something strange were overwhelming you. Instead, continue to rejoice, for you, in a measure, have shared in the sufferings of the Anointed One so that you can share in the revelation of his glory and celebrate with even greater gladness!*

1 PETER 4:12–13 TPT

I've observed a principle: The pathway to leadership almost always takes us through the valley of adversity. We see this principle not only in the story of Joseph, who endured thirteen years of adversity, but also in the lives of many other leaders in both the Old and New Testament.

Moses was raised in the royal splendor of Pharaoh's household in Egypt, but he was forced to flee and spend forty years in desert exile before God spoke from a burning bush and called him to lead the Hebrew people out of slavery. Joshua spent the years of his youth as a slave in Egypt and his middle-aged years wandering in the desert at Moses' side. He was well acquainted with adversity when God called him to lead Israel's armies in the conquest of Canaan. And we see this same pattern played out in the lives of David, Isaiah, Amos, Hosea, and other Old Testament leaders.

Every leader God has used often went through a time of adversity to fulfill the larger story of their life.

## Question

Do you find yourself in the midst of a university of adversity?

*Father, thank you for building me into a man of God through my experiences.*

# Isn't This Joseph's Son?

*All bore witness to Him, and marveled at the gracious words which*
*proceeded out of His mouth. And they said, "Is this not Joseph's son?"*
LUKE 4:22 NKJV

Jesus grew up in a small community in Nazareth where people knew him to be the son of Joseph, the carpenter. He was also becoming known as a rabbi who thought and did things "outside the box." So, when the public ministry side of his life began to surface, the first observations were, "Isn't this Joseph, the carpenter's son?"

This is not unlike what happens when God calls us into a more public ministry. "Isn't that John, the CPA, or Bill, the restaurant manager, or Jim, the bank executive?" The first question among our critics is "When did John, Bill, or Jim get religion?"

The religious spirit in the workplace reveals itself in many ways. The religious spirit can best be defined as an agent of Satan assigned to prevent change and maintain the status quo by using religious devices. The religious spirit seeks to distort a genuine move of God through deception, control, and manipulation. It was the primary force against Jesus designed to intimidate and turn his relationship with God into a set of rules and regulations. Satan does not want Jesus in the workplace because that is where the authority lies to change a workplace, city, or nation. God desires you to bring his presence with you into the workplace every day.

## Question

Do you ever let the devil shame you into alienating your faith from your work life?

*Father, thank you that my work is a ministry and calling.*

# Keeping Oaths

*"This we will do to them: we will let them live, lest wrath be upon us because of the oath which we swore to them."*

JOSHUA 9:20 NKJV

Joshua and the people of Israel were in the promised land. They were winning battles and were feeling good about their progress. One day a band of Gibeonites came by dressed as travelers in order to fool Joshua. They wanted to make Joshua believe they were merely travelers instead of enemies. The Gibeonites asked Joshua to make a peace treaty with them. Since Joshua chose to believe their story, he did just that. That was a mistake on Joshua's part. The Bible says Joshua did not inquire of the Lord about the Gibeonites. This forced Joshua to uphold the peace treaty with the Gibeonites even though it was made under false pretenses.

Keeping our oaths before the Lord is a serious matter. One might think that Joshua had every right to consider the agreement with the Gibeonites null and void since it was done under false pretense. However, Joshua knew how God viewed oaths. He knew that a man's word, once it was given, should be good as done. There was no reversing it.

Whenever we become a child of God, we represent him. When his children follow unrighteousness, he takes this personally. Unrighteousness opens us up to Satan's attack. God's protection shield is removed. So, Joshua knew that if he did not honor his oath, he would be subject to God's judgment.

## Question
Is there any unfulfilled oath you have made to anyone?

*Heavenly Father, show me my unfulfilled commitments and help me fulfill them. I do not want to be subject to your judgment for my unrighteousness.*

# Comforting Others

*He is the Father of tender mercy and the God of endless comfort. He always comes alongside us to comfort us in every suffering so that we can come alongside those who are in any painful trial. We can bring them this same comfort that God has poured out upon us.*

2 CORINTHIANS 1:3–4 TPT

I was fourteen years old in September 1966. I was home watching *I Dream of Jeannie* on television when the program was interrupted by a news bulletin: "Three prominent local businessmen have died in a plane crash in the mountains of Tennessee." That's how I learned of the death of my father.

It was difficult and painful growing up without a father. I loved and needed my dad. I couldn't understand why God would take him away from me so suddenly.

In the years since my father died, God brought a number of men across my path who have lost fathers at an early age. Because of my own loss, I had an instant connection with others who suffered similar losses. We shared an experience that many other people couldn't fully understand.

God can take our adversity—a heart attack, cancer, an automobile accident, violent crime, bankruptcy, a marriage crisis, the loss of a loved one— and transform that pain into encouragement for the people around us. We come out of those experiences stronger and better able to comfort others.

Although adversity may never be a blessing, God in his grace can bring blessing out of our adversity. The key is releasing the hurt and pain to the Lord so he can bring the needed healing to our lives.

## Question
Have you experienced a tragedy in your life?

*Father, I pray you will use my adversity to bless others.*

# Failing Forward

*Brethren, I do not count myself to have apprehended; but one thing I do, forgetting those things which are behind and reaching forward to those things which are ahead, I press toward the goal for the prize of the upward call of God in Christ Jesus.*

PHILIPPIANS 3:13–14 NKJV

Back in the 1970s, Tom Watson was the up-and-coming golfer on the PGA Tour. But time after time, when Tom led a tournament coming into the last round, he would choke, bogey a few holes, and finish in the middle of the pack. Soon, the media began calling him a "choker." That kind of criticism only increases the pressure and the tendency to choke.

Tom Watson said in an interview, "Everybody has choked. In the 1974 U.S. Open, I kept hitting the ball right to right. My nerves wouldn't allow me to adjust. That's what choking is—being so nervous you can't find a swing or a putting stroke you can trust."[21]

How did Watson overcome his tendency to choke? "Byron gave me the best cure for it," Watson recalled, referring to Byron Nelson, the legendary golf pro of the 1930s and '40s. "Walk slowly, talk slowly, deliberately do everything more slowly than you normally do. It has a way of settling you down."[22] That advice helped Tom Watson overcome his nervousness. He went on to win many tournaments, including five British Opens.

Everybody fails. It's part of the process. Most successful entrepreneurs have been through a number of failures in life, but they usually don't think of their failures as defeats.

## Question

Have you failed at something? If you hope to succeed, learn everything you can from your failures.

*Father, help me to fail forward and learn valuable lessons for future success.*

# God's Financial System

*"I have given you a land for which you did not labor, and cities which you did not build, and you dwell in them; you eat of the vineyards and olive groves which you did not plant."*

JOSHUA 24:13 NKJV

Earlier I talked about God's economy and how the Israelites gained the promised land because of their love and obedience to him versus sweat and toil.

When God transitioned me from a business to a nonprofit ministry, I discovered God's economy of receiving. Let me share two examples.

I love to play golf, and I love to go to the beach. I've played golf since I was eleven years old and was a professional for a short time in my early twenties. I went through a financial crisis in 1994 and could not afford certain things during a seven-year period. One of those things was a golf membership. Out of the blue a friend who owned a golf course came to me and gave me a free membership. I never discussed my situation with him. The free membership was extended to me for ten years!

I once considered buying ocean front property but could not afford it after my financial crisis. While visiting a friend at the beach, I was introduced to a Christian couple who owned five oceanfront condos. When they heard my story, they were touched. They have been providing me a week at the beach free of charge for the last ten years.

God's economy often measures back to us in tangible ways when we give our lives and service to him. And it is often very personal to what we enjoy most.

## Question
What is something God has given you that you never had to pay for?

*Father, thank you that you love to give to your sons and daughters.*

# The Cost of Unbelief

*Without faith living within us it would be impossible to please God. For we come to God in faith knowing that he is real and that he rewards the faith of those who passionately seek him.*

HEBREWS 11:6 TPT

How is your faith quotient? On a scale of one to ten, where would you rank yourself? Every day, I marvel at the faith most of us exercise without even thinking about it.

We drive our cars sixty to seventy miles per hour with an oncoming car doing the same while only a yellow line and six to eight feet separate us. We place our faith in the belief that all the other cars will not cross into our lane. We fly on airplanes that take us over oceans, trusting the pilots with our very lives. We ride on thrilling amusement rides that take us several stories into the air and travel fifty to seventy miles per hour down a winding slope. We trust the builders and operators of that ride with our own mortality.

There is a great irony in the fact that we can place our faith in such things but cannot place our faith in the hands of our Creator. What consequence have you suffered from a lack of faith? Jesus is always looking for faith on the earth.

God often calls us to put our toe in the water before he will part the water. Faith requires us to "see it" before we experience it.

## Question

Is there an area in your life where you have not been able to trust God? Why not repent of your unbelief and place your faith totally in his hands today?

*Father, give me the faith to trust you in every area of my life.*

# Considering the Risk and Reward

*"What shall be done for the man who kills this Philistine and takes away the reproach from Israel? For who is this uncircumcised Philistine, that he should defy the armies of the living God?"*

1 SAMUEL 17:26 NKJV

Every entrepreneur must determine the risk and reward before entering a venture. We must determine if God is leading us after we consider all factors. We also must consider if the timing is right to proceed.

When David heard about Goliath and that no one in the Israelite army was willing to fight him, he was angry. However, he didn't just respond out of pure emotion. He asked a very important question. "What will be done for the man who kills this Philistine and removes this disgrace from Israel?" He got the answer he was hoping for: "The king will give great wealth to the man who kills him. He will also give him his daughter in marriage and will exempt his family from taxes in Israel" (1 Samuel 17:25 NIV).

The religious spirit always tries to make the business side of faith evil. Money and profit are not evil. It is the love of money and the pride of life that get man into trouble. David understood the proper balance of these coexisting to accomplish God's purposes.

## Question

Ask God four questions before you proceed in any venture:

1. Is the Holy Spirit leading me?
2. Is this the time to be involved?
3. Is the risk worth the reward?
4. Do I have what is necessary to be successful with God's help?

*Father, give me wisdom to determine my course of action in all my endeavors.*

# Three-Phase Obedience

*Jesus answered him, "'Love the Lord your God with every passion of your heart, with all the energy of your being, and with every thought that is within you.'"*
MATTHEW 22:37 TPT

Y ears ago, I went through what I call my "Joseph Pit" experience. It was during this time of great adversity and great growth that I wrote *TGIF: Today God Is First*, and God birthed many of the things I am doing today. During this season, I discovered a spiritual truth about how most believers experience three distinct phases of their growth toward obedience in their Christian walks.

When we first begin our spiritual journey, we often make decisions from a goal of convenience. We decide what outcome we want and then make decisions based on the perceived outcome.

God desires that each of us live an obedience-based life. In order to transition us from an outcome-based process to an obedience-based process, he will often bring a crisis into our lives. This crisis is designed to create pain that motivates us to seek him to alleviate the pain. We have all heard of "foxhole" Christianity. There is place of obedience for everyone! However, this is not where God desires us to remain.

Ultimately, God desires us to live a life of obedience and intimacy rooted in conviction. We obey his commands from a heart of love and devotion. During the crisis phase, we discover the personal love of God in our lives that we had never experienced before.

The Christian life can be summed up in one word: *love*. God's desire for each of us is to know him intimately and to love him with all of our heart.

## Question
Have you told your heavenly Father you love him today?

*Father, help me walk in obedience to your commands.*

# Giving Him the Key

*Behold, I stand at the door and knock. If anyone hears My voice and opens the door, I will come in to him and dine with him, and he with Me.*

REVELATION 3:20 NKJV

A friend of mine tells the story of an encounter he had with a very important government official—the head of state for a country. In the course of some meetings with my friend, the official came up to him and said, "I perceive that there is a difference between you and me. Is it because I come from a different denomination?" My friend began to explain why there was a difference.

"If you were to come to my home, I would invite you in as an honored guest. As my guest, you would enjoy everything I had in my home. However, you would still be a guest. You would not have the keys to the home, and your authority in that home would be merely as a guest. However, if I said to you that I am turning over my home to you and you now have the keys to my home, I would be your servant." My friend continued, "This is the difference between you and me. You have merely invited Jesus into your home as a guest. I have given Jesus the keys to my home [heart], and I am his servant. All you have to do is invite him in as the new owner." The man did this and is now allowing Jesus to rule and reign in every detail of his life.

So often many of us enter a relationship with God that brings us salvation. But God also wants us to experience his power and presence every day of our lives and to see his hand at work in us. This only happens when we give him the key to our life; he must be more than an honored guest.

## Question

Where are you today? Has your life with God been more like an honored-guest relationship, or does he have the key to your life?

*Father, today I yield my life to you as my Lord and Savior.*

# Power Repentance

*As Jesus left Capernaum he came upon a tax-collecting station, where a Jewish man named Matthew was collecting taxes for the Romans. "Come, follow me," Jesus said to him. Immediately Matthew jumped up and began to follow Jesus.*
MATTHEW 9:9 TPT

Are you playing Christianity, or are you having an encounter daily with the living Christ? Imagine living a life in which you were hated and despised, and one day you decide to completely change the course of your life. That is what we see in the life of Matthew. Not many would change the course of their life just because a perfect stranger invited them to. My guess is that Matthew had heard about this man named Jesus. Jesus' reputation had preceded him. So, when Jesus took a special interest in Matthew, he had already been prepared in his heart to respond to Jesus. This encounter changed Matthew's life. No longer did he steal from the citizens. No longer did he take advantage of others. His life was radically changed by his encounter with Jesus.

Whenever we move from playing Christianity to having a genuine encounter with the living Christ, we are confronted with our own humanity and sin compared to the unmerited love and power of Jesus Christ that is personally directed to us.

## Question
How about you? Do you need a personal encounter with Jesus today?

*Father, reveal your power in my work life today.*

# Are You a Problem Solver?

*Jesus then took the barley loaves and the fish and gave thanks to God. He then gave it to the disciples to distribute to the people. Miraculously, the food multiplied, with everyone eating as much as they wanted!*

JOHN 6:11 TPT

Have you ever considered how Jesus' fame spread throughout the land? It was because he solved problems in people's lives. He solved Peter's fishing problem. He solved Peter's tax problem when he told him to go catch a fish to get the money to pay their taxes.

He solved the blind man's problem. He fed the five thousand and solved the food problem. He solved the prostitute's problem by preventing her from being stoned. He solved Lazarus' problem—he raised him from the dead. Every time he solved a problem, his influence and reputation grew.

A young servant girl worked for the king of Israel. The general had contracted leprosy. She told her queen that Elijah could heal him. Elijah gave instructions for the general to go wash in a lake. The general did, and he was healed. How do you think the general viewed that servant girl after this? Her "stock" went way up!

Do you desire to have more influence in the lives of others or to have greater impact in your workplace? If so, begin solving problems. Culture does not care who solves their problem—they just want their problem solved. Start being a problem solver, and your personal stock value will begin to grow among your associates and employer, and your spiritual authority will grow.

## Question
What problem has God called you to solve?

*Father, thank you for making me a problem solver.*

# Receiving Bad News

*"A great multitude is coming against you from beyond the sea, from Syria; and they are in Hazazon Tamar"...And Jehoshaphat feared, and set himself to seek the LORD, and proclaimed a fast throughout all Judah.*

2 CHRONICLES 20:2–3 NKJV

Have you ever had someone bring you really bad news? It was so bad that when you heard it, your stomach immediately became upset. You went into a crisis mode. I once received a letter that brought such fear upon me I could hardly stand up.

King Jehoshaphat had just been informed that his country was going to be attacked by an army much larger than his. However, instead of panicking, he immediately turned to the Lord by calling for a time of fasting and prayer. The people from every town in Judah responded.

King Jehoshaphat prayed and reminded God of his promise to Israel. Then he asked God for strategy. It came through the prophet, Jahaziel, son of Zechariah. He said, "Listen, King Jehoshaphat and all who live in Judah and Jerusalem! This is what the LORD says to you: 'Do not be afraid or discouraged because of this vast army. For the battle is not yours, but God's'" (2 Chronicles 20:15 NIV).

God supernaturally wiped out their enemies that day. They didn't even have to fight. God caused the enemy to fight themselves when they began to praise God on the battlefield (see 2 Chronicles 20:22–23).

Jehoshaphat immediately did four things in response to bad news: (1) He called for prayer, (2) he called for fasting, (3) he asked for God's strategy, and (4) he began his battle by praising God in the midst of the fight.

## Question
### Have you gotten some bad news lately?

*Father, help me to follow the example of Jehoshaphat to pray, fast, ask, and praise.*

# Two Types of People

*By your hand save me from such people, Lord,*
*from those of this world whose reward is in this life.*
PSALM 17:14 NIV

There are two types of people in the world. There are those whose activities are designed to generate a reward in this lifetime, and there are those who live to generate a reward when they meet our Lord in heaven.

Not every Christian models the latter. How can we judge whether we are living for the future reward versus the earthly reward? There are several key indicators.

Future-reward people tend to be givers. They make their time and resources available for kingdom purposes. They realize their sowing will ultimately be rewarded at the judgment seat of Christ where what they have done on earth will be judged and rewarded by God (2 Corinthians 5:10).

Future-reward people live a life based upon obedience-based decisions. They don't make decisions based on their perceived outcome. They realize a decision based on obedience alone may not result in an immediate outcome. Jesus was obedient to the cross, but the immediate outcome was his own death on the cross.

Future-reward situations show up in daily life in a number of ways. Perhaps God calls you to sow money into a ministry or another person's life without expectation of return from them. Perhaps you are called to serve another person without expectation of any earthly reward. The situations we might encounter are unlimited.

## Question
Are you living a life based on a future reward or short-term reward?

*Father, help me evaluate how I make decisions and how I allocate my resources.*

# Hanging Out with Sinners

*When Jesus reached the spot, he looked up and said to him,*
*"Zacchaeus, come down immediately. I must stay at your house today."*
LUKE 19:5 NIV

Jesus modeled four things when he lived on the earth that allowed him to impact other people's lives. I call them the four *B*s of transformation.

First, he *built a relationship* with other people. In the marketplace, it is rare that you can impact a person without building a relationship first. The adage that people don't care what you know until they know that you care is especially true in the workplace. Jesus built relationships with the people around him.

Jesus *blessed them*. He tried to meet whatever physical need they had. Many times he healed them first then told them to go and sin no more. He listened to their concerns.

The third thing Jesus did was he *began praying* for them. He often prayed for deliverance for a person who was demon possessed. He prayed they would know the Father.

Finally, he *brought the kingdom of God* into their lives. He invited people to believe in him as the Savior of the world and to partake of eternal life.

I decided to test this model with an acquaintance. I intentionally refused to talk about Jesus to this person until I had accomplished the first three steps in my relationship with him. After I had fulfilled the first three steps, I presented Christ to my friend. He received Christ immediately because the soil was prepared and he was ready to receive.

## Question
Are you prepared to follow these four stages of relationship building before you present Christ to others?

*Father, help me follow Jesus' example of loving and caring for others.*

# Do Not Reach for Power

*We are those who boast in what Jesus Christ has done,*
*and not in what we can accomplish in our own strength.*
PHILIPPIANS 3:3 TPT

Years ago, I was asked by a large organization to meet with them about doing some cooperative projects in the faith-at-work area. I visited their headquarters and, after several meetings, concluded that we should proceed on a joint conference.

During my overnight visit, I was awakened at 5 a.m. and led to read Exodus 33:15. Moses said he could not go any farther if God did not promise that his presence would go with him. I sensed this was to be our theme for the conference.

Later that morning, when I shared this with the leader of the organization, he did not take it seriously. I was a bit irritated, and my pride was hurt, but I decided to follow a principle that I had been walking in for a few years: "Act like you have the authority but do not reach for the power." I realized that if God had truly spoken his words into my heart, I would not have to exercise my authority to make it happen. God would orchestrate it.

More discussion was given to the theme, but nothing was decided. Hours later the conference theme came up again. I turned to a friend and read Exodus 33:15 aloud, and he got excited about using that verse as the theme. The leader, to my amazement, chimed in as well and said, "Yes, that should be the theme of the conference." It was a big lesson for me.

## Question
Do you reach for the power or allow God to guide and direct?

*Father, help me realize my spiritual authority but to never reach for the power.*

# Thinking outside the Box

*This He said to test him,*
*for He Himself knew what He would do.*
JOHN 6:6 NKJV

Jesus and the disciples had just crossed the Sea of Galilee, and multitudes followed him because of the miracles they saw him do. He was about to speak to them when Jesus realized it was dinner time, and the people would be hungry. There were more than five thousand people who needed to be fed.

Jesus already knew what he was going to do in this situation. However, he was testing the disciples to see if they would think beyond themselves to find a God-solution to the problem. They failed the test. They immediately thought like most of us would think. The disciples looked in their pocketbooks and realized they did not have adequate resources to purchase enough food for the crowd.

It is when we come to the end of our resources that God comes in with his. It is when this happens that we should manifest God's power in our problem. That's what Peter did when the crippled man asked him for money in Act 3. He told him he did not have money, but what he did have was the power of God. The man was healed.

## Question
When a problem arises in your work life,
do you think of only the most logical solution?

*Father, help me to go outside the box and see the glory of God manifested in my problem!*

# Team Building

*"You shall receive power when the Holy Spirit has come upon you;
and you shall be witnesses to Me in Jerusalem, and in all Judea and Samaria,
and to the end of the earth."*

ACTS 1:8 NKJV

Building a good team is key to the success of any enterprise. Jesus chose twelve unique individuals to build his world-changing enterprise. He intentionally chose several who had similar backgrounds—Peter, James, and John were fisherman. However, Matthew the tax collector and Simon the Zealot were probably worlds apart in their experiences and worldview. Matthew came from an industry many considered corrupt. It is clear Jesus chose those who had a skill set first, then he changed the character of the individual. He mentored each one.

A good team needs to have team members with different viewpoints as well as those who are specialists in a particular area. It is noteworthy that Jesus chose someone with expertise in handling money. Taking a team of twelve around the country required money and the ability to manage it. I'm sure Jesus changed Matthew's perspective on the proper use of money throughout their time together.

Once the team was formed, Jesus spent time molding his team into a cohesive unit. He corrected them when they needed to be corrected. He taught them what it meant to love one another. He washed their feet. He taught and modeled servant leadership. Before you put a team together, sit down and make a list of the skills you want represented on your team. Then recruit and invest spiritually into your team. Who knows, your team might just change the world too!

## Question
Are you responsible for managing a team?

*Father, show me how to be a person of character equal to my skills.*

# Receiving What God Gives

*"A person can receive only what is given them from heaven."*
JOHN 3:27 NIV

John the Baptist was in the business of bringing sinners to the place of repentance by baptizing them and teaching them about the coming Messiah. Over time, he had developed quite a group of disciples. Yet when the promised Messiah showed up—the fulfillment of John's business plan—true to form, his coworkers (or disciples) went to John to complain that the one about whom he had testified was stealing all of their "customers." "Rabbi," they said, "that man who was with you on the other side of the Jordan…look, he is baptizing, and everyone is going to him" (John 3:26 NIV). John's response showed clearly that he understood his purpose and role in life in the above verse.

John understood that we receive by understanding our purpose and what God desires us to receive in light of our purpose. We need not worry about what others receive. Many of us try to receive things God never intended us to receive or to be someone God never intended us to be.

We are to receive from God based on our obedience and by doing our work unto the Lord. He is the source of our increase and provision in life and work. God provides the principle of sowing and reaping so that we understand we must participate in the process by sowing (working) and receiving fruit from our work-life calling.

## Question

Do you model receiving only what God has given to you through obedience?

*Father, help me to receive only what you desire me to receive.*

# Mourning for Your City

*So it was, when I heard these words, that I sat down and wept, and mourned for many days; I was fasting and praying before the God of heaven.*
NEHEMIAH 1:4 NKJV

Nehemiah lived in the world of politics. He was a high-ranking worker in the government of Babylon. His official title was cupbearer for King Artaxerxes. He would be considered the modern-day US Secret Service agent who made sure the king was safe from being poisoned. Judah had been driven into exile, and some of his friends had just returned with news about his fellow brothers and sisters in Jerusalem.

I was in Shushan the citadel, that Hanani one of my brethren came with men from Judah; and I asked them concerning the Jews who had escaped, who had survived the captivity, and concerning Jerusalem. And they said to me, "The survivors who are left from the captivity in the province are there in great distress and reproach. The wall of Jerusalem is also broken down, and its gates are burned with fire." (Nehemiah 1:1–3)

Nehemiah's response upon hearing the news is the kind of response that is necessary for a Christian leader to impact his or her city. He responded by weeping for the condition of his beloved city. He immediately went into prayer and asked for God's direction for how he could be a positive impact on his city. He developed a strategy to rebuild the wall of Jerusalem. He accomplished the task in only fifty-two days.

God is calling forth men and women from the marketplace today to be catalysts to impact their cities.

## Question
### Do you weep for your city?

*Father, help me to pray for my city and to be a catalyst to rebuild its spiritual walls.*

# Thinking Big

*"Most assuredly, I say to you, he who believes in Me, the works that I do he will do also; and greater works than these he will do, because I go to My Father."*

JOHN 14:12 NKJV

It was 4:00 a.m. in Cape Town, South Africa, in July 2000 when businessman Graham Power was awakened by a vision from God that came in three distinct parts. In the first part of the vision, God instructed Graham to rent the forty-five-thousand-seat Newlands rugby stadium in Cape Town for a day of repentance and prayer for that city. In the second part of the vision, he saw the prayer movement spreading to the rest of South Africa for a National Day of Prayer. In the final part of the vision, he saw the prayer effort spread to cover the rest of the continent.

It was only thirty days earlier that a man named Gunnar Olson stood in front of a podium at the conclusion of a marketplace conference in Johannesburg, South Africa, and proclaimed Isaiah 60 over the continent of Africa and that God was going to use Africa to bless the nations.

Graham was obedient to the vision, and on March 21, 2001, a capacity crowd gathered in the Newlands rugby stadium for prayer and repentance. Soon after, a notorious gangster in the city was saved. News of the first gathering spread quickly, and in 2002, eight cities in South Africa hosted a day of prayer. The events were broadcast on television.

By June 2006, what began as Transformation Africa became the Global Day of Prayer with participation from two hundred nations from seven continents around the world.

It all started from the obedience of one businessman.

## Question
What might God want to do through your life?

*Father, help me to be sensitive to the leading of the Holy Spirit in my life.*

# God Owns My Business

*"Therefore if you have not been faithful in the unrighteous mammon, who will commit to your trust the true riches?"*

LUKE 16:11 NKJV

Stanley Tam was an innovator in the reclamation of silver in the photographic process but is best known for his commitment to Jesus Christ. A large sign adorning the home of United States Plastic Corporation proclaims, "Christ Is the Answer," and Tam's widely read book, *God Owns My Business,* describes how he arrived at the conviction that he should legally make God the literal owner of his business.

Tam, who has traveled throughout the country and world to testify about his Christian faith, is one who is willing to "put his money where his mouth is." Although his business success could have made him a millionaire many times over, he and his wife, Juanita, draw only modest salaries from US Plastics. All profits are channeled through his foundation, with those funds designated for a variety of Christian ministries, primarily overseas missions.

In the fall of 1954, Tam was speaking at a revival meeting in Medellin, Colombia, when God confronted him in a supernatural way. God let him know he wanted him to turn the business over to him completely and become his employee. So, on January 15, 1955, Stanley Tam ceased being a stockholder in either of his companies, States Smelting and Refining Corporation or United States Plastic Corporation. "I don't think there is such a thing as a part-time Christian; we are all in full-time ministry," says Tam.[23]

## Question

Does God own your business or your work life? If not, why not make that decision today and let him use your work life for his glory.

*Father, I submit all my work and business to you to use for your purposes.*

# Hearing God on the Job

*"I am the good shepherd; I know my sheep and my sheep know me...*
*My sheep listen to my voice; I know them, and they follow me."*
JOHN 10:14, 27 NIV

Tom Fox is a successful financial investment manager who heads up a workplace ministry in the Twin Cities, Minnesota, area. He used to be troubled when he heard Christians say, "The Lord told me..." He certainly had never heard God speak to him like that. "What is different about those people and me?" he wondered. Tom had read that Jesus had said that his sheep hear his voice, but he didn't understand how they could do that. His pursuit to answer that question began his quest to discover how to hear God's voice himself.

Fortunately, Tom discovered how to hear God's words of guidance in his daily life by spending time in God's Word and being more aware of his direction in his life. He practiced this in the day-to-day operations of his business, and he is teaching others how to hear God's voice as well.

Many people wrongfully believe God does not speak today. Yet the Bible says, "My sheep hear my voice" (John 10:27 ESV). Jesus promises to reveal himself the more we seek him: "He who has My commandments and keeps them, it is he who loves Me. And he who loves Me will be loved by My Father, and I will love him and manifest Myself to him" (John 14:21 NKJV).

We are to seek Jesus with all of our heart. When we do this, we will discover that quiet voice inside, a prompting, a knowing inside that the God who made us is directing our steps. Proverbs 3:5–6 says that we are to trust the Lord with all of our heart and lean not on our own understanding. And if we acknowledge him, he will direct our steps.

## Question
### Do you struggle to hear God's voice?

*Father, thank you that you speak to me—even on the job.*

# Live as Though You Are Dead

*Since you are now joined with him, you must continually view yourselves as dead and unresponsive to sin's appeal while living daily for God's pleasure in union with Jesus, the Anointed One.*

ROMANS 6:11 TPT

How will I know when I am going to come out of my adversity pit?" the man asked me.

"When it doesn't matter anymore," I replied.

It brought back memories of when I also had sat across from a mentor who said to me, "The only problem you have, Os, is you are not 'dead' yet. You need a good funeral." He was talking about my carnal flesh life. He was encouraging me to lay aside my old life to live a new life in Christ, letting the old life die.

When Joseph was elevated to be ruler over the entire kingdom of Egypt after years of slavery and imprisonment, my guess is that it didn't really matter that much to him. I believe Joseph had become dead to his circumstances. It does not mean we can't have a longing for better days, but there is a godly contentment that allows us to remain in any condition with a peace that passes all understanding.

The Bible says we are to live as though we are dead. This does not mean we do not have emotions or dreams. "Then He said to them, 'My soul is exceedingly sorrowful, even to death'" (Mark 14:34 NKJV). That sounds like anxiety to me, yet we know Jesus never sinned. So, we can conclude that we can have concerns and emotions without crossing over into sin. God has given us his Spirit to allow us to operate inside the storms of life without sinning.

## Question
Have you become dead to anxiety and fear of the future?

*Father, thank you for calming the storms in my life.*

# Spiritual Life Is Caught

*Elisha then left his oxen and ran after Elijah.*
1 KINGS 19:20 NIV

There is a man in my life whom I consider my mentor. He came into my life during a crisis period and helped me understand my situation. I have learned a great deal from him though I have rarely spent more than a few hours in his presence at any one time. I mostly *caught* what I have learned. He never took me through a Bible study. He never sent me articles or things to read. I learned by being around him.

One day I had a crisis arise. I remembered what my mentor did in a crisis in his life. I decided to apply the same faith principle to that issue. Amazingly, a miracle occurred because I applied faith, just as my mentor had, to my crisis. This is what I mean by catching the faith of another. Spiritual truth is learned through the atmosphere that surrounds us, not through intellectual reasoning.

When Elijah handpicked Elisha as his successor, Elisha immediately killed his twelve sets of oxen and ran after Elijah just to be with him. No doubt he knew what a great privilege it was to be selected by the great prophet. However, it was not enough for Elisha to be handpicked. He also wanted a double portion of Elijah's anointing. It appears that God answered this prayer.

If you want to grow in your Christian life, ask God to lead you to a man who is far ahead of you spiritually and simply start hanging out with him to catch what he has.

## Question
Do you have a mentor in your life?

*Father, lead me to a mentor in my life that can be a source of encouragement and wisdom for me.*

# Speak to Your Mountain

*"Have faith in God. For assuredly, I say to you, whoever says to this mountain,
'Be removed and be cast into the sea,' and does not doubt in his heart,
but believes that those things he says will be done, he will have whatever he says."*
MARK 11:22–23 NKJV

I recently taught on the principle of using our authority to speak to our mountains in our work life. A man wrote me after reading my testimony.

I own a video company that shoots a variety of projects. One day, my editor discovered a videographer's worst nightmare—a garbled mess of video picture and little or no audio on tapes that I had shot the weekend before. Four tapes of raw footage from two separate events were ruined.

I laid my hands on the tapes and prayed for restoration…God had told me that the tapes would be fine in a day. My associate challenged me to put in the tape anyway and not wait. I put a tape in the editing deck, and right before our eyes, the tape now had a perfectly clear picture and audio where there had been no sound moments before.

The next morning, I put in one of the remaining damaged tapes…I prayed aloud over the ruined footage and reassured my wife…

Suddenly, before our eyes, the tape began to clear up. Just as my pastor announced how God intimately loves us on the video, I turned to look at my wife and saw the tears streaming down her face. Apparently, God had designed this moment to touch her deeply on issues that only the two of them knew about. Not only did God save my business, but he also ministered to my family through this crisis-fixing miracle.

## Question
What type of mountain might God want you to speak to today?

*Father, thank you for giving us the authority to move our mountains.*

# The Real Deal

*God kept releasing a flow of extraordinary miracles through the hands of Paul. Because of this, people took Paul's handkerchiefs and articles of clothing, even pieces of cloth that had touched his skin, laying them on the bodies of the sick, and diseases and demons left them and they were healed.*

Acts 19:11–12 TPT

We have an expression in America that says, "He's the real deal." What we are saying is that the person in question is really who they appear to be. They are not trying to be or to convince you that they are someone they are not. It is a compliment when someone says, "You are the real deal."

The apostle Paul was the real deal. God began using Paul in amazing ways. There arose people who saw this power and wanted to do the same acts as Paul.

> Then some of the itinerant Jewish exorcists took it upon themselves to call the name of the Lord Jesus over those who had evil spirits, saying, "We exorcise you by the Jesus whom Paul preaches." Also there were seven sons of Sceva, a Jewish chief priest, who did so. And the evil spirit answered and said, "Jesus I know, and Paul I know; but who are you?" Then the man in whom the evil spirit was leaped on them, overpowered them, and prevailed against them, so that they fled out of that house naked and wounded. (Acts 19:13–16 NKJV)

It is impossible to be the real deal without tapping into the real power source. The Holy Spirit is our power source.

## Question

Do you want to experience miracles in your walk with God?

*Father, reveal your power in and through my work life.*

# Four Types of Christians

*When you yield to the life of the Spirit, you will no longer be living under the law, but soaring above it!*

GALATIANS 5:18 TPT

In his book *Anointed for Business*, Ed Silvoso provides a thoughtful look at the four types of Christians in the workplace. The following four categories provide an excellent tool for self-assessment:

1. The Christian who is simply trying to survive.
2. The Christian who is living by Christian principles.
3. The Christian who is living by the power of the Holy Spirit.
4. The Christian who is transforming his or her workplaces for Christ.[24]

Category one: Christians who are simply trying to survive have no purpose or zeal for integrating their faith at work. They have not seen the power or presence of God in their work lives. Such Christians segment their faith life from their work life.

Category two: The second type of Christian in the workplace includes those who are living by Christian principles. Twelve-step programs can be helpful to change bad habits, but they may not yield the spiritual change God requires.

Category three: Christians who are living by the power of the Holy Spirit understand the importance of developing a heart toward God through prayer, study of the Word of God, and obedience.

Category four: A wonderful by-product of living by the power of the Holy Spirit is that you can transform your workplace for God. Christians who passionately seek the manifestation of God's kingdom here on earth will be able to realize this transformation in their workplaces.

## Question
What category of believer are you?

*Father, show me see how I can transform my workplace today.*

# Asa, a Model King Until...

*"Because you have relied on the king of Syria, and have not relied on the LORD your God, therefore the army of the king of Syria has escaped from your hand."*

2 CHRONICLES 16:7 NKJV

Asa was a godly king of Judah. There were two kingdoms during his reign—Judah and Israel. Israel's king was Baasha, who was a wicked king. To the east of Judah was Damascus, whose king was Ben-Hadad. Asa was an amazingly faithful and righteous king for thirty-five years. He got rid of the idol worship and even deposed his mother for idol worship. God blessed his rule by allowing peace in the land for thirty-five years.

When Asa came into power, the nation was lost. There was no godly ruler. There were many wars, and the people began to cry out to God for deliverance. God sent them Asa.

However, thirty-five years later, Asa began to move away from trusting God and decided he could buy the favor of his enemy, the king Ben-Hadad. Asa sent gold and silver to him as a bribe, asking Ben-Hadad to cancel his treaty with King Baasha and go to war on behalf of Asa and Judah. Asa's strategy worked, and he defeated Israel. However, there was a cost.

What we learn from Asa is that whenever we place our trust and obedience in the Lord, God becomes our source of security and prosperity. However, when we move away from trusting God, that security is removed, and we fail to receive those things God intended us to have.

## Question
Where are you placing your trust today?

*I am grateful, Father, that I can put my complete trust in you.*

# The Integrity Test

*Yahweh, who dares to dwell with you?*
*Who presumes the privilege of being close to you,*
*living next to you in your shining place of glory?*

PSALM 15:1 TPT

Lack of integrity is nothing new. The Bible is full of examples. One of these involves Gehazi, the assistant to the most famous prophet of his day, Elisha. It's hard to imagine that anyone working with such an anointed man, who saw firsthand the power of God, would fail the integrity test. But he did.

When Elisha healed Naaman, a general in the army, from leprosy, he didn't expect to be compensated, and he didn't ask for money. When Naaman insisted that Elisha take some form of payment, the prophet answered, "As surely as the LORD lives, whom I serve, I will not accept a thing" (2 Kings 5:16 NIV).

Gehazi, however, did not agree with his employer and took matters into his own hands. "Gehazi, the servant of Elisha the man of God, said to himself, 'My master was too easy on Naaman, this Aramean, by not accepting from him what he brought. As surely as the LORD lives, I will run after him and get something from him'" (v. 20 NIV).

As a result of his sin, God judged Gehazi. Elisha fired him, and God struck him with leprosy, and his life was never the same. He was removed from serving one of God's most extraordinary prophets.

Each of us has the potential of being a Gehazi if we do not have a foundation built into our lives that makes us willing to receive only what God gives us through the fruit of our obedience.

## Question
### Would you pass the integrity test?

*Father, keep my motives pure in all I do.*

# Can Your Boss Say This?

*Pharaoh said to his servants, "Can we find such a one as this,
a man in whom is the Spirit of God?"*
GENESIS 41:38 NKJV

God has uniquely gifted you to bring his presence and power in the area of your calling. Once you begin to realize this, God will use you just as he did Joseph with his employer, Pharaoh. Your life should be a testimony of the power, creativity, and servanthood of Jesus that it impacts your employer to the degree that he says the same thing Pharaoh said about Joseph: "Can we find anyone like this man, one in whom is the Spirit of God?"

When God accomplishes this in your life, he gives you authority in your workplace. You will begin to see others drawn to you. You may begin to be ostracized as well. This, too, is part of your call. Do not fear this. Embrace it.

We should not be seeking to remove ourselves from the pressure cooker of life but using that pressure cooker to reveal the power and grace of God through our lives to others. It is here that we will receive our inheritance as we fulfill our purposes in and through our work-life call.

## Question
Do people say you are a person filled with the Spirit of God?

*Father, I pray for supernatural wisdom and discernment to manifest your presence and power in my work life.*

# Balance the Natural and Spiritual

*Even if the best warrior went to battle, he could not be saved simply by his strength alone. Human strength and the weapons of man are false hopes for victory; they may seem mighty, but they will always disappoint.*

PSALM 33:16–17 TPT

The Bible tells us not to put our confidence in things the world considers to be our protection, defense, or strength. However, the man or woman who does not perform well on the job is left behind in today's competitive world. Not only is this typical of the world at large, but even many Christians promote the importance of identifying our strengths and encourage us to move in them to accomplish God's will. Yet, we are discouraged from depending upon our own strengths. Instead, we are urged to rely totally upon the Lord.

God wants us to depend upon him, and he demonstrates this throughout Scripture. For example, in Judges 7, God wouldn't let Gideon fight against another army until he reduced his own from twenty-two thousand soldiers to a mere three hundred so that Gideon could not boast about his army's strength. In Joshua 6, God told Joshua to walk around Jericho seven times and blow trumpets instead of relying upon his mighty army to overpower his enemy. In 2 Samuel 24, God judged David when he counted his troops to determine the size of his army's strength, apparently because David took the census out of pride or overconfidence in the strength of his army.

Today, bring every project and endeavor before the Lord as you ask for his power and grace to accomplish it using both your natural gifts and God's Spirit working together.

## Question
### Where are you placing your faith today?

*Father, I trust you to accomplish your work through me today.*

# The Fertile Pasture

*Shepherd Your people with Your staff, the flock of Your heritage,
who dwell solitarily in a woodland, in the midst of Carmel;
let them feed in Bashan and Gilead, as in days of old.*
MICAH 7:14 NKJV

There are a people who live isolated in a wasteland of stressful workplaces and seemingly endless pressure trying to make sense of their daily life. They don't realize it, but deep down inside, they long for a shepherd who will help them discover their own purpose and reason for living. They are the lost majority in the marketplace who are living lives as though they are a child, lost and aimless in a deep, dark forest.

Though most do not know it, they long for a pastor who will reveal to them their destinies. Your staff, which represents your vocation, is the means by which God is going to use you to pastor those in your sphere of influence in the workplace. This is where you will derive your inheritance. The people you serve will be the spiritual inheritance God has allotted to you.

This forest is more fertile than all other potential fields because the power and authority represented by this forest have the potential to impact far greater fields. This forest has CEOs, presidents of nations, entertainment moguls, media tycoons, and educators, to name just a few. They are the shapers of society who have yet to meet their maker.

## Question

Are you willing to use your staff to be a shepherd to those in the fertile pasturelands?

*Father, help me to pastor others in the workplace.*

# Promoted beyond Your Anointing

*The anointing which you have received from Him abides in you, and you do not need that anyone teach you; but as the same anointing teaches you concerning all things, and is true, and is not a lie, and just as it has taught you, you will abide in Him.*
1 JOHN 2:27 NKJV

Have you ever done a job so well that you were promoted outside your skill set? The exceptional salesman gets promoted to manager and fails as a manager. The secretary gets promoted to office manager but fails for lack of management skills. Understanding your anointing will enable you to know when you are moving in a direction away from that which God has intended for your life. Sometimes God will place you in situations in which you have no natural gifting. In these cases, God puts you there to experience his power in order to accomplish your tasks.

An organization hired a career consulting company to take all its employees through a series of tests to determine if each employee fits into his or her proper job function. When the results for one employee were shared with the rest of her team, her profile revealed that one of her greatest weaknesses was a lack of organization and focus. Her boss didn't believe the results of this assessment and publicly acknowledged that this employee was the most detailed and organized individual on the entire team. "How could that be true?" he asked.

The consultant said, "Her personality profile would indicate she would normally be weak in the areas described, but she has overcome her natural weaknesses by learning to be focused and detailed."

## Question
Are you allowing the Holy Spirit to reshape you and your gifts?

*Father, reshape and develop me in areas where I need to be reshaped by your Holy Spirit.*

# New Paradigms

*"Yes, he has hidden himself among the supplies."*
1 SAMUEL 10:22 NIV

If you want to experience something you've never done, you must do something you've never done. In *Experiencing God: Knowing and Doing the Will of God*, Henry Blackaby writes, "You can't stay where you are and go with God at the same time."[25]

God often has to radically change us if we are going to fulfill his purposes in our lives. Saul was about to be anointed by Samuel as the first king of Israel. Samuel said to Saul, "The Spirit of the Lord will come powerfully upon you, and you will prophesy with them; and you will be changed into a different person" (1 Samuel 10:6 NIV). Up to this point, Saul had never prophesied or led a group of people.

Saul took a big step of faith right away and prophesied with the prophets just as Samuel said he would. Yet, when Samuel called the entire nation of Israel together to announce him as Israel's first king in history, Saul was nowhere to be found. This part of the story is humorous. When they called Saul's name, he didn't even come forward. So, the people "inquired further of the LORD, 'Has the man come here yet?' And the LORD said, 'Behold, he is hiding himself among the baggage'" (v. 22 NASB).

Your greatest setback can be thinking that there's no way that God can use "little me." However, the reality is that he can and will if we respond to the new places he takes us.

## Question
Is God moving you into a place that is not comfortable?

*Father, help me respond in faith to wherever you take me.*

# The Workaholic

*You did not receive the spirit of bondage again to fear,*
*but you received the Spirit of adoption by whom we cry out, "Abba, Father."*
ROMANS 8:15 NKJV

Living a balanced life is evidence of a Spirit-led life. People work long hours for many reasons, which can lead to significant problems in our lives.

One reason people overwork is that they often think they must work longer hours to keep up with their workload. Like any compulsive behavior, there is usually something beneath this behavior. As a former workaholic myself, I can tell you the root of overworking is often (1) a fear of loss or lack and (2) a need for self-acceptance created by performance.

The fear of loss or lack can be a fear of what will happen if we don't work long hours. A fear that there may not be enough money if we don't put in extra time can drive us to overwork. Often an inaccurate view of what is enough makes us drive ourselves to greater levels of achievement, believing a financial reward will insure us against potential financial disaster.

The second reason people work long hours is their need to gain self-acceptance and esteem from their jobs. However, when we begin to be driven to work more, it becomes an unhealthy condition. We are looking to gain self-esteem from our performance instead of being secure in our position in Christ.

So, in order to avoid letting work become an idol and a compulsive behavior, we must maintain a balance that allows us to spend quality time with the Lord, our families, and fellow believers.

## Question

Do you ever work long hours for either of the two reasons described above?

*Father, help me to trust you to be my provider.*

# Closed on Sunday

*"Observe the Sabbath, because it is holy to you."*
EXODUS 31:14 NIV

Can a business have a Christian testimony without ever saying a word?

Atlanta-based Chick-fil-A, Inc., is America's largest quick-service chicken restaurant chain. The company's stated corporate purpose is "to glorify God by being a faithful steward of all that is entrusted to us, and to have a positive influence on all who come in contact with Chick-fil-A."[26] The company is a great example of a business that is modeling Christian values and producing a quality product in the competitive fast-food industry. Chick-fil-A is one of the fastest-growing chains nationally, with over $11 billion in annual sales in 2019.[27]

One of the defining distinctions of Chick-fil-A is that the restaurants are not open on Sundays. From the time Truett Cathy, the company's founder, started in the restaurant business in 1946, he believed that God wanted him to honor the Sabbath by keeping the stores closed on Sundays. Although he was challenged on this idea many times by shopping mall operators, Truett always held that Chick-fil-A can have more sales in six days than those that are open for seven.[28] This has proven to be true.

Chick-fil-A demonstrates the faith of its people through kingdom values without having to preach. They model the character of Christ through the training of their staff and management. They provide extraordinary customer service and offer an exceptional product. They uphold quality in every area and train their staff to be friendly, personable, and meticulous in how they serve their customers. I've personally witnessed this through my interaction with their leadership and staff as a speaker at their headquarters in Atlanta and as a customer.

## Question
How is your faith translated in the way you do your work?

*Father, help me reflect your values in the way I do my work.*

# Faithful to the Truth

*Behold, you desire truth in the inward parts.*
*You teach me wisdom in the inmost place.*
PSALM 51:6 WEB

Kenneth Lay was the chairman and CEO of Enron, a multibillion-dollar energy corporation that went bankrupt at the hands of its executives because of mismanagement and misrepresentation of its financial practices. Many people lost their retirement investments or their life savings as a result.

In 1996, Kenneth Lay made a comment in a book entitled *Business as a Calling* by Michael Novak.

> In my own case I grew up the son of a Baptist minister. From this background, I was fully exposed to not only legal behavior but moral and ethical behavior and what that means from the standpoint of leading organizations and people. I was, and am, a strong believer that one of the most satisfying things in life is to create a highly moral and ethical environment in which every individual is allowed and encouraged to realize their God-given potential. There are few things more satisfying than to see individuals reach levels of performance that they would have thought was virtually impossible for themselves.[29]

Something went very wrong from the time Kenneth Lay wrote those words and the time he was convicted of securities and wire fraud in May 2006.

The Scriptures are full of men and women who did great things for God but did not finish well toward the latter part of their lives.

## Question
How can you pursue truth in your work today?

*Father, protect me from pride that can lead to ethical failure.*

# The Black Hole

*"My grace is sufficient for you."*
2 CORINTHIANS 12:9 NKJV

If you are older than thirty-five, you may recall the early days of the space program. I remember the early spacecraft launch with John Glenn. One of the most exciting and tense moments of his return to earth was his reentry to the earth's atmosphere. There was a blackout period for several minutes in which mission control had no radio contact with Glenn's capsule. He was in the "black hole." Then, mission control shouted with joy when they reestablished contact with the spacecraft. It was a time of rejoicing.

Have you ever had a time when you were in a spiritual black hole in your life? I have. The pressure was unbearable. No sense of God's presence. No sense of anything going on around me. God was about as far away as the man in the moon—at least from my perspective. I think every Christian who is called to make a significant difference in this world experiences times like these. These are the times when we question the reality of God, the love of God, the personal care of God. And he demonstrates to us that he was there all the time. These times are needed in order to know that we have the "heat shield" that can withstand the incredible heat that comes when we follow God with a whole heart—a heart that is radical in its commitment to fully follow his ways.

The apostle Paul asked God to remove the heat from his own life one time (see 2 Corinthians 12). God's answer was not what he wanted to hear. He told him his grace would be sufficient.

## Question
How's your heat shield today? Can it withstand the heat that would want to burn up everything in your life not based in him?

*Father, I pray your grace can be my heat shield today.*

# Trinity of City Transformation

*Now while Paul waited for them at Athens, his spirit was provoked within him when he saw that the city was given over to idols. Therefore he reasoned in the synagogue with the Jews and with the Gentile worshipers, and in the marketplace daily with those who happened to be there.*

ACTS 17:16–17 NKJV

In order to transform a city or nation, the work must take place in two areas: the local church and the marketplace. Paul was burdened for Athens when he saw all of the idols in his city. So, he began a strategy to win back his city by preaching in both the synagogue to the religious leaders and Jews and those in the marketplace every day.

Over the years I have worked in city-reaching movements. I found there is a "trinity" of relationships required to impact a city. This group is made up of intercessors who pray for the city, churches that have a passion for serving the city by solving problems, and marketplace leaders who make positive changes with their finances and influence through businesses in that city. These three must work in tandem by identifying and solving problems in their city in order to see real change. People don't care who solves their problems; they just want their problems solved. When you do that, you gain more influence in the city.

God is moving today in cities across the world through collaborative coalitions made up of intercessors, priests, and kings. This is a city transformation trinity that the Holy Spirit is forming to rid our cities of idols and restore the spiritual foundations.

## Question
Are you called to impact your city for Christ?

*Pray that God raises up godly workplace leaders who will lead with a biblical worldview.*

# Beware of Unusual Circumstances

*Each believer is given continuous revelation by the Holy Spirit*
*to benefit not just himself but all.*
1 CORINTHIANS 12:7 TPT

Whenever something unusual happens in daily life, these are often signs that God is up to something. We must have a heightened sense of awareness of what God may want to do in these situations. My mentor once shared how he was upgraded on an airline unexpectedly. A woman sat down next to him who was very troubled. He began to quietly pray for the woman, and God gave him supernatural insights that her problem was related to the fact that she had not forgiven her mother in a family-related issue. He decided to politely share his insight. The woman was shocked. My mentor began to minister to her on the airplane and ultimately led her to Christ.

God is raising the spiritual bar for Christians who want to impact the world for Christ today. He wants to break through into people's lives supernaturally by giving them insights into the needs of people in order to bring them to Christ.

Jesus often spoke supernaturally into the lives of others based on the circumstance of the moment. He often spoke of their current condition in life and invited them to make a change.

Be aware that God is always working around you.

## Question
Are you available to speak into the lives of others?

*Father, make me sensitive to daily opportunities to minister to those with whom I come in contact.*

# Your Promised Land

*"I have said to you, 'You shall inherit their land, and I will give it to you to possess, a land flowing with milk and honey.' I am the LORD your God, who has separated you from the peoples."*

LEVITICUS 20:24 ESV

God called the people of Israel to leave Egypt and come out of slavery in order to enter their own promised land. It meant they had to change the way of life they had always known. Instead of being told what to do every day by a taskmaster, they were now being led by the cloud of God into the desert with the ultimate goal of entering their own promised land.

Every believer has a promised land in his life. It is the place where you receive all God intends for you to receive. However, many of us are still living in Egypt, where we sweat and toil in response to the taskmaster of production dictated by our workplaces and our lifestyles of busyness.

We will know when we are beginning to experience our promised land when we experience God's rest while we are fulfilling our work-life call. We will begin to give testimony to what Joshua says in the above verse. We will begin to receive things we never built or planted. We begin to experience a level of rest in our working lives that is not characterized by sweat and toil. Things become easier because we are receiving them as a fruit of our call instead of a goal.

## Question
Are you living in your promised land? Be obedient to his voice.

*Father, show me the steps to take to receive my promised land.*

# What's Your Brand?

*The one who calls you is faithful, and he will do it.*
1 THESSALONIANS 5:24 NIV

Companies spend millions of dollars making their brands known in business. They want you to recognize their brand, associate it with positive thoughts, and have it influence your next purchasing decision. Companies like Coca-Cola, Nike, Mercedes, and Walmart are brands that have built a reputation over many years. The idea is that when you think of their brand, you will associate their brand with their product.

Every individual has a personal "brand," whether you want one or not. Cultures have a brand. Your brand is defined by your conduct. If you are always late, you'll soon develop a brand or reputation for being late. Others will even show up late because they know you will be late. If you are a person who exaggerates the truth, others will soon learn not to take you seriously.

However, the opposite can also be true. Your brand can be incredibly positive. By being a man of your word, who is consistent in dealing fairly and honestly with others, your brand becomes known as someone who is faithful in all aspects of life.

God's "brand" is his faithfulness. Faithfulness means one is true to fulfilling his promises to others within the time to which he commits. God is faithful to fulfill all his promises to his children.

## Question

What is your brand among your peers? Is it a positive brand, or does it need improvement?

*Lord, today make me a faithful brand that others can trust.*

# Faith Is Spelled R.I.S.K.

*Peter got down out of the boat, walked on the water and came toward Jesus.*
*But when he saw the wind, he was afraid and, beginning to sink, cried out,*
*"Lord, save me!"*

MATTHEW 14:29–30 NIV

Jesus told Peter to get out of the boat. There is always a risk when we attempt something no one has ever done before. Naysayers seem to come out of the woodwork. Why? Because it's not their vision; it's yours. Sometimes we fail the first time out. It's a fact that most entrepreneurs fail before they are successful.

"Success," as Winston Churchill is often credited with saying, "is going from failure to failure without loss of enthusiasm." Everybody fails. It's part of the process that leads us to maturity and success. Most successful entrepreneurs don't think of their failures as defeats. They think of them as lessons.

If you hope to succeed, learn everything you can from your failures. In *The Three Success Secrets of Shamgar*, Orlando Magic executive Pat Williams observed, "Our experiences may not all be triumphs and successes, but so what? Failure is usually a far better teacher than success—if we are willing to learn the lessons. As Houston Astros pitcher Larry Dierker observed, 'Experience is the best teacher, but a hard grader. She gives the test first, the lesson later.'"[30]

Someone once said, "When your memories are bigger than your dreams, you're headed for the grave." God wants to give us new dreams that are bigger than anything that has ever happened to us in the past.

## Question
Have you ever let failure keep you from trying again?

*Father, help me to use my failures to fail forward so I can succeed in the future.*

# A New Kind of Army

*Proclaim this among the nations: Prepare for war! Rouse the warriors! Let all the fighting men draw near and attack. Beat your plowshares into swords and your pruning hooks into spears.*
JOEL 3:9–10 NIV

God is raising up a new kind of army in these last days. It is the remnant in the body of Christ that has the greatest potential for societal transformation of any segment of society—men in the workplace. It is a remnant that has been largely silent.

Plowshares and pruning hooks are agricultural instruments that farmers use in their work. The prophet Joel says these very instruments will be used in the last days as weapons of war. However, it won't be a war against man and an enemy but against the kingdom of darkness.

As we enter the last days, men will begin to see their vocations as instruments to defeat the forces of evil and usher in the kingdom of God. You will see Christ glorified in the marketplace like never before. You will see hundreds and thousands become part of a new harvest of souls in the "nine-to-five window"—where many have yet to experience the saving knowledge of Jesus Christ—as men share the gospel with coworkers and experience God in new and dramatic ways in their work-life calling.

You are a spiritual warrior in a worker's uniform. God has called you to transform your view of yourself and your work. He desires to use you and your work life to impact your workplace, city, and nation.

## Question
Are you ready to beat your plowshare into a sword and your pruning hook into a spear?

*Father, help me to use my work-life call as a weapon of love.*

# Recognizing the Religious Spirit

*"Woe to you, scribes and Pharisees, hypocrites! For you pay tithe of mint and anise and cummin, and have neglected the weightier matters of the law: justice and mercy and faith. These you ought to have done, without leaving the others undone."*

MATTHEW 23:23 NKJV

Living according to rules and regulations and by our own human efforts is a trap set by the religious spirit that we can all fall into in the workplace. Here are some characteristics of how the religious spirit manifests itself in believers:

- Workers may have difficulty praying and applying God's promises to everyday work encounters.
- Workers may believe that biblical truths apply only to their personal lives, families, and churches, not to their jobs.
- Workers may focus on evangelizing coworkers but fail to do their work with excellence.
- Workers may give greater priority to religious activity and events than to relationships with others at work.
- Workers maintain an "us" versus "them" attitude when relating to non-Christians in the workplace.
- Workers may refuse to join a workplace prayer group or Bible study because they feel that the group will try to replace the role of their local church. Workers don't see a need for such activity in the workplace.
- Workers feel the need to compartmentalize faith activities to their local church alone.
- Workers discount the idea that Christianity could transform a workplace, city, or nation as "overzealous," "naive," or even doctrinally wrong.

## Question
Do you model your faith at work?

*Father, help me to be available 24/7 as a representative of the kingdom of heaven.*

# Noah's Building Plan

*Noah did everything just as God commanded him.*
GENESIS 6:22 NIV

When God chooses to do something on the earth, he uses a man or woman to accomplish it. It is a partnership that is very one-sided. God gets the worst part of the deal.

God got to a very bad place with the human race. He decided to start over. He was going to wipe out the entire population and begin afresh. He chose one man upon which to base his entire strategy. Can you imagine that? God placed his entire plan around one man. Why? Because he could trust him. The Bible says Noah did everything just as God commanded him. He didn't argue with God. He didn't take shortcuts. He listened, and he obeyed.

Who was this man called Noah? "Noah was a righteous man, blameless among the people of his time, and he walked faithfully with God" (Genesis 6:9). When it came time to execute God's plan, he chose Noah to build a big boat. However, living in the desert, Noah had no idea what a boat was or how to build one. So, God told him how to build it. He gave him the dimensions: the height, width, space requirements—everything he needed to complete the task.

God will instruct us in performing our work too. God is in partnership with us in our working life. He has given us the tools, the creativity, and the drive to accomplish what he placed us on earth to do.

## Question
Do you need God to show you how to succeed in your call?

*Father, I ask for wisdom and understanding that you promise to give generously (James 1:5).*

# Prayer at Work

*Epaphras, who is also from Colossae, sends his loving greetings. I can tell you that
he is a true servant of Christ, who always labors and intercedes for you.*
COLOSSIANS 4:12–13 TPT

Many of us have been entrenched in the "secular versus sacred" model for so long that it can be difficult for us to view our work as a ministry and workplace believers as missionaries in the nine-to-five window. However, God tells us clearly that we are to glorify God in all that we do (see Colossians 3:17, 24). Having people pray for us to fulfill our purpose and calling in our workplaces is consistent with the will of God for every individual.

While the idea of a workplace intercessor may be a new concept for us, we need to remember the examples we find in the New Testament of believers praying for one another, such as Epaphras in the Scripture above.

Colin Ferreira is a friend, a board member for our ministry, and the owner of an optical business in Trinidad. I first met Colin in 2001 when he invited me to speak at a Caribbean workplace conference that he was organizing. I have watched Colin develop into a kingdom business leader.

Through a series of struggles common to most businesses, Colin began to recognize the need for more prayer coverage. One of the organizations for which he had been supplying financial and leadership support maintained a prayer ministry. Colin asked the minister who headed the organization to intercede for him and his company on an ongoing basis, and she gladly agreed.

The two met periodically to discuss prayer needs and critical issues developing within the organization, which the minister then prayed for.

## Question

Is prayer a regular part of your time with God? Are you in relationship with others who are praying for you?

*Father, help me make prayer a priority in my life.*

# The Ultimate Performance Review

*If anyone's work which he has built on it endures,*
*he will receive a reward.*

1 CORINTHIANS 3:14 NKJV

Have you ever had a job performance review? If you are in the workplace, you will likely have had one. Employers want to see if you have done what was requested of you and whether you have done it in the prescribed way that has produced the anticipated results. If you do well, you will be affirmed and may even get a pay raise. If you fail to live up to expectations, you could even get fired.

The Bible has its own performance review. It is called the judgment seat: "For we must all appear before the judgment seat of Christ, that each one may receive the things done in the body, according to what he has done, whether good or bad" (2 Corinthians 5:10).

The generation that came out of Egypt with Moses is going to have a bad day at the judgment seat because we already know God's view on the matter. "Therefore I was angry with that generation, and said, 'They always go astray in their heart, and they have not known My ways'" (Hebrews 3:10). The Bible says, "There is a way that seems right to a man, but its end is the way of death" (Proverbs 14:12).

There is a way in which God wants you and me to operate on the earth. He has given us his Word—our instruction manual—in order to know his ways of doing things.

## Question

How well do you know the instruction manual?

*Father, help me be a student of your Word.*

# Wanted: Dead or Alive

*Our struggle is not against flesh and blood, but against the rulers, against the authorities, against the powers of this dark world and against the spiritual forces of evil in the heavenly realms.*

EPHESIANS 6:12 NIV

In the Old West, it was common to see a poster on the wall of the town jail or post office with a man's picture below the words *Wanted: Dead or Alive!* These depicted the most notorious criminals who posed the greatest danger to society.

Let me ask you some personal questions. Is there a "Wanted: Dead or Alive" poster in hell with your name on it? Are you a real danger to hell? Do you cause problems for Satan's legion of demons? Are you pushing back Satan's agenda on planet earth? Are the unsaved in danger of receiving salvation through you? Will someone receive healing because you dared to pray for them? Will someone's life be impacted because you chose to pray for them in your workplace during a difficult time? Will a city be impacted for Jesus Christ because of you?

Millions of believers sit on the sidelines every day, having no impact on the kingdom of darkness. Their names will never appear on a wanted poster in hell because Satan sees that they are no threat. However, God wants you to be a threat to Satan's kingdom.

What are some things you can do that will pose a threat to Satan's agenda? Perhaps you can begin praying for one of Satan's most notorious talk show personalities. Or maybe you are called to visit a retirement home to bring the love of Christ into a lonely place. There are many ways you can earn a reputation in hell.

## Question

Are you willing to be a force that Satan's legions will have to reckon with?

*Father, help my life be feared by the kingdom of darkness.*

# Uriah

*"Wherever two or three come together in honor of my name,
I am right there with them!"*
MATTHEW 18:20 TPT

My friend Rick shared a story about an encounter he had when praying with a couple whose business was struggling financially.

> I waited for a few moments until a word popped into my mind. The word was Uriah. I knew that Uriah was the husband of Bathsheba and that King David had ordered Uriah to be sent to the front lines of a battle where there was a high likelihood that he would be killed. That is exactly what happened. Essentially David murdered Uriah so that he could take Bathsheba away from him. Wow! What did all this have to do with the couple who was seated in front of me?
>
> I told the couple about the word that just popped into my mind. When I spoke that word, Uriah, the wife immediately dissolved into tears. "Oh Lord," she cried, "I knew that you were going to make me confess all of these sins." She went on to describe how she had been married previously. At work she fell in love with another man (her current husband) and colluded with that man to extricate her from her marriage to her first husband. Once the first husband was out of the way (divorced, not murdered), the two now in front of me were free to become husband and wife…In short, they didn't have a business problem—they had a sin problem!

## Question
Do you have a problem in your workplace?

*Father, thank you for knowing the source of and solution to every problem.*

# Graduate-Level Christianity

*"Love your enemies and pray for those who persecute you."*
MATTHEW 5:44 NIV

There was a man who had become a friend and mentor to me, but a conflict arose between us that we were unable to resolve. I never imagined that this man would go from being one of my best friends to an enemy. I asked God to show me how I should treat this man, and the words of Jesus came to mind: *Love your enemies and pray for those who persecute you.*

*Lord,* I said, *surely you don't mean I'm to* love *this man! Not after the way he's hurt me and refused to reconcile!*

As I argued with God, I remembered that Jesus, before he was betrayed, got down on his knees and washed the feet of Judas Iscariot, his enemy. The moment that scene came to my mind, I knew what God was calling me to do. I had to wash the feet of my Judas.

This man had once been my friend and mentor. He was a Christian author and speaker, and I decided to bless this man by continuing to promote his ministry and his books.

Did he ever come back to me and reconcile? Yes, seven years later. But even if he had never reconciled with me, I knew that I did what God called me to do. I washed the feet of my Judas. I passed the test.

God doesn't promise that, if we forgive, there will be a happy ending. He doesn't promise that the man who refuses to pay a bill will suddenly write a check. The "Graduate-Level Test" is not about getting the results we want. Those whom God calls to leadership are often required to embrace a higher standard of obedience that may have a personal cost to it.

## Question

Are you willing to be an imitator of Jesus?

*Father, help me acquire the nature of Christ in all that I do.*

# Why the Workplace?

*Stop imitating the ideals and opinions of the culture around you, but be inwardly transformed by the Holy Spirit through a total reformation of how you think.*

ROMANS 12:2 TPT

I often receive requests from the media for interviews about the faith-at-work movement. One day a writer from the *New York Times Magazine* called. After several interviews, the reporter asked me, "Can you point me to someone who can demonstrate what this looks like in a daily workplace?" I told the writer to give my friend Chuck a call. Chuck was a banker who is a great example of a Christian impacting his workplace and city for Christ.

I told Chuck that the reporter would be calling him, and Chuck and I immediately began praying for the writer. A few days later, Chuck called me and said the Lord was going to use this article not only for the workplace movement but also in this writer's life.

The writer visited Chuck and the bank for two days and attended community meetings, interviewed all the employees of the bank, and watched Chuck pray for many people at the bank.

Afterward, Chuck asked the writer about his own relationship with God, which led to him praying to receive Christ. Two weeks later, photographers came to take pictures for the article, and they, too, prayed to receive Christ.

When the article was published, it was one of the best, most extensive, and balanced articles on the faith-at-work movement that has been written from a secular viewpoint.

## Question
How might God use you to impact your workplace?

*Father, thank you for choosing me to represent you in the workplace.*

# Manipulation in the Workplace

*The acts of the flesh are obvious: sexual immorality, impurity and debauchery; idolatry and witchcraft; hatred, discord, jealousy, fits of rage, selfish ambition, dissensions, factions.*

GALATIANS 5:19–20 NIV

The envelope arrived in my mailbox with the exciting announcement on the outside: "You've just won $1 million dollars!" Of course, like you, I have gotten so many of these over the years that I automatically filed it in my nearby deep file—the trash can. The sensational headline is used to get you to open the envelope only to discover they are trying to sell you magazines with an opportunity to be entered into a sweepstakes drawing that could allow you to win a million dollars.

Every day we are exposed to manipulative ploys in the workplace. Some might even call it "bait and switch." An offer is made that appears to say one thing, but it is actually asking you to do something else.

Whenever you do something that has the appearance of giving something for nothing with the intentional goal of coercing someone to take action through deceptive practices, you have engaged in manipulation. You see this take place in advertising, marketing, and even Christian ministries.

In order to avoid engaging in manipulative practices in the workplace, ask yourself if you are attempting to persuade others to buy your product by using deceptive practices. Make sure you are conveying the truth about your product or service and what it professes to do. Don't use gimmicky sales approaches to engage others.

## Question

Are you promoting your products or services with truth and integrity?

*Father, help me be truthful in all my marketing efforts.*

# Godly Forefathers

*The Angel of the L*ORD *admonished Joshua, saying, "Thus says the L*ORD *of hosts:*
*'If you will walk in My ways, and if you will keep My command, then you shall*
*also judge My house, and likewise have charge of My courts; I will give you places*
*to walk among these who stand here.'"*

ZECHARIAH 3:6–7 NKJV

In a Wednesday morning prayer, the speaker, commonly believed to be George Washington, entreated God with these words: "Almighty and eternal Lord God, the great Creator of heaven and earth, and the God and Father of our Lord Jesus Christ; look down from heaven in pity and compassion upon me Thy servant, who humbly prostrates myself before Thee."

On another occasion he said, "To the distinguished character of a patriot, it should be our highest glory to add the more distinguished character of a Christian."[31]

America was founded as a Christian nation. The Founding Fathers had deep faith in Jesus Christ. Today, there is a movement designed to remove God from our history and our foundations. When we do this, America will no longer be good. And when America ceases to be good, we will cease to be great.

## Question
Are you standing in the gap for revival to come to our nation?

*Father, I pray that this generation might acknowledge and embrace its godly heritage and that you will raise up other leaders who lead from a godly foundation.*

# When Doing Right Ends Wrong

*My fellow believers, when it seems as though you are facing nothing but difficulties, see it as an invaluable opportunity to experience the greatest joy that you can! For you know that when your faith is tested it stirs up in you the power of endurance.*

JAMES 1:2–3 TPT

Sports can teach us a lot of valuable life lessons if we let them. I played sports growing up and was a golf professional for three years in the 1970s. Sometimes we buy into the idea that if we will do all the right things and execute the perfect golf swing or the perfect baseball pitch or the perfect whatever, we are guaranteed success. Sometimes this is true: the outcome matches the execution and the goal. However, in sports, as well as in life, success is not guaranteed.

Sometimes you can make the perfect golf swing and end up in a divot or bunker, while other times you can make a great baseball pitch, and the batter will hit a home run. The examples are limitless.

So, what do we do when the outcome is bad? We must accept that in sports, as in life, outcomes don't always end the way we hope.

Jesus came to be the Savior of the world. He was a perfect human being without sin. He did all the right things. The result was death on the cross because a short-term positive outcome was not God's plan for the situation. He had a bigger picture in mind.

## Question

Have you ever done everything right and still had an enterprise turn out really bad?

*Father, give me the grace to accept bad outcomes that occur even when I have done all the right things.*

# Wrestling with God

*The sun rose above him as he passed Peniel, and he was limping because of his hip.*
GENESIS 32:31 NIV

Jacob connived and manipulated his way to get what he wanted. It was a generational stronghold passed down through his mother, who encouraged her son to play a trick on his father, Isaac, by pretending to be Esau. This trick resulted in Isaac giving the family blessing to Jacob, which meant Jacob would eventually inherit the land God had promised to Abraham's seed.

Jacob's crisis came years later when he was faced with the prospect of meeting his brother, who said he would kill him the next time he saw him. Esau had built his own clan and was about to meet Jacob and his clan in the middle of the desert. Jacob was fearful, so he retreated. There he met a messenger from God who wrestled with him. Jacob clung to God and refused to let go of this angel. It is the place where Jacob was given a painful but necessary spiritual heart transplant. From that point on, Jacob would walk with a limp because God had to dislocate his hip in order to overcome Jacob's strong will.

For workplace believers, God often has to "dislocate our hip" through failure and disappointment. Our nature to control and manipulate is often so strong that it takes a catastrophic event to wake us up. Yet God did not reject Jacob for these character traits. In fact, God blessed him greatly because he saw a humble and contrite heart beneath the cold and manipulative exterior. Jacob's encounter with the messenger was marked by Jacob getting a new name, Israel. For the first time, Jacob had a nature change, not just a habit change.

## Question
What will God have to do in your life to gain your complete consecration to his will and purposes?

*Father, reveal any area in my life that is not under your control.*

# Are You Becoming Secularized?

*This is why God lifted off his restraining hand and let them have full expression of their sinful and shameful desires. They were given over to moral depravity, dishonoring their bodies by sexual perversion among themselves—all because they traded the truth of God for a lie.*

ROMANS 1:24–25 TPT

When describing the condition of our country, I often use the analogy of the frog in the kettle. When a frog sits in warm water and the water begins to increase in temperature, the frog adjusts to the temperature until it does not recognize how hot it has gotten, and eventually, it dies.

Societies suffer from this same condition when we fail to call sin, sin. Changes in public opinion about sexuality, abortion, and euthanasia and a lack of Christian influence are adopted gradually into the culture. Eventually, the people wake up one day and realize the country they once loved has radically changed and that it's too late to return. They realize the freedoms they once had no longer exist. It didn't happen overnight but over many decades. Gradually we begin to see secular ideology penetrate the educational systems, and these values are further reflected in business, media, arts, and entertainment.

America is being influenced by socialistic and Marxist ideology today. The only way this trend will be reversed is if there is a heart change in the people. Our nation is in desperate need of revival. Pray that God will move in our nation and the other nations of the world.

## Question
Is your faith relevant to the world in which you are living?

*Father, allow me to be salt and light to the culture in which I live.*

# Two Grocers

*"You shall have a perfect and just weight, a perfect and just measure, that your days may be lengthened in the land which the LORD your God is giving you."*

DEUTERONOMY 25:15 NKJV

A few hundred years ago, there were two Christian grocers in London. One of them said to the other, "You know, as Christians, we're supposed to have honest scales. It says so in the Bible. So how should we do that?"

"Well, I'll tell you what," said the other grocer. "I'll come and check your scales on Wednesdays to make sure they're accurate, and you come on Sundays and check mine. We'll make sure they're accurate." The two grocers developed a list of twelve principles that they felt should guide the way they were to do business.

People preferred to buy from them because they knew they would get a good product at a fair price and weighed on honest scales. Other grocers who were Christians decided to join in, and they formed an association of Christian grocers. In those days it was actually called the Most Worshipful Company of Livery Merchants.

This group led to other industries adopting a similar idealism known as Livery Companies in the City of London. The rulers of Britain began to see the effect of these companies and said, "What we need to do is make it a law for the whole nation. So instead of just these grocers having their honest scales, every scale in Britain needs to weigh accurately." The government's Weights and Measures Department, which is still in existence today, can trace its history back to the day when these two grocers decided to keep themselves accountable for biblical principles."[32]

## Question

Are you operating based on honest weights and measures?

*Father, I pray you raise up more godly companies around the world.*

# David Fulfilled His Purpose

*"For David...served the purpose of God in his own generation."*
ACTS 13:36 ESV

Imagine for a moment that you have just died and you are about to come before the judgment seat of Christ. Jesus is speaking to his angel about you. He then says these words: "John served the purpose of my heavenly Father for his generation."

Will God be able to say you served your purpose in your generation? Imagine being able to say that. God was able to say this about the life of David even though David made some incredibly bad choices in his life that led to long-term consequences. However, because David repented each time he erred, his purpose was accomplished on earth as God had designed it.

Success is fulfilling the complete purpose for which God made you. It has nothing to do with wealth, accomplishments, stature in life, or standard of living. It has to do with living a life of obedience to the Father. And when we live a life of obedience to the Father, we will fulfill the purposes that God had in mind when he made you and me.

## Question
Is God using you to fulfill an assignment on earth?

*God, help me fulfill my purposes for my life in this generation.*

# Freedom and Boundaries

*The LORD God commanded the man, saying, "Of every tree of the garden you may freely eat; but of the tree of the knowledge of good and evil you shall not eat, for in the day that you eat of it you shall surely die."*

GENESIS 2:16–17 NKJV

Everyone needs the gift of freedom and boundaries in their work to succeed. God set up the ultimate work environment in the garden of Eden. He gave Adam and Eve the responsibility to manage the animals, the agriculture, and every activity. He gave them specific instructions as to how things were to be done but gave liberty of expression for fulfilling their tasks.

He also told them what was off-limits. They could not eat from the tree of good and evil because he knew it would be bad for them. He was not trying to withhold from them; he was trying to protect them.

If you are a manager, it is your responsibility to clearly define the job responsibilities of those under your care. They should know without a doubt what their freedoms and their boundaries are in carrying out their duties. They should be given adequate freedoms with authority to enforce their decisions that will impact whether they can be successful or not.

Once freedoms and boundaries are established, this allows healthy accountability to take place between management and worker.

## Question

Do you have a clearly defined job description with measurable goals outlined? Are your freedom and boundaries clearly defined so you know what you can and cannot do within the scope of your job? If not, you are setting yourself up for failure.

*Father, thank you for providing freedom and boundaries in my life.*

# Spirit-Led Creativity

*David gave his son Solomon…the plans for all that he had by the Spirit, of the courts of the house of the LORD, of all the chambers all around, of the treasuries of the house of God, and of the treasuries for the dedicated things.*

1 CHRONICLES 28:11–12 NKJV

George Washington Carver would get up early in the morning each day to walk alone and pray. He asked God how he was to spend his day and what God wanted to teach him that day. Carver grew up at the close of the Civil War in a one-room shanty on the home of Moses Carver—the man who owned his mother. The Ku Klux Klan had abducted him and his mother, selling her to new owners. He was later found and returned to his owner, but his mother was never seen again.

Carver grew up at the height of racial discrimination, yet he had overcome all these obstacles to become one of the most influential men in the history of the United States.

He made many discoveries with the use of peanuts and sweet potatoes. However, after he recommended to farmers that they plant peanuts and sweet potatoes instead of cotton, he was led into his greatest trial. The farmers lost even more money due to the lack of market demand for peanuts and sweet potatoes. Carver prayed, "Mr. Creator, why did you make the peanut?" Years later, he shared that God led him back to his lab and worked with him to discover some three hundred marketable products from the peanut. He made over one hundred discoveries from the sweet potato. These new products created a demand for peanuts and sweet potatoes, and they were major contributors to rejuvenating the Southern economy.[33]

## Question
Have you asked God what he wants to create through you?

*Father, thank you for using me to create things that will be useful for others.*

# Managing Money

*He who loves silver will not be satisfied with silver;*
*nor he who loves abundance, with increase.*
*This also is vanity.*
ECCLESIASTES 5:10 NKJV

A successful businessman once confided in another businessman known for his wisdom. "I've made a lot of money. I will soon be able to retire comfortably and do just about anything I want."

"John," the wise businessman replied to the man, "I've noticed that nearly every time someone thinks they've built a tree that is so tall it almost reaches heaven, God decides to shake the tree."

Money is mentioned more than two thousand times in the Scripture. Jesus referred to it many times in illustrating an important lesson to his disciples. He often spoke of being a good steward of the resources he entrusts to us. He wants a return on his investment, and he wants us to stay away from making money an idol in our lives.

As we look at our relationship to our heavenly Father and our use of money, it is clear that we, like Jesus, are here to do the will of the Father in all areas of life. This means seeking to live a life that is totally yielded to his purposes—even in the financial area.

Money, independence, and security are often the reasons many start their own businesses or change jobs. Check your motives today and see if your financial life can stand Jesus' scrutiny.

## Question
Are you operating as a faithful steward of the financial resources he has entrusted to you?

*Father, help me be a good steward of all you entrust to me.*

# Recalibrating Route

*The crooked places shall be made straight
and the rough ways smooth.*
LUKE 3:5 NKJV

I love the GPS in new cars. A voice comes on and tells me how far I have to go and when to turn. However, sometimes I get off course, and the voice says, "Recalculating route." The GPS is telling me I have gone off course, and it is now recalculating the best route based on my wrong turn. Sometimes we can make wrong turns in our spiritual lives. We think we are going the right direction only to discover it was never God's will to enter that relationship, make that business deal, hire that person—the examples are limitless.

There is an amazing thing about God. He can make our crooked places straight. He has the ability to make whatever blunder you make turn out right. It may mean there might be some consequences to those decisions, but he will always allow our actions to work together for good for those called according to his purposes if we repent and seek him fully to make things right.

God's omnipotence is always one step ahead of our incompetence. Do you think he knew you would make that misstep? Absolutely. Do you think your life was planned even with that misstep figured in? Absolutely.

Isn't it comforting to know you cannot plan God out of the equation no matter how bad you mess up? He will always turn crooked places into straight places for those who are humble and contrite.

## Question
Do you need a crooked place straightened out today?

*Father, I pray you straighten the course so I can flow in your perfect will.*

# Trained for War

*Blessed be the LORD my Rock,*
*who trains my hands for war,*
*and my fingers for battle.*

PSALM 144:1 NKJV

You'll never experience God in powerful ways by acquiring Bible knowledge alone. It is only when that knowledge is used in the heat of battle that you will know the reality of what you've learned intellectually. Otherwise, it remains only an exercise in spiritual gymnastics that yields little fruit.

David became a great warrior and leader of a nation at an early age. His training ground was his job as a shepherd in the open fields. When bears and lions sought to take his sheep, he personally fought them. This was his early preparation for future battles. Goliath was the real competition amongst a discerning audience to reveal how well his training prepared him.

Today, our local churches often look more like luxury cruise liners designed to tickle the ears, entertain their members, and make them feel good instead of a battleship designed to train an army for war. The average member still watches from the sidelines.

In sports you discover how well you handle pressure by competing. You can practice all you want, but you never know how you will do until you enter the game and test what you've learned and practiced when there is pressure added to the equation. In battle you discover how well you are trained by what you actually do on the battlefield.

## Question

Have you ever prayed with someone in public? Have you ever personally led someone to Christ? Have you ever served others for the sake of the gospel? Have you ever taught a Bible study? Get engaged in the game.

*Father, give me the grace to step onto the battlefield.*

# A Conversation in Heaven

*I will raise up for Myself a faithful priest*
*who shall do according to what is in My heart and in My mind.*
1 SAMUEL 2:35 NKJV

I once imagined a meeting in heaven between the angel Gabriel and Jesus. It went something like this: "Gabriel, I chose twelve men from the workplace to build my church. They were an unlikely group. But I wanted a people to express my life where they spent most of their time and experienced most of their challenges. However, today we have a problem. My church is not being represented in the workplace. So, I've decided to call several people to serve me in this arena.

"There is a man who reminds me of my servant Jacob. Boy, what a manipulator and controller he was before I did my work in him. Now you recall that Jacob became one of the patriarchs! This businessman has the same potential. He is our man to awaken my servants. However, I must remove some things he relies upon. This will draw him to me. It will be painful at first but necessary. It will take seven years. But I plan to restore all I take from him.

"The result will be quite amazing. He will engage many others. He'll usher in a whole new focus in my church that has been lost since those early days. I plan to do this with many others as well. My plan is designed to raise up an army in these last days before I return. Gabriel, it is time for you to go now. You know what you must do. Be gentle but firm with my servant."

## Question
What kind of conversation might Jesus and an angel have about your life?

*Father, do whatever is needed for me to fulfill my destiny while living on this earth.*

# Seven Needs

*The weapons of our warfare are not carnal but mighty in God for pulling down strongholds, casting down arguments and every high thing that exalts itself against the knowledge of God, bringing every thought into captivity to the obedience of Christ.*

2 CORINTHIANS 10:4–5 NKJV

Jerry had grown up with a father who was a successful businessman but a workaholic. Although Jerry lacked for nothing materially, he never sensed much warmth or compassion from his parents. Then, when Jerry was still in his early teens, his father died very suddenly. His large family was left with little support. Vowing to himself that he would never experience financial need again, Jerry worked hard at his business. A stronghold of insecurity and fear brought reliance on the wealth he had accumulated rather than a prayerful dependence on God.

Jerry renounced the strongholds of insecurity and fear that had made money his idol. The Holy Spirit began to restore balance and intimacy with God and others as a result.

God created human beings with seven primary needs, as represented in Genesis 1 and 2. Each of us has a need for (1) dignity, (2) authority, (3) blessing and provision, (4) security, (5) purpose and meaning, (6) freedom and boundary, and (7) intimate love and companionship.[34]

Whenever we seek to meet one or more of these basic needs outside God's design, we set the stage for the development of a generational stronghold. Jerry discovered that he was attempting to me his needs through a demonic stronghold of insecurity and fear.

## Question
Do you have any generational strongholds impacting your life?

*Father, help me remove any strongholds that keep me from experiencing these seven needs.*

# Confront and Support

*Paul insisted that they should not take with them the one who had departed from them in Pamphylia, and had not gone with them to the work. Then the contention became so sharp that they parted from one another.*

ACTS 15:38–39 NKJV

Conflict in the workplace, ministry, or even marriage is inevitable because you are working closely with one another. God has wired each of us with different personalities that can view circumstances differently. One person can see a situation and conclude something totally different from another.

There are times when differences and conflicts just cannot be resolved. It doesn't mean that one person or the other is evil or sinful. It just means that the difference of opinion or the personality clash has no solution. John Mark had disappointed Paul once before, and Paul didn't want to give him another chance even though Barnabas wanted John Mark to join them on a later journey. In the end, Paul and Barnabas agreed to disagree about including John Mark, and they parted company.

There's a postscript to this story. In 2 Timothy 4:11, Paul wrote from his prison cell in Rome and told Timothy, "Get Mark and bring him with you, because he is helpful to me in my ministry" (NIV). Sometime after the disagreement between Paul and Barnabas, John Mark redeemed himself and became a valued partner in Paul's ministry. In fact, as Paul faced execution in Rome, he wanted his friend John Mark at his side.

Whenever there is disagreement, make sure you maintain the support of the person at the same time you disagree with their position. Avoid personal attacks and implying the motive behind someone else's position. This will allow you to disagree and still maintain a relationship.

## Question
Is there someone with whom you have a conflict?

*Father, help me handle conflict while still supporting the relationship.*

# The Place of Nothingness

*Be still, and know that I am God.*
PSALM 46:10 NKJV

Do you find yourself in a place of nothingness? There is a time in our walk with God when he sets us in a place of isolation and waiting. It is a place in which all past experiences are of no value. It is a time of such stillness that it can disturb the most faithful if we do not understand that he is the one who has brought us to this place for only a season. It is as if God has placed a wall around us. No new opportunities—simply inactivity.

During these times, God is calling us aside to fashion something new in us. It is a place of nothingness designed to call us to deeper roots of prayer and faith. It is not a comfortable place, especially for a task-driven workplace believer. Our nature cries out, "You must do something," while God is saying, "Be still, and know that I am God."

Many people live a very planned and orchestrated life where they know almost everything that will happen. But for people in whom God is performing a deeper work, he brings them into a time of quietness that seems almost eerie. They cannot see what God is doing. They just know that he is doing a work that cannot be explained to themselves or to others.

## Question
Has God brought you to a place of nothingness?

*Father, help me to remain still and know that you are my God and the source of all I need today.*

# You Need Power

*"I promise you this—the Holy Spirit will come upon you, and you will be seized with power. You will be my messengers to Jerusalem, throughout Judea, the distant provinces—even to the remotest places on earth!"*

ACTS 1:8 TPT

D. L. Moody was a shoe salesman until God moved him into a full-time preaching ministry, often in the streets of Chicago. There came a point in his journey with God when he realized he needed more in his life than what he was experiencing:

> At the close of the Sabbath evening services I remember two holy women they would say to me, "We have been praying for you. You need power."
>
> I need power? I said to myself. Why, I thought I had power. I had a large sabbath school and the largest congregation in Chicago. I was in a sense satisfied. But then came these two godly women who prayed for me, and their earnest talk about "the anointing for special service" set me thinking. They prayed that I might receive the anointing of the Holy Ghost. And there came a great hunger into my soul. I knew not what it was. I began to cry as I never did before. The hunger increased. I kept on crying all the time that God would fill me with his Spirit. Well, one day, in the city of New York—Oh, what a day! I cannot describe it; I seldom refer to it; it is almost too sacred an experience to me.
>
> I went to preaching again. The sermons were no different; I did not present any new truths, and yet hundreds were converted. I would not be placed back where I was before that blessed experience if you would gave me all Glasgow.[35]

## Question

Are you experiencing God's power in your Christian life?

*Father, may the Holy Spirit be free to live through me in all areas of my life today.*

# Practicing the Presence of God

*Enoch walked with God.*
GENESIS 5:24 NKJV

The true test of a person's spiritual life and character is not what he does in the extraordinary moments of life but what he does during the daily grind of everyday life when there is nothing tremendous or exciting happening.

In the 1600s, there was a monk named Brother Lawrence who was a dishwasher in his monastery. He made a profound discovery that is true for every believer in the workplace today. "For me the time of activity does not differ from the time of prayer, and in the noise and clatter of my kitchen, while several persons are calling together calling for as many different things, I possess God in as great tranquility as when upon my knees at the blessed Sacrament."[36]

You see, he found no urgency for retreats because, in the most common task, he met the same God to love and worship as he did in the stillness of the desert. Enoch was a man who practiced the presence of God. The Bible does not give a detailed account of his life. All we know about him is that "He walked with God." In fact, it says in Genesis 5:22 that Enoch walked with God for three hundred years! Wow! That is faithfulness.

## Question

What does it mean to practice the presence of God daily? It means we are constantly talking to our heavenly Father about the issues in our day. It means praying about things as they come up. It means standing in line at the grocery store and praying for the person God brings to mind. It means singing a song of praise in your car while you are sitting in traffic. That is practicing the presence of God.

*Father, live through me every day and every moment of my life.*

# Why Does God Allow Evil?

*Lord, if you measured us and marked us with our sins,*
*who would ever have their prayers answered?*

PSALM 130:3 TPT

One of the most common questions every person wrestles with in life is this: "God, if you are loving, just, and all-powerful, why do you allow good people to suffer?" Billy Graham addressed this question in *Answers to Life's Problems*:

> We do not know all the reasons why God permits evil. We need to remember, however, that He is not the cause of evil in this world, and we should therefore not blame him for it. Remember that God did not create evil, as some believe. God created the world perfect. Man chose to defy God and go his own way, and it is man's fault that evil entered the world. Even so, God has provided the ultimate triumph of good over evil in Jesus Christ, who on the cross, defeated Satan and those who follow him. Christ is coming back and when He does, all evil will be ended forever and righteousness and justice will prevail.
>
> Have you ever thought about what would happen if God suddenly eliminated all the evil in this world? Not one person would be left, because we are all guilty of sin.
>
> Whenever we suffer, we should remember that the Son of God went before us, drinking the cup of suffering and death to the dregs. Because Christ is fully man and fully God, we know that God understands our fears, sorrows and suffering. He identifies with us.[37]

## Question
Do you sometimes struggle with why evil exists in the world?

*Father, help me to trust you for the answers to life's questions.*

# Block Logic

*Thus says the L<small>ORD</small> of hosts, the God of Israel:*
*"Houses and fields and vineyards shall be possessed again in this land."*
JEREMIAH 32:15 NKJV

In the Scriptures we discover a difference in the way the Hebrew mind viewed things compared to the way many Westerners relate to God. Hebrews used something called Block Logic. "That is, concepts were expressed in self-contained units or blocks of thought. These blocks did not necessarily fit together in any obvious rational or harmonious pattern."[38]

Greek logic, which has influenced the Western world, was different. "The Greeks often used tightly contained step logic, whereby one would argue from a premises to a conclusion, each step linked tightly to the next in coherent, rational, logical fashion."[39]

This is why some Bible stories don't make sense to the Western mind. "It is particularly difficult for Westerners—those whose thought patterns have been influenced more by the Greeks and Romans than by the Hebrews—to piece together the block logic of Scripture."[40]

Consider Jeremiah and God's instruction to purchase land at a seemingly inopportune time. If I asked you to purchase some land when you knew that the country you were living in was about to be invaded and you were sure to be placed under arrest, how wise do you believe such an investment would be? Do you believe God would lead you to make such an investment? That is exactly what God told Jeremiah to do. However, God had a good reason for having Jeremiah make such a purchase. It was to be a testimony and a promise that God was going to restore the Jews to their land.

## Question
Do you obey God even when it makes no sense?

*Father, give me the faith to obey even when I don't understand the logic behind the instruction.*

# Place Your Confidence in God

*Now Satan stood up against Israel,*
*and moved David to number Israel.*
1 CHRONICLES 21:1 NKJV

God always requires total trust in him alone for our victories in life. Throughout Scripture, we are cautioned not to place our trust in the strength of horses, other men, or our own abilities. David's decision to take a census was a failure to keep his trust totally in the Lord.

David's purpose in counting his population was to assess his military strength, much like the second census taken under Moses (Numbers 1:2–3). David found eight hundred thousand men eligible for military service in Israel and five hundred thousand men in Judah (2 Samuel 24:9), more than double the previous head count.

David's commander evidently recognized the grave error that his king was about to make. "But Joab replied, 'May the LORD multiply his troops a hundred times over. My lord the king, are they not all my lord's subjects? Why does my lord want to do this? Why should he bring guilt on Israel?'" (1 Chronicles 21:3 NIV).

This census displeased the Lord. David was falling into the temptation of trusting in the size of his army rather than in the Lord. God punished David and reduced his forces by bringing a plague that killed seventy thousand men (vv. 14–15).

## Question

How do we do this in our lives today? We trust our bank accounts, our skills, and the security of our workplace. When we begin placing our faith in these things instead of in the provider of these things, we get into trouble with God. What a lesson this is for each of us!

*Father, help me to trust you with every detail of my life.*

# Oaks of Righteousness

*"The Spirit of the Lord GOD is upon Me, because the LORD has anointed Me to preach good tidings to the poor; He has sent Me to heal the brokenhearted, to proclaim liberty to the captives, and the opening of the prison to those who are bound."*

ISAIAH 61:1 NKJV

It was the worst time in my life. Feeling betrayed by God, I stormed out the door and walked up the heavily wooded hill behind my house. Reaching the hilltop, I raged at God. "God!" I shouted, "Is this how you treat someone who is faithful to you? I've waited and waited. I've worked and prayed. And for what? For this? I hate you, God! I hate you!"

I sat down on an old oak tree that had broken at the base and was lying on the ground. For the next three hours, I sobbed uncontrollably, unable to speak, unable to pray. I wondered how God could abandon me. I wondered if he even existed. Maybe I had wasted my life believing in a myth.

Finally, I got up to leave. When I looked over at the fallen oak that I had sat on, I noticed something interesting. The fallen tree was pointed toward the base of another oak tree—a tree that stood strong and tall with wide-spreading branches. At that moment, I heard a quiet voice inside me say, *Today, like this broken oak tree, you are a broken man. But this brokenness was needed in order for you to become like the large, strong oak tree that stands before you.*

Years later, I would look back and know that God himself had spoken to me out of my period of darkness and silence.

## Question
Do you find yourself in a dark place?

*Father, I entrust my circumstance to you to fulfill your purposes through them.*

# The Eternal Sales Call

*If you publicly declare with your mouth that Jesus is Lord and believe in your heart that God raised him from the dead, you will experience salvation.*

ROMANS 10:9 TPT

I once had a conversation with a technology company CEO. He began receiving my *TGIF* devotional a few weeks earlier, compliments of his mother-in-law. Each morning he read the daily message and found that it really helped him.

He felt his technology product might assist our ministry. I could tell he probably did not know the Lord personally. So, I asked, "Could you tell me more about your spiritual journey and where you feel you are?" He told me of his background in which he was raised in a particular Christian tradition. I shared how Christ came not to give us a religion but to have a personal relationship with us.

"So, what do you think keeps you from making such a commitment?" I asked after sharing the gospel.

"Well, quite frankly, I feel that I can't let go of control. I fear what might happen."

I appreciated his honesty. I helped him understand that every person has a control issue to overcome. However, Christ requires us to give up control in order to give us real life.

"So, now that we have dealt with that issue, is there any reason you would not be prepared to make that commitment to Christ?"

"Well, now that you put it that way, no, I guess there isn't," he responded. The CEO prayed with me, and what he intended to be a typical sales call became a call for eternity.

## Question

Is there an opportunity today to use your work as a channel to share the love of Christ with someone who is waiting to receive salvation through you?

*Father, make me an instrument of your love for someone today.*

# Saved from Such Men

*By Your hand save me from such people, Lord,*
*from those of this world whose reward is in this life.*
PSALM 17:14 NIV

Whenever I travel over the ocean, I am always reminded of the seemingly insignificant time we have on this earth. I often imagine dropping a glass of water out the window of the jet into the huge body of water below. The Lord then reminds me that this is how my life is compared to eternity—a mere drop in the ocean.

Yet every day, millions of people will go to work seeking to gain that elusive thing called success. The rewards of this life continue to provide the incentive for sixty-hour weeks or the extra weekend away from the family. Sometimes we get entrenched in the message of the world. This message is an appealing, seductive call to sell out eternity for the temporal.

As a Christian businessman, I fell for this for many years until the Lord allowed me to wake up. It took some severe wake-up calls, but they did their job. I'm so grateful the Lord cares enough to give us these wake-up calls. He knows what real life is about. We think we know what it is only to learn once again that real life is found only in what we build on eternity.

## Question

How does the verse above line up with where you are today? Are you building around a world whose reward is in this lifetime or an eternal one? Do those with whom you associate live in such a way that they demonstrate their reward is not concerning this life?

*Father, give me the grace to seek first your kingdom and know that all these things will be added.*

# Confronting Evil

*The LORD sent Nathan to David.*
2 SAMUEL 12:1 NKJV

When God judges a situation, he often uses his servants as vessels for communicating to the guilty party. Such was the case with David, who tried to conceal his sin of sleeping with Bathsheba and then orchestrated a cover-up plot that included intentionally setting up her husband to be killed.

There are times when God may want to use you to be the instrument to judge unrighteousness. Sherron Watkins was a finance president at Enron, the now infamous Houston-based energy company that went bankrupt because of financial fraud by top-level executives. She was the one who became suspicious of her company's accounting practices.

She thought she might lose her job if she confronted other top-level managers. Yet, if she did not do something, it could impact the entire company and its employees. Sherron was a Christian and knew God was calling her to do something.

At first, she decided to use constructive ways to bring the problem to her superiors. Eventually, she met with CEO Kenneth Lay and outlined the elaborate accounting hoax that she believed was going on in the company. He ignored her concerns. Months later, the company collapsed when the problems came to light, and Lay was convicted on ten counts of conspiracy.

Sherron Watkins served as a modern-day Esther in the corporate world to expose a scandal that would destroy a company. She was recognized as *Time* magazine's "Person of the Year" in 2002 for her role in exposing the scandal.[41]

## Question
Are you willing to be the instrument of God, if necessary, to expose unrighteousness?

*Father, give me the courage to stand against unrighteousness when I encounter it.*

# Getting Picked

*"You didn't choose me, but I've chosen and commissioned you
to go into the world to bear fruit."*
JOHN 15:16 TPT

I will never forget the day in junior high school when I went to the gymnasium to view the list of those who made the basketball team. Several of us went excitedly to see who was on the list and who was not. I made it! The feelings of exhilaration were beyond description for a fourteen-year-old. Those who didn't make it were sad and downcast.

Most of us growing up either landed on the "picked" or the "unpicked" side of life. I often heard friends say, "I never got picked for anything. I wasn't very good in sports or music."

It is awesome to be picked by the God of the universe to be on his team. When God chose you, he knew what he was doing. God doesn't always pick those who have the greatest skill, the greatest aptitude, or even the greatest personality. However, he always has something in mind for those he picks.

There is one thing he requires of those he picks. They are not to be fruit-makers but fruit-bearers. Our goal should not be to bear fruit. Our goal should be to know the one who chose us and makes the fruit. When we really know the one who chose us, the fruit will be a natural by-product.

Today, as you begin your workday, consider where you will drop some fruit. It might be by praying for a coworker. It might be by simply greeting someone cheerfully during lunch. It might be by leading someone to the Savior today. Share your fruit freely.

## Question
Are you bearing fruit wherever you go?

*Father, make me a bearer of fruit through my life.*

# Jesus, the Carpenter

*Therefore, my brothers and sisters, make every effort to confirm your calling and election. For if you do these things, you will never stumble, and you will receive a rich welcome into the eternal kingdom of our Lord and Savior Jesus Christ.*

2 PETER 1:10–11 NIV

In the film *The Passion of the Christ*, produced by Mel Gibson, there is a wonderful scene that shows Jesus working as a carpenter. It is my favorite scene in the movie, and it gives us a rare glimpse of what his everyday life might have been like before his public ministry began.

Admittedly, God's strategy for sending the Savior of the world seems a little odd. Jesus was born into a working-class family. He worked with his father Joseph in his carpentry business until age thirty, so most of his adult life was given to "secular" labor. To build his church, he chose twelve men who had come straight from the workplace and who had no religious credentials for ministry.

Jesus' ministry focused on the marketplace, where people spent most of their time. Of his 132 public appearances in the New Testament, 122 of them were in the marketplace, and forty-five of his fifty-two parables had a workplace context. It is also interesting to note that of the forty divine encounters and miracles listed in the book of Acts, thirty-nine occurred in the workplace.[42] Jesus spent most of his adult life in the marketplace, not the synagogue.

## Question

When was the last time you experienced God's activity in your work life?

*Father, thank you that my work is a holy calling from you.*

# The Power of One

*Judah said to Simeon his brother, "Come up with me to my allotted territory, that we may fight against the Canaanites; and I will likewise go with you to your allotted territory." And Simeon went with him.*

JUDGES 1:3 NKJV

After the death of Joshua there arose a wicked king named Adoni-Bezek who was creating havoc in the land. He prided himself on defeating his enemies and cutting off their big toes and thumbs. He had done this to seventy kings. Now, without Joshua to lead them, the people wondered how they were to defeat this wicked king. Until this time, every king had attempted to defeat Adoni-Bezek themselves and had lost. The Lord told them they were to join forces with the other tribes in order to defeat this wicked king.

Today, God is calling the body of Christ together in cities to operate in unity in order to defeat the wickedness in our cities. However, the key to victory is a willingness of churches, workplace leaders, and intercessors to work together as a unified army.

Jesus said, "I in them, and You in Me; that they may be made perfect in one, and that the world may know that You have sent Me, and have loved them as You have loved Me" (John 17:23). God calls each of us individually and corporately to represent Christ to the world, but our independence, pride, and individualism often prevent us from becoming unified in the purposes of Christ. The marketplace and the church must come together to bless the city with practical initiatives that benefit the city.

## Question

Are you involved in any initiative to touch your city for Christ?

*Father, I pray for the peace of my city.*

# Responses to Adversity

*Though the fig tree may not blossom, nor fruit be on the vines; though the labor of the olive may fail, and the fields yield no food; though the flock may be cut off from the fold, and there be no herd in the stalls—yet I will rejoice in the LORD, I will joy in the God of my salvation.*

HABAKKUK 3:17–18 NKJV

When we experience adversity, we generally respond in one of three ways: (1) we become angry, (2) we try to gut it out, or (3) we accept it with joy.

*Getting Angry:* When adversity comes our way, we say, *Why me, Lord?* We become bitter and resentful and blame God and others for our problems. We view ourselves as victims and demand that God answer our accusing questions: *Why don't you love me, Lord?* We feel entitled to life, health, wealth, and happiness.

*Gutting It Out:* Another way we respond is by repressing our emotions. We lie to ourselves and say, *I'm pushing through this. I'm demonstrating endurance.* In reality, we are merely isolating ourselves with a shield of false bravado. We don't meditate on God's love, pray, or believe God really has anything good planned for us.

*Accepting It with Joy:* This is the response God seeks from us. When adversity comes, we rest in his love and trust that he knows best. We realize that nothing can happen to us without his permission. Habakkuk knew that Israel was about to suffer intense adversity as part of God's loving discipline through the looming national tragedy, and he faced this with an attitude of acceptance with joy.

## Question
Is there a situation that is challenging you to trust with joy?

*Father, help me to have the faith of Habakkuk and embrace my circumstance with faith.*

# The Spiritual Realm

*Here's what I've concluded. I will pray in the Spirit,*
*but I will also pray with my mind engaged.*
*I will sing rapturous praises in the Spirit,*
*but I will also sing with my mind engaged.*
1 CORINTHIANS 14:15 TPT

How real is the spiritual realm? My lawyer friend from Nigeria, Emeka, tells a personal story of how he was preparing for an important case he would present before his country's supreme court. He knew that he must be prepared to argue five separate points.

As he neared his court appearance, he began to pray about how he was to argue the case. He spent much time in legal preparation and intercessory prayer. As he went to court, the Spirit spoke to him and said, *Do not argue point one, point two, point three, or point four. Only argue point five.* Imagine my friend's struggle of faith. If he were understanding this wrong, the shame and professional fallout would be devastating.

When the time had come to present the case, my friend said, "Judge, I wish to withdraw points one through four. I wish to argue only point five."

The opposing counsel stood up. "Your honor, he cannot do that!"

"Objection overruled, counsel," said the judge.

My friend went on to present his case around point five only and then sat down. When the opposing counsel stood to present his case, he stood speechless for twelve minutes. He had not prepared for point five.

Emeka won the case.

## Question

When was the last time you had something happen that could only be explained as "God"?

*Father, help me live a supernatural life as my "natural" life.*

# Following His Will

*Yahweh, you can scrutinize me. Refine my heart and probe my every thought.*
*Put me to the test and you'll find me true.*
PSALM 26:2 TPT

Throughout the Old Testament, we see many situations in which God tests his people in order to determine if they will follow him or follow the systems of this world.

The nation of Israel was tested many times during the forty-year sojourn in the wilderness. "God led you all the way these forty years in the wilderness, to humble you and test you, to know what was in your heart, whether you would keep His commandments or not" (Deuteronomy 8:2 NKJV).

You might ask, "Why does God test us? Doesn't he know everything?" Yes, God knows, but we don't know ourselves. God doesn't test us in order to find out something he doesn't already know. He tests us so that we can learn about ourselves and his love, power, and faithfulness.

God tested Abraham by commanding him to sacrifice his son Isaac on a mountain in the land of Moriah. Isaac was Abraham's only son by his wife Sarah—the son God had promised to Abraham. By demanding that Abraham sacrifice Isaac, God seemed to be nullifying his covenant of making a great nation of Abraham. How could God's promise be fulfilled if Isaac were dead?

God tested Abraham to reveal whether or not Abraham truly trusted his promise. Yes, God knew what Abraham would do, but he wanted Abraham to know as well. So, God put Abraham to the test, and Abraham passed. As Abraham raised the knife to sacrifice his own son, God stopped him and provided a sacrificial ram instead.

## Question
Are you obedient to his will, or are you self-willed?

*Father, help me pass the test of obedience.*

# Being Led by God

*"Then your light shall break forth like the morning, your healing shall spring forth speedily, and your righteousness shall go before you; the glory of the Lord shall be your rear guard. Then you shall call, and the Lord will answer; you shall cry, and He will say, 'Here I am.'"*

Isaiah 58:8–9 NKJV

One of the great paradoxes of walking with God is discerning the difference between a "natural idea" versus a "God idea." One of my mentors challenged me one day to make sure that my ideas and the actions I take are directed by God and not from my own reasoning. But being in a marketing profession, there is a constant rub between the "natural" and the "spiritual."

There are three places from which a thought or idea originates: (1) our natural mind, (2) Satan, and (3) the Holy Spirit. There are a few ways to discern from which place a thought is coming. If a thought comes to you that you know would be something you would not normally consider doing, this is likely God speaking.

I once participated in a conference when an offering was being taken to make up for a poorly organized event that left the organizers very short on funds. It was clearly a case of poor management. Nevertheless, I prayed. I assumed I would give a token gift. However, the figure that suddenly came into my mind was $1,000. I argued with God and struggled with my attitude. I thought he must have two zeros out of place! But I obeyed—as I knew that was not my idea. Unfortunately, the event had to be canceled, but we helped the leader recover from her losses. Sometimes things don't turn out as planned, but we must embrace God's promise that "in all things God works for the good of those who love him, who have been called according to his purpose" (Romans 8:28 NIV).

## Question
Do you submit your plans to the Lord for confirmation from God?

*Thank you, Holy Spirit, for directing my every step.*

# Come out of Babylon

*"'Come out of her, my people,' so that you will not share in her sins, so that you will not receive any of her plagues; for her sins are piled up to heaven, and God has remembered her crimes."*

REVELATION 18:4–5 NIV

There is a day when God is going to judge the system of Babylon around the world. What is Babylon? Babylon is a system of doing business. The stronghold of the workplace is mammon and pride. Dependence on money and misplaced trust are at the core of a Babylonian philosophy of life. Revelation 18 describes a time when God will judge this Babylonian system. It is the one place where we see a system destroyed in one day, even one hour. I do not believe Babylon is a particular city but a world system. "Therefore in one day her plagues will overtake her" (Revelation 18:8). "Woe! Woe to you, great city, you mighty city of Babylon! In one hour your doom has come!" (v. 10).

As Christian workplace believers, we are called to acknowledge the signs of the times. When the Soviet Union fell, many knew it was going to happen because they could recognize the signs of the times. God has a way of shaking things up. These shakings force us to determine who and what we will place our trust in. God says that we are to "Love the Lord your God with all your heart and with all your soul and with all your mind" (Matthew 22:37).

## Question

Are you still living in Babylon in the way you do business? If so, expect to share in the sins of Babylon when God decides to judge her.

*Father, show me where I might be operating in a "Babylonian" system of work.*

# Dissolving a Partnership

*Lot chose for himself all the plain of Jordan, and Lot journeyed east.
And they separated from each other.*
GENESIS 13:11 NKJV

When Abraham and Lot realized their families and livestock could no longer live off the same land, there had to be a separation. The question was, how should the separation take place? Abraham told Lot to choose where he wanted to live. Sodom seemed to be the most fertile and logical place to locate. So, Lot chose Sodom.

My friend Bill had come to the decision that the Lord desired him to dissolve his partnership. The partner questioned Bill, "How are we going to divide our accounts?"

"That's easy. I want you to choose the accounts you want, and I will take what you don't want." This was quite a step of faith for Bill, but he felt the leading of the Lord.

The partner chose the very best clients they had and left Bill with accounts that generated less than 20 percent of the revenue. Bill was surprised but accepted his offer. He told his partner, "I can see the decision you have made. You have made a very poor decision that God will not bless. Because of your decision, I believe you can be assured that the value of your clients will go down in the coming months." Bill had no basis for making this assumption other than the story of Abraham and Lot and the Holy Spirit's prompting inside of him.

Months passed, and Bill had some lean months. However, over time, those small accounts gradually increased in value, and the accounts of his partner decreased. It was a profound lesson for Bill and his former partner.

## Question
Are you honoring those you work with?

*Father, help me serve others as I would want to be served.*

# Resurrected Faith

*Abraham stretched out his hand*
*and took the knife to slay his son.*
GENESIS 22:10 NKJV

There are times in our lives when God brings a test to see if we are ready to put to death the very thing that God promised we would have. Such was the case in the life of Abraham with Isaac. Isaac was the promised son. Yet, God said to sacrifice him in obedience to God.

When God brings such a test into our lives, we usually have a choice. Neither choice is attractive. One choice will often salvage some aspect of the vision. The other choice will totally kill the vision from our perspective. However, that is the faith decision. That is the only decision from God's perspective.

If we choose the faith decision that kills the vision, we will witness the resurrection of the vision supernaturally by God. Our own faith will be launched into a whole new dimension. He will raise us up in order to speak through our lives in that experience.

However, if we choose the lesser decision, we will reside in a lesser walk with God. God will accept the decision, but there will be consequences to our faith journey. He cannot trust us with a bigger vision because he sees our obedience is moveable based on our perceived consequences.

If we choose the lesser decision, then God will often orchestrate other events in our lives that are designed to develop our faith to a level that will allow us to make the right decision the next time.

## Question

Do you have resurrection faith that will trust God to raise your situation from the dead?

*Father, thank you for being a resurrection God in my life.*

# Horizontal or Vertical

*Woe to those who are wise in their own eyes,*
*and prudent in their own sight!*
ISAIAH 5:21 NKJV

Many of us have been trained to make decisions and respond to problems in a horizontal way instead of vertically. Operating from a horizontal basis means we try to fix the problem through our own self-efforts by bringing greater pressure upon it through our reasoning or our natural skills. Operating from a vertical position means we are seeking God for the answer and waiting for him to affect the problem. Perhaps you have a business partner who is careless about managing money or a boss who is overly critical or an employee whom you clash with. When we operate horizontally, we attempt to fix things through our flesh.

Our responsibility is to ask God for help to solve the problem and to rely on him for the outcome. The minute we take on the responsibility, God quietly stands by to let us experience failure until we decide to seek him for the answer.

One of the best examples of the contrast between a vertical and horizontal dimension in Scripture is that of King Saul and David (see 1 Samuel 25). King Saul thought the way to preserve his kingdom was to kill David. While in pursuit of him, there were several occasions when David had the opportunity to kill Saul, but David chose to wait upon God's timing and await his own deliverance because he understood authority.

Saul thought David was the problem and sought to get rid of him through force. He lost his kingdom because he chose to rule horizontally instead of vertically.

## Question
Are you trusting God for outcomes in your life?

*Father, help me to stay vertical with you.*

# Moving Ahead of God

*Sarai said to Abram, "See now, the LORD has restrained me from bearing children. Please, go in to my maid; perhaps I shall obtain children by her." And Abram heeded the voice of Sarai.*

GENESIS 16:2 NKJV

Have you ever felt that you were supposed to receive something from God, but it just hasn't materialized? You wait and wait until, finally, you decide that maybe God wants you to help out the situation. This is exactly what happened in the case of Abraham and Sarah.

God had promised them a son, but as years passed by, they were still without a child. They took their eyes off the one who had made the promise and decided to take matters into their own hands. So, Abraham lay with Sarah's maidservant, Hagar, and she bore a son, Ishmael (see Genesis 16). The son of promise, Isaac, came later through Sarah, just like God had promised. However, many today see the modern-day conflict between the Arabs and Israelis as the fruit of this act of disobedience that occurred centuries ago.

The way to avoid making "Ishmael" decisions is to seek God fully on the matter in prayer, be in an accountable relationship with your spouse and close associates who know you well, and gain agreement through two or more people. The Bible says, "The heart is deceitful above all things and beyond cure. Who can understand it?" (Jeremiah 17:9 NIV).

Whenever we want something strongly, it is a dangerous place because we no longer look at the matter objectively with a willingness to change our viewpoint. We have to approach a matter impartially, as if we were "dead" to the issue.

## Question
Are you struggling to get a breakthrough with God?

*Father, help me to trust you for the breakthrough I need in my life.*

# Listen to God

*"For My thoughts are not your thoughts, nor are your ways My ways," says the Lord.*
*"For as the heavens are higher than the earth, so are My ways higher than your*
*ways, and My thoughts than your thoughts."*
ISAIAH 55:8–9 NKJV

God speaks to his children in many ways. God has said that his ways are not our ways. If left to our reasoning, we will fail to walk in the full counsel of God, which leads to poor decisions.

Thus, our goal is to avoid being deceived and to develop a listening ear that hears the voice of God with confidence. Our goal is to have such intimacy with God that we can walk in the full blessing of our decisions and be assured they are not based on our own reasoning alone. This does not mean that we do not use the intellectual and logical skills that he has equipped us with.

J. Oswald Sanders explains his method of receiving guidance from God for decisions; "I try to gather all the information and all the facts that are involved in a decision, and then weigh them up and pray over them in the Lord's presence, and trust the Holy Spirit to sway my mind in the direction of God's will. And God generally guides by presenting reasons to my mind for acting in a certain way."[43] Discerning his voice is the first step toward making the right choices in life.

## Question
Do you have a decision to make? Submit that decision to the Lord.

*Father, make the desires of my heart the same desires that you have for me. Help me wait for your perfect timing on this matter.*

# Removing Hindrances

*Love never brings fear, for fear is always related to punishment.*
*But love's perfection drives the fear of punishment far from our hearts.*

1 JOHN 4:18 TPT

I was in another country and had just completed a teaching on how spiritual strongholds (2 Corinthians 10:4) can hinder us from fulfilling our destinies. A woman approached me at the end of the meeting and asked me if I could join her and her friend for lunch so that she could learn more. I noticed how bold the woman was and perceived she would not take no for an answer. I agreed to join them.

Before she began asking me questions, I asked her to tell me about the relationship she had with her father. "I have an awful relationship with my father. He says I'm fat and that I'll never amount to anything."

I responded gently to her statement: "Jennifer, you have a generational stronghold of rejection. You try to mask it by trying to be successful in business. Your aggressive nature is rooted in a fear of failure because you've lived your whole life trying to win the approval of your father through performance. I want you to know you are totally loved and accepted by your heavenly Father. You can stop trying to win his favor."

Immediately, she began to weep in the middle of the restaurant. "No one has ever told me this, but what you say is true." We prayed for God to destroy the stronghold of fear and rejection in her life through the blood of Jesus Christ. She walked out of the restaurant that day with a new sense of love and acceptance.

## Question
Are there hidden strongholds that keep you from being free?

*Father, reveal any strongholds that may be hindering my life.*

# Is Perception Reality?

*He said, "I have been very zealous for the LORD God of hosts; because the children of Israel have forsaken Your covenant, torn down Your altars, and killed Your prophets with the sword. I alone am left; and they seek to take my life."*

1 KINGS 19:14 NKJV

The CEO walked into his manufacturing plant only to observe an employee standing by idly, not working. Angrily, he walked over to him, peeled off a one-hundred-dollar bill, and gave it to him: "Here, go spend your time elsewhere!" The man looked at the CEO somewhat puzzled but left with the one hundred dollars. "How long has that man worked for us?" said the CEO to the employee standing nearby.

"Well, sir, that man does not work for us; he is only the delivery man."

Perception is not always reality. Elijah was in a crisis. Jezebel wanted to kill him. The nation was falling to Baal worship. From his vantage point, it was all over. He was the only prophet remaining in all the land who had not bent his knee to the idol of Baal. He wanted to die.

Then, the Lord sent his angel to correct Elijah's perception: "Yet I reserve seven thousand in Israel—all whose knees have not bowed down to Baal and whose mouths have not kissed him" (1 Kings 19:18 NIV). There were seven thousand Elijah knew nothing about! Elijah's perception was not reality.

Often we cannot see God's plan that may be being orchestrated behind the scenes. He is accomplishing his purposes. But we need a fresh perspective on our situation.

## Question
Do you need a reality check on your situation?

*God, refresh my perspective and help me to see the truth.*

# Paul's Disagreement with the Prophet

*When he had come to us, he took Paul's belt, bound his own hands and feet, and said, "Thus says the Holy Spirit, 'So shall the Jews at Jerusalem bind the man who owns this belt, and deliver him into the hands of the Gentiles.'"*

ACTS 21:10–11 NKJV

In Acts 21, we find an interesting scene involving Paul, the disciples, and a prophet named Agabus. Agabus tied Paul's hands and feet to dramatize the word of prophecy he was going to give Paul that he would be bound and persecuted in Jerusalem. The leaders concluded from this that Paul was not to go to Jerusalem.

However, Paul disagreed. "Why are you weeping and breaking my heart? I am ready not only to be bound, but also to die in Jerusalem for the name of the Lord Jesus" (Acts 21:13 NIV).

Was Paul acting in disobedience to the counsel of others and even the Holy Spirit's confirmation by other believers? If so, does that mean that Paul was not to go? Paul knew something the others didn't. He didn't disagree with the prophecy, but he disagreed with the interpretation.

It is always the individual's responsibility to interpret the meaning and action required from counsel from others. Prophecy was the messenger, but the recipient needed to determine the action required from the message.

The important lesson for us is to understand that doing the will of God does not always have a positive outcome. If it did, we would make decisions based only on perceived outcomes. Jesus was obedient to the cross.

## Question
Have you ever let others sway you from doing what you know you should do?

*Father, help me remain steadfast in obeying your voice to me.*

# Understanding Our Own Calling

*"If I want him to remain alive until I return,*
*what is that to you? You must follow Me."*
JOHN 21:22 NIV

Jesus was talking to Peter after he had just had a very important encounter with him—one of the last meetings the two would have. This was the third time Jesus had shown himself to the disciples after his resurrection. It is the famous dialogue between Jesus and Peter in which Jesus asked three times if Peter loved him. Jesus followed by commanding, "Feed my sheep" (v. 17). Jesus went on to foretell Peter's death. As they were walking together, John was with Peter and Jesus. Peter asked Jesus about John and whether he would die also. Jesus reacted sharply to Peter's comment, telling him not to worry about what John's role or purpose was in life. All Peter had to do was worry about fulfilling his own purpose.

As workplace believers, we tend to measure our success by whether we have achieved a certain position or stature in life. Even as Christians, we are always confronted with the temptation to believe that certain people are blessed if they have achieved prominence. In his discussion with Peter, Jesus was getting at the very heart of a person's calling. Peter was worried about whether his friend John was going to get the same lot in life as he was. Jesus told him it should not be his concern. He was to concern himself only with one thing: his own calling before God.

## Question

Are you tempted to compare yourself with where others are in their lives? Are you dissatisfied with where God has you right now? Be of good cheer. Paul says to be "confident of this, that he who began a good work in you will carry it on to completion until the day of Christ Jesus" (Philippians 1:6).

*Father, help me to live vertically with you so I might fulfill my purpose.*

# Three Things

*I pray that the light of God will illuminate the eyes of your imagination, flooding you with light, until you experience the full revelation of the hope of his calling— that is, the wealth of God's glorious inheritances that he finds in us, his holy ones!*
EPHESIANS 1:18 TPT

Paul's letter to the Ephesians exhorts believers to experience three important things in their spiritual lives that he experienced personally. As a good mentor, he desires those he is leading to follow his example.

First, God wants you to have the eyes of your heart enlightened in order to know the hope to which he has called you. God has called each of us to a future and a hope. Some do not ever realize the dreams they envision for their lives. Paul prays they will experience this.

Second, God wants you to know there is an inheritance for each believer in Jesus Christ. There are riches to be had—not financial riches—but spiritual riches that are laid up for every saint. There will be a reward for your faithfulness.

Third, God desires you to tap in to the power that is available to every believer. Paul often exhorted believers not to look at his persuasive words but the demonstration of the power of God in his life. He wants you to know this same power is available to you. After all, Jesus said we would do even greater works than he did after he sent the Holy Spirit to us.

## Question
Are you experiencing the power of God in your life?

*Father, I pray you reveal the hope that exists inside of me and help me to know that there is an inheritance awaiting me.*

# Coming out of Egypt

*Thanks be to God, for in the past you were servants of sin,*
*but now your obedience is heart deep,*
*and your life is being molded by truth through the teaching you are devoted to.*
ROMANS 6:17 TPT

Becoming a new person in Christ is part of a lifelong journey that begins at conversion. Before coming to Christ, we were living (in a metaphorical sense) in Egypt, in the land of bondage. Just as the people of Israel toiled as slaves in Egypt, we were slaves to sin and worldly ambition.

Greed can be a cruel taskmaster. We may have had all the trappings of power in the business world—a corner office, a staff of our own, profit sharing, a company car—but we were living as slaves in the land of Egypt. We didn't run our career; our career ran us.

Jesus once said, "No one can serve two masters…You cannot serve both God and money" (Luke 16:13 NIV). In the original language, the word translated as "money" was an Aramaic word, *mammon*. This does not refer merely to money as a medium of exchange but also to a demonic spirit designed to promote a mindset of ambition for riches, power, and worldly gain. The people of Jesus' day thought of mammon as a false god. Jesus was saying that those who spend their lives seeking worldly gain are idolaters.

The only way we can be free from this idolatry is to turn away from mammon and allow the one true God to transform us into a different person.

## Question
Is your life best represented as Egypt or the promised land?

*Father, I repent of any idolatry of mammon today and ask you to help me make only you the Lord of my life.*

# Baptism at the Red Sea

*Sharing in his death by our baptism means that we were co-buried with him, so that when the Father's glory raised Christ from the dead, we were also raised with him. We have been co-resurrected with him so that we could be empowered to walk in the freshness of new life.*

ROMANS 6:4 TPT

When Moses led the people of Israel out of Egypt, he took them to the edge of the Red Sea. The people saw the sea before them and heard the chariots of the Egyptians behind them. They knew they were trapped—and they lost their faith in God. In panic and despair, they turned on Moses and said, "Why did you bring us out into the desert to die? When we were slaves in Egypt, didn't we tell you, 'Just leave us alone and let us continue serving the Egyptians.' Better to live as slaves than to die out here!" (Exodus 14:11–14, author paraphrase).

They couldn't imagine that God's path to freedom actually led straight into and through the deep waters! The waters of the Red Sea, like the New Testament sacrament of baptism, are a symbol of death.

Like the people of Israel in their journey, we panic and cry out to God, "Did you bring me out into this desert of adversity to die?" We would rather live as slaves than die to self and yield control of our lives to God. But God takes us through the depths so that we can emerge as new people, ready to enter the promised land.

Often the greater and higher the calling, the more intense the adversity.

## Question
### Do you find yourself in deep water?

*Thank you, Father, that you are preparing me for a life that is designed to impact many.*

# Shedding Former Things

*They remained where they were…until they were healed. Then the LORD said to Joshua, "Today I have rolled away the reproach of Egypt from you."*

JOSHUA 5:8–9 NIV

God is calling you out of Egypt, out of your old life of bondage. He's calling you to a new person, living out his plan for your life in the promised land, a land flowing with milk and honey. God wants you to take your place in the financial marketplace, the corridors of commerce, the capitals of information and entertainment, and the halls of government.

When the people of Israel crossed over the Jordan River and set foot upon the land of promise, God told Joshua to make flint knives and revive a ritual that had fallen into disuse: circumcision.

The rite of circumcision is the surgical removal of the foreskin. This rite was established as a sign of God's covenant with Abraham in Genesis 17, but it had not been practiced during the forty years that Israel wandered in the wilderness before reaching the promised land. Joshua obeyed God's command and had all the Israelite men circumcised at a place they called Gibeath Haaraloth (a rather graphic name that means "hill of foreskins").

The rite of circumcision is painful, bloody, and personal, and the Israelite men were incapacitated until their wounds had healed. This represented putting aside the old way of life and entering the promised land with confidence and power.

Circumcision was a prophetic act of demonstrating a new heart and commitment to follow God.

## Question
Have you been circumcised in heart for God's calling?

*Father, lead me into my promised land for your glory.*

# Josiah, God's Leader

*Now before him there was no king like him, who turned to the LORD with all his heart, with all his soul, and with all his might, according to all the Law of Moses; nor after him did any arise like him.*

2 KINGS 23:25 NKJV

What type of person does God raise up when a nation becomes synonymous with idol worship and sin? God raised up a leader who had the courage to destroy the evil and bring the nation back to God. His name was Josiah.

Manasseh's son Amon reigned for twenty-two years after him and was also wicked. However, Amon's son was named Josiah and became king at eight years old after his father was assassinated.

"[Josiah] did what was right in the sight of the LORD, and walked in all the ways of his father David; he did not turn aside to the right hand or to the left" (2 Kings 22:2 NKJV). He was a courageous leader.

God responded to the godly reforms that Josiah brought to his nation. "Because your heart was responsive and you humbled yourself before the LORD…Therefore I will gather you to your ancestors, and you will be buried in peace. Your eyes will not see all the disaster I am going to bring on this place" (vv. 19–20 NIV). Judgment always follows the sin of a nation. If there were ever a time we needed God to raise up Josiahs in our cities and nations, it is now.

## Question
Does your country need godly leaders?

*Father, bring forth godly leaders into my city and nation.*

# Desert Training

*O God of my life, I'm lovesick for you in this weary wilderness. I thirst with the deepest longings to love you more, with cravings in my heart that can't be described. Such yearning grips my soul for you, my God!*
PSALM 63:1 TPT·

The desert holds a special place in God's Word. The Scriptures portray the desert as a place of inspiration and exaltation—a place where people met God in a powerful new way. King David wrote Psalm 63 while in exile in the desert of Judah. He was hiding from his son Absalom, who wanted to replace him as king of Israel.

For Joseph, a deep pit in the desert was the first stop on a thirteen-year journey through desolation and despair. That thirteen-year desert experience served to break Joseph's self-will and self-confidence. It taught him that he could not control anything and that he needed to rely on God to manage the events in his life. Joseph's desert trial prepared him by scorching the youthful pride and arrogance out of his young life so that when he was thirty years old, he could rule Egypt at Pharaoh's side in a spirit of humility and servanthood.

Before becoming king of Israel, David was a shepherd. Part of his training for leadership involved hand-to-claw combat with the beasts of the wilderness, including the lion and the bear. Elijah learned the principles of spiritual leadership while in the wilderness of Gilead. And Jesus was tempted and tested for forty days in the desert before he began to preach.

## Question

Has God given you a dream, but now it seems that your dream has withered and died under the scorching desert sun?

*Father, give me the grace to walk through any desert season you bring into my life to fulfill your destiny.*

# Hearing God

*"My own sheep will hear my voice and I know each one,*
*and they will follow me."*

JOHN 10:27 TPT

I have discovered a pattern in the way God speaks to me when I'm faced with major decisions. I will spend a great deal of time seeking direction from him and asking him to speak to me regarding a decision. I spend time in prayer and Bible study. Many times I have suddenly had a rush come over me with an overwhelming feeling of his presence. The feeling is usually so intense I will begin to cry, sometimes uncontrollably. (Thank God this doesn't happen too often because it is rather embarrassing in a public setting.)

One night as the famous Bible teacher F. B. Meyer stood on the deck of a ship approaching land, he wondered how the crew knew when and how to safely steer to the dock. It was a stormy night, and visibility was low. Meyer, standing on the bridge and peering through the window, asked, "Captain, how do you know when to turn this ship into that narrow harbor?"

"That's an art," replied the captain. "Do you see those three red lights on the shore? When they're all in a straight line, I go right in!"

Later Meyer said, "When we want to know God's will, there are three things which always occur: the inward impulse, the Word of God, and the trend of circumstances. Never act until these three things agree."[44]

## Question
Do you seek God in every decision you have to make?

*Father, thank you for your Holy Spirit that directs me in all my decisions through prayer.*

# Spouses and Making Decisions

*A fool is in love with his own opinion,*
*but wisdom means being teachable.*
PROVERBS 12:15 TPT

When John Benson decided to make some financial investments in a new business venture, he was very excited about the possibility of a handsome financial return. His business and financial background had served him well. John felt strongly that his wife, Jenny, would not understand the complexity of his investment, so he only casually mentioned it to her. When she asked a few simple questions, John became defensive and justified his plans for investing in the venture.

A year later, after investing a large sum of money, John received a phone call from the investment company. All the investors who had put money in the company were going to lose their investment with no ability to recoup it.

This story is experienced by many across the world. God's principles for making decisions require input from both spouses, regardless of their level of expertise. Whenever I am faced with a major decision, I first consult the Lord, and then I consult my wife. I've even said to Christian audiences, "It's amazing how similar, at times, the voice of my wife is to the voice of the Holy Spirit." She may disagree totally with something that seems very straightforward to me, but I have learned not to move forward if we are not in agreement.

In marriage, this stewardship of decisions requires two people. God blesses this union by honoring the decisions made with the motive of glorifying God and relying on his Spirit to lead in our decision-making process.

## Question

Before you make a major decision, do you get confirmation for your decision from your spouse?

*Father, help me see my wife as a valued partner in making decisions.*

# Time Management

*"Lord, help me to know how fleeting my time on earth is. Help me to know how limited is my life and that I'm only here but for a moment more."*
PSALM 39:3–4 TPT

David accomplished a great deal in his lifetime. However, he also understood life had an end to it, and he wanted to make the most of it. He learned to use his time wisely. And so should we.

Peter Drucker was a renowned management consultant to major corporations and authored many best-selling business books. He suggested three activities that might help busy executives better manage their time.

First, do not start with the task. Start with your time. Determine where your time is going. Then, attempt to manage that time and cut back unproductive demands on your time. Consolidate your 'discretionary' time into the largest possible continuing time units.

Drucker refers to the second step as time management. After listing the activities to which we devote our time, he suggests that we ask three questions about each of these activities to help us minimize the amount of time we waste:

1. "'What would happen if this were not done at all?' And if the answer is, 'Nothing would happen,' then obviously the conclusion is to stop doing it."[45]
2. Next, "Which of the activities on my time log could be done by somebody else just as well, if not better?"[46]
3. Thirdly, what do I do that wastes my time without contributing to my effectiveness?[47]

## Question
Have you evaluated how you are spending your time?

*Father, I pray you help me better use my time.*

# How's Your Joy Quotient?

*He said to them, "Go your way, eat the fat, drink the sweet, and send portions to those for whom nothing is prepared; for this day is holy to our Lord. Do not sorrow, for the joy of the LORD is your strength."*

NEHEMIAH 8:10 NKJV

One of the overriding pieces of evidence that someone has a genuine relationship with our living Savior is his consistent attitude of joy and outlook on life. A follower of Jesus should not be a person who always looks at life as if the glass is half empty. Instead, we should be the most positive people on earth. We should see opportunity in the midst of challenges.

The light that resides in you should be like the beam of a lighthouse to a ship that is seeking direction. Our lives should have the fragrance of Christ. People should be attracted to our lives just as the bee is attracted to the nectar in the colorful flower.

The apostle Paul understood this when he said,

Now thanks be to God who always leads us in triumph in Christ, and through us diffuses the fragrance of His knowledge in every place. For we are to God the fragrance of Christ among those who are being saved and among those who are perishing. To the one we are the aroma of death leading to death, and to the other the aroma of life leading to life. And who is sufficient for these things? (2 Corinthians 2:14–16)

## Question

How would others describe your joy quotient? On a scale of one to ten, where would they rank you?

*Father, help me greet every circumstance knowing that the joy of the Lord is my strength.*

# One Body

*By one Spirit we all were immersed and mingled into one single body.*
1 CORINTHIANS 12:13 TPT

Imagine with me for a moment that you have won a very expensive car. However, in order to receive your prize, you must agree to an unusual requirement. You must agree to remove one major component in that car in order to receive the gift.

Which component will you remove?

Will it be the steering wheel? Perhaps it will be the left front tire or the front seat or the two headlights. My illustration may seem ridiculous, but you get the point. Unless you have the complete car and have the ability to use all of its components, your ability to benefit from that car is going to be severely limited. The Bible says you and I are part of a larger body—the body of Christ. We each have our own body, but we are also made up of a larger body that has a unique function to play. When you are not functioning as God intended, the entire body suffers because you are not fulfilling your prescribed role.

Jesus knew the key to fulfilling his mission was getting his larger body to work as one. "I pray also for those who will believe in me through their message, that all of them may be one, Father, just as you are in me and I am in you. May they also be in us so that the world may believe that you have sent me" (John 17:20–21 NIV).

## Question

What is your part in the overall mission? Are you fulfilling your prescribed function as designed by the manufacturer?

*Father, help me walk in unity with the rest of the body of Christ for your kingdom purposes.*

# Your Calling's Depth and Width

*If we are distressed, it is for your comfort and salvation; if we are comforted, it is for your comfort, which produces in you patient endurance of the same sufferings we suffer.*

2 CORINTHIANS 1:6 NIV

God must love you a lot! He doesn't allow someone to go through the kinds of adversity you have experienced unless he has a special calling on your life." Those were the words said to me by two different mentors at two different times within a three-year period. Later I would learn another related truth from a respected man of God—a man who lives in another country, a man whom God uses throughout the globe. "The depth and width of your faith experiences are directly proportional to your calling." What were these men of God saying?

They were describing a process of preparation that God takes each of his leaders through when he plans to use them in significant ways. A "faith experience" is an event or "spiritual marker" in your life about which you can say, "That is where I saw God personally moving in my life." It is an unmistakable event in which God showed himself personally to you. It was the burning bush for Moses, the crossing of the Red Sea or the Jordan River for the nation of Israel, Jacob's encounter with the angel. It was the feeding of the five thousand for the disciples. It was the time when you saw God face-to-face in your life.

If God has plans for using you in the lives of many others, you can expect that he is going to allow certain faith experiences to come into your life in order to build a foundation that will be solid. That foundation is what you will be able to look back on to keep you faithful to him in times of testing. Each of us must have personal faith experiences in which we meet God personally so that we can move in faith to whatever he may call us.

## Question

Do you need a personal faith experience right now in your life?

*Father, I pray you reveal yourself to me.*

# The Lord Is Not in It

*He said, "Go out, and stand on the mountain before the LORD." And behold, the LORD passed by, and a great and strong wind tore into the mountains and broke the rocks in pieces before the LORD, but the LORD was not in the wind; and after the wind an earthquake, but the LORD was not in the earthquake.*

1 KINGS 19:11 NKJV

I don't believe that God is in it," I said to my friend. A situation had arisen in which a friend was about to engage in something he felt God was leading him into. Later, the truth of the situation was revealed, and our friend made a bad mistake. God was not in it.

Elijah was in a crisis in his ministry. God had just corrected him about his perspective of his situation. If any man needed a touch from God, it was Elijah because he was in such distress he wanted to die.

The Lord intervened and told Elijah that he was coming to talk to him. However, God did not tell Elijah how he was going to reveal himself. It was up to Elijah to tell whether God was in the situation about to take place.

God's ways are not always highly visible. Sometimes he chooses to come as a soft, gentle whisper. It is sometimes difficult to recognize it as the Lord because he shows himself in such subtle ways.

We need to be able to discern when God is actually part of our situation. Only then can we avoid being deceived into thinking God is not behind our projects.

## Question
Is there a situation where you need to know if God is in it?

*Father, I ask you for wisdom in knowing when you are involved in my activities.*

# He Had Such Great Potential

*Jacob gave Esau bread and stew of lentils;*
*then he ate and drank, arose, and went his way.*
*Thus Esau despised his birthright.*

GENESIS 25:34 NKJV

Nearly everyone has heard someone say, "Oh, he had such great potential. He never lived up to it though."

Esau was the brother of Jacob. He was a man who had great potential. He was skilled in almost everything he did. He was a hunter. He was a leader. He came from a godly patriarch family. The problem was that he put his energies into all the wrong enterprises. He was promiscuous and married outside the tribe. His parents were greatly saddened.

Esau made the greatest mistake of his life when he traded away his birthright for a simple meal. He had just returned from a time of hunting, and he was hungry. His brother was making stew but would not give him any. Esau was angered by this and negotiated for what he wanted by agreeing to give Jacob his family inheritance. It seems almost unbelievable that Esau would do such a thing.

Esau had not understood the value of his birthright or his future in God. He could only see the immediate pleasures available to him. His appetites were driven by his flesh. And his choices led to a life in which even God said he despised Esau. Every day there are Esaus living out their calling in the same way. The Bible says there is a way that seems right but only leads to death.

## Question

Are you living for the larger story of your life?

*Father, I pray for those still living as Esaus and ask you to move on their behalf in order that they fulfill their godly heritage.*

# Allowing God to Promote

*The fame of David went out into all lands,*
*and the LORD brought the fear of him upon all nations.*

1 CHRONICLES 14:17 NKJV

We live in a day of self-promotion. Marketing firms are hired today to persuade others to view a person or situation in the way they want you to. There are millions of dollars spent annually by sports companies, personality agents, and marketing firms to create fame for their clients and products. They negotiate sponsorship deals and try to get the most money for the most exposure. The ultimate goal is fame and notoriety.

There is a great danger in self-promotion. Self-promotion is trying to move from the place where you are to a place ahead of where God may want you. It is not wrong to become famous, popular, or desired by others as long as it happens as a fruit of your calling. However, when you begin to orchestrate things in an effort to inflate who you are for the sake of gain, you have crossed the line.

David's fame was a result of his fulfilling his mission in life. When he failed, he repented. When he was successful, he acknowledged the Lord. Never do you see David exalt himself over the Lord. Yes, he made some selfish decisions that led to sin. But David could not be criticized for self-promotion.

We all must carefully balance the difference between marketing designed to inform and educate versus marketing intended to manipulate. Proverbs says, "Let another praise you, and not your own mouth; someone else, and not your own lips" (Proverbs 27:2 NET).

Following this principle will keep you from moving beyond God's method of promotion.

## Question
Are you careful about self-promotion?

*Father, help me trust you for my advancement.*

# Strongholds over Industries

*The LORD said to Joshua, "This day I have rolled away the reproach of Egypt from you." Therefore the name of the place is called Gilgal to this day.*

JOSHUA 5:9 NKJV

A longtime *TGIF* subscriber, Bill, called and asked for my help. I met him in Lake Tahoe, and over a three-hour lunch, he confided to me some of his struggles in his industry. He said that he'd often been lied to and exploited by others in his business. The Holy Spirit prompted me to say, "That's because the ruling spirit in this industry is mammon and deceit. I believe that God has called you to play a part in cleaning up your industry."

"But how?" he said. "I've got a federal lawsuit on my back. I'm being driven out of business."

"Bill," I said, "God has put you in a season of preparation in order to remove the 'Egypt' from your working life so as to bring his kingdom into your industry."

God desires to bring his kingdom into every sphere of life. When Jesus wanted to bring his kingdom into the corrupt tax system in Jerusalem, the first thing he did was recruit Matthew, the tax collector. He began investing in Matthew's life. Jesus' presence brought conviction to anyone who was operating in an ungodly manner.

## Question
Do you need the presence of Jesus in your industry? Invite him in today.

*Father, help me bring God's kingdom into my working life.*

# Teaching versus Imparting

*The people were awestruck by his teaching, because he taught in a way that demonstrated God's authority, which was quite unlike the religious scholars.*
MARK 1:22 TPT

It is not enough to simply teach; you must also impart to others," said my mentor one day. One of the spiritual gifts God has given to me is the gift of teaching (Romans 12:7). However, the Lord does not desire for teachers to only impart knowledge to others. Knowledge alone will not empower others to be mature disciples of Christ.

The people recognized there was something different about Jesus. He was a teacher of the law as a rabbi. However, whenever he taught, there was an authority that went beyond the conveying of information. He was imparting truth through the authority of his life. His words impacted others profoundly.

A Bible teacher who wants to have the greatest impact on those he teaches should teach transferable life application from the Scriptures that he has lived out personally. This is what gives you the authority to teach. I rarely teach a concept that I have not personally lived out and have an accompanying testimony. Paul believed and lived this principle as well: "When I came to you, I did not come with eloquence or human wisdom as I proclaimed to you the testimony about God" (1 Corinthians 2:1 NIV).

Each of us has been given the authority to impart the message of the kingdom to others. Some of us have a particular anointing that God uses in the lives of others.

## Question

Are you a teacher in any capacity? If so, make sure you impart life into your listeners.

*Father, I ask you to reveal your anointing in me so I can impart it to others.*

# Who Should Be in Charge?

*When the righteous are in authority, the people rejoice;*
*but when a wicked man rules, the people groan.*

PROVERBS 29:2 NKJV

We hear a lot these days about being "politically correct." It seems we must be sensitive to every group, no matter how that group might negatively impact our lives or violate ethical or moral laws. When God created the earth, he did not care what people thought of his policies. His policy was *the* way!

But his primary motive was not to control but to bless mankind, his creation. His nature was only good. In Jeremiah 9:24, we find God's nature described: "'I am the LORD, who exercises kindness, justice and righteousness on earth, for in these I delight,' declares the LORD" (NIV).

He laid down rules in the garden of Eden for Adam and Eve to follow. As long as they followed the rules, they would reign over every living creature. They were representing the Creator in all aspects. God's government was being expressed through his creation in humans, nature, and animals. He was and is the ultimate righteous ruler.

God's desire was to extend this mandate across the earth through godly leaders who could represent and legislate his kingdom in all spheres of life. This is why he said in Deuteronomy: "The LORD will make you the head, not the tail. If you pay attention to the commands of the LORD your God that I give you this day and carefully follow them, you will always be at the top, never at the bottom" (28:13 NIV).

God desires to raise up godly leaders who can represent his interest on the earth.

## Question
Has he called you to be one of his righteous representatives?

*Father, make me your faithful representative in the marketplace.*

# From Adversity to Blessing

*"My son, do not despise the chastening of the LORD, nor be discouraged when you are rebuked by Him; for whom the LORD loves He chastens, and scourges every son whom He receives."*

HEBREWS 12:5–6 NKJV

Although God takes no pleasure in our pain, we have to acknowledge that he sometimes allows painful circumstances to occur to make us more like Christ.

I once came across the following poem written by an anonymous Confederate soldier. The lines of this poem express the soul of a man who has learned to view his times of adversity from a different perspective.

I asked God for strength, that I might achieve.
I was made weak, that I might learn humbly to obey.
I asked God for health, that I might do greater things.
I was given infirmity, that I might do better things.
I asked for riches, that I might be happy.
I was given poverty, that I might be wise.
I asked for power, that I might have the praise of men.
I was given weakness, that I might feel the need of God.
I asked for all things, that I might enjoy life.
I was given life, that I might enjoy all things.
I got nothing that I asked for—but everything I had hoped for.
Almost despite myself, my unspoken prayers were answered.
I am, among men, most richly blessed.[48]

## Question
Do we trust God to lead us even though we can't see the pathway?

*Father, help me to use darkness to bring light to my soul.*

# God Restores

*"I will repay you for the years the locusts have eaten—the great locust and the young locust, the other locusts and the locust swarm—my great army that I sent among you."*

JOEL 2:25 NIV

Solomon tells us that God has made everything beautiful in its time and that there is a time for everything and a season for every activity under heaven. (See Ecclesiastes 3:1, 11.)

God brings about both the good and the bad. The seasons of famine have a divine purpose in our lives. They accomplish things that only these hard places can accomplish. But there is a time when those hard places have accomplished their purpose, and he begins restoration. God did this with the nation of Israel after a season of famine and devastation.

> Be glad, people of Zion,
> rejoice in the LORD your God,
> for he has given you the autumn rains
> because he is faithful.
> He sends you abundant showers,
> both autumn and spring rains, as before.
> The threshing floors will be filled with grain;
> the vats will overflow with new wine and oil. (Joel 2:23–24)

God wants each of us to know that there is a time when he will restore in order to demonstrate his gracious hand in our lives. He is a loving Father who tenderly guides his children through the difficult places.

## Question

Has God taken you through a time of leanness? Know that he is the restorer of that which the locusts have eaten.

*Father, give me grace to wait patiently for you to bring this about in my life.*

# Higher Education

*The Spirit gives to one the gift of the word of wisdom.*
*To another, the same Spirit gives the gift of the word of revelation knowledge.*
1 CORINTHIANS 12:8 TPT

I walked out of the church parking lot after participating in a training class on hearing the voice of God. As I was talking to a friend, I looked over at a woman who was talking to her friend. The words *higher education* popped into my mind.

We had just learned that whenever something pops into our minds that seems foreign to our normal thinking, it is often the Holy Spirit speaking to us. We must connect the thought to an action the Holy Spirit may be desiring us to take.

I decided to be bold and walked over to the woman. "Pardon me, can I ask you if you, by chance, have had a good bit of education in your life?"

The woman responded immediately, "Why, yes. I have two MBAs." I was encouraged to proceed.

"I believe the Lord wants to encourage you that he has directed you in your education, and although you cannot see the results of that investment in time and money, he is going to use it for his purposes. He wants you to be encouraged to know this."

The woman was very encouraged by the words I spoke to her. I walked away feeling good about being obedient to his prompting.

Every believer has been wired to hear the Holy Spirit's promptings in our lives. One of the primary ways he encourages believers is through other believers. However, many of us have been duped into thinking we cannot hear God's voice.

## Question
Are you listening to the Holy Spirit during your day?

*Father, help me be sensitive to your voice during my daily activities.*

# Defining Moments

*Moses stretched out his hand over the sea; and the Lord caused the sea to go back by a strong east wind all that night, and made the sea into dry land, and the waters were divided.*

EXODUS 14:21 NKJV

History often remembers people because of a defining moment that took place in their life. There are good defining moments and bad defining moments. September 11, 2001, was a bad defining moment for the United States of America. Many people's lives were changed as a result. Israel had a defining moment when they crossed the Jordan River and stepped onto the promised land. Moses had a defining moment when he parted the Red Sea with his staff. We could go on.

How would you like to be remembered? Is there a defining moment in your life with which others will associate your name? Thomas, one of the disciples of Jesus, is remembered as "Doubting Thomas." What a shame. I wonder what other good things Thomas did. However, because Thomas doubted that Jesus had truly come back from the dead and needed Jesus to show the nail marks on his hands and side, he will forever be associated with this question posed to the Savior when he saw him after he was resurrected.

For most of us, we can still define our moments for the future. God may yet have a defining moment when you will discover something new or see the work of God in your life in a unique way. I think God likes defining moments. He wants you to have an experience with him that is memorable.

## Question
Have you had your defining moment?

*Father, reveal your glory to me so that I can have a defining moment.*

# Getting Refueled

*The next morning, Jesus got up long before daylight, left the house while it was dark, and made his way to a secluded place to give himself to prayer.*

MARK 1:35 TPT

How do you get refueled? When our cars run low on fuel, we simply drop by the local filling station to get more fuel. When our bodies are hungry, we feed them. How do we refuel our spiritual lives? We can learn from the example Jesus modeled in his life.

In the New Testament we see that Jesus had a very demanding schedule. He traveled from town to town, often walking many miles between the towns. He spent a lot of time with people. As a speaker and teacher, I can tell you that it is very draining to minister for extended periods. Your body and your spirit become fatigued.

The day before the above Scripture was recorded, Jesus had a full day of ministry (Mark 1:29–37). The following day it says Jesus got up before the sun rose and went to pray. The disciples were wondering where he was. Jesus knew one of the key ways to refuel his mind, body, and spirit was by spending time in prayer to his heavenly Father.

This is a critical discipline for every follower of Jesus if you expect to have power and victory in your Christian walk. We each need to find a solitary place to focus upon the Lord, his Word, and his input for our lives.

## Question

Are you getting refueled by spending quiet time with God?

*Father, help me make time for you every day.*

# Defining Your Self-Worth

*I thank you, God, for making me so mysteriously complex!*
*Everything you do is marvelously breathtaking.*
*It simply amazes me to think about it!*
*How thoroughly you know me, Lord!*
PSALM 139:14 TPT

What measurements do you use to define your self-worth? Do you define it based on your financial assets? Is it based on what you have achieved professionally? Perhaps you define your value based on the number of children you have.

There are many things we can use to define our self-worth. However, the Scriptures tell us there is only one measure for our self-worth. Each of us has self-worth because we are made in the image of God. And because we are made in the image of God, we are valuable. Whenever you and I place a value in ourselves that is based on some other performance criteria, we have moved beyond God's view of our worth as human beings. You are never more valuable to God than you were the day you were born.

Basing our self-worth on how much money we have or our achievements is an easy trap. We are bombarded with messages that say we are defined by what we drive, where we live, how many toys we own, and the size of our investment account. The media message is designed to create dissatisfaction and lust for what we don't have.

Paul said the purpose of his existence was to know Christ, "the power of His resurrection, and the fellowship of His sufferings, being conformed to His death" (Philippians 3:10 NKJV).

## Question
By what terms do you define yourself? Is it based on knowing Christ alone?

*Father, thank you that my worth is rooted in knowing you alone.*

# God's Tests of the Heart

*They were left, that He might test Israel by them, to know whether they would obey the commandments of the LORD, which He had commanded their fathers by the hand of Moses.*

JUDGES 3:4 NKJV

There is a spiritual truth God revealed in the conquest of the promised land recorded in Judges 3: "These are the nations the LORD left to test all those Israelites who had not experienced any of the wars in Canaan" (v. 1 NIV).

They didn't pass the test. "The Israelites did evil in the eyes of the LORD; they forgot the LORD their God and served the Baals and the Asherahs" (v. 7 NIV).

Martin Luther said there are three things necessary to create a successful minister of God: prayer, meditation, and temptation. You'll really never know the strength and reality of your faith until you experience difficulty in life. You'll never know for sure whether God can be trusted or if you'll fall into temptation.

The apostle Peter thought his faith in Christ was solid until the temptation came to deny him. Jesus knew Peter was not mature yet and that he would deny Jesus three times in one day. Peter didn't believe it. Sure enough, Peter denied Jesus three times. He needed to be placed in a situation to reveal his true condition. God allows circumstances to develop around your life to give your faith the opportunity to be proven. It is only when we are tested in battle that we become skilled warriors.

If you fail the test, do not think you are lost. Learn from it and grow through the experience, just as Peter did.

## Question

Has God brought a test recently to let you see how you might respond?

*Father, give me the grace to pass the tests you bring my way.*

# Crying Out to the Lord

*When the children of Israel cried out to the Lord, the Lord raised up a deliverer for the children of Israel, who delivered them: Othniel the son of Kenaz, Caleb's younger brother.*

JUDGES 3:9 NKJV

I often receive requests to help someone whose life is in a difficult place. After a few questions I am able to discern if the Lord has called me to get involved. More often than not, I am not to be involved. Many times I find these people have not experienced enough pain to want to do anything about their situations. Until they are ready to cry out to the Lord for a solution to their situation, they will simply talk about desiring change but never take the necessary steps needed for change.

If you invest time into someone who has not yet come to the place of wanting a spiritual solution to his problem, you will become emotionally exhausted. The apostle Paul understood this principle when he actually turned such people over to Satan for the destruction of their flesh (see 1 Corinthians 5:5).

The people of Israel were finally in enough pain to cry out to God for relief from their oppression. Like so many times throughout the Scriptures, God answered by raising up a deliverer (see Judges 3:8–11).

## Question

Are you in a difficult place in your life? Are you only talking about changing, or are you ready to cry out to the Lord for a solution?

*Father, help me seek you with a whole heart for the solution to my problem.*

# God Delays

*Now even though Jesus loved Mary, Martha, and Lazarus,*
*he remained where he was for two more days.*
JOHN 11:5–6 TPT

"Why doesn't God heal me? I have prayed and prayed, and I am still sick. Do I not have enough faith? I am so tired of this," said my friend who had gone more than three years battling his illness.

Mary and Martha were very close to Jesus. The Bible says Jesus loved Mary, Martha, and Lazarus. Lazarus, Mary and Martha's brother, had become terminally ill. Jesus was away in Jerusalem during the time of Lazarus' illness.

After Jesus heard the news that Lazarus was ill, instead of running to the aid of Mary and Martha, Jesus waited two days. Lazarus died and was placed in a tomb. Jesus' response to the news was: "This sickness will not end in death. No, it is for God's glory so that God's Son may be glorified through it" (John 11:4 NIV). Jesus had to look beyond Mary and Martha's current grief in order to fulfill God's purpose for this sickness.

Mary was in deep mourning over the death of her brother. When she finally went to see Jesus, she immediately cried out to him, "Lord, if you had been here, my brother would not have died" (v. 32 NIV). There was a preordained plan for the purpose of Lazarus' death. But only Jesus knew this. Jesus raised Lazarus that day.

When we experience sickness and do not see a breakthrough, we can only seek Jesus for our healing and leave the outcome to him. A day will come when Jesus reveals his purposes in your situation.

## Question
Are you trusting God for the healing of a loved one? Stand firm.

*Father, you are the great healer. I trust you to heal my loved one in your timing.*

# A Lack of Provision

*"It will be that you shall drink from the brook,
and I have commanded the ravens to feed you there."*
1 KINGS 17:4 NKJV

The prophet Elijah pronounced a drought upon the land because of the sin of Ahab and the nation of Israel. There was only one problem. Elijah had to live in the same land as Ahab.

"Then the word of the LORD came to Elijah: 'Leave here, turn eastward and hide in the Kerith Ravine, east of the Jordan. You will drink from the brook, and I have directed the ravens to supply you with food there'" (vv. 2–4 NIV). God provided for Elijah in a supernatural way. The ravens brought bread in the morning and meat in the evening. His water came from the brook.

God often uses money to confirm direction for our lives. Many times, God uses a lack of provision to move us into new directions. It is a catalyst to encourage new ideas and strategies. Many times, the loss of a job becomes the greatest blessing to our lives because it provides the catalyst to do things we simply would never do without taking the step to get out of our comfort zone.

Friend, if you are fully following the Lord in your life and seeking direction from him, and if you have no unconfessed sin in your life, there is no way he will allow you to miss his provision for you.

## Question
Are you puzzled by a lack of direction in your life?

*Father, thank you for promising to direct my steps.*

# Finish the Job

*It came to pass, when Israel was strong, that they put the Canaanites under tribute,*
*but did not completely drive them out.*
JUDGES 1:28 NKJV

Have you ever hired a contractor to do some work and ended up having to spend time and energy to get him back to finish the job? The small unfinished projects simply irritate you and create ill will between you and your contractor. If you have been involved in a building project, you have surely had this experience.

God wanted his people to finish the job. He often told the Israelites to remove their enemies from the promised land. However, many times they would not finish the job, and the remnant that was left would come back and create difficulties. Often the people of Israel would intermarry with the enemies they failed to vanquish, which enticed God's people into their enemies' way of living. Other times they had to enslave their enemies, which took time away from their mission.

Whenever we fail to complete a job, it creates ill will from those we are serving. It also violates a basic biblical mandate for every believer to do his work with excellence. The Bible says that Daniel and his friends did their work ten times better than anyone else. They were known for their excellence.

It is often said of American football that the hardest place to score from is the one-yard line. That is because the defenses are greatest where there is the most resistance. Sometimes completing a job is like this. If a project is not completed 100 percent, you will be known for what you did not finish rather than for what you did finish.

## Question
Have you completed 100 percent of the projects you started?

*Father, help me be a person who completes 100 percent of my assignments.*

# You Were Made to Fly

*"Naked I came from my mother's womb, and naked shall I return there.
The LORD gave, and the LORD has taken away; blessed be the name of the LORD."*

JOB 1:21 NKJV

Can a caterpillar fly? If you said, "No," you would be partially correct. Actually, a caterpillar can fly, but it must have a transformation first.

The butterfly begins life as a caterpillar, a wormlike larva that spins a cocoon for itself. There is a process that must be completed for a butterfly to fly. We might be tempted to help this process by tearing open the cocoon— but that's the worst thing we could do. The struggle makes it strong and enables it to fly. Butterflies need adversity to become what God intended them to be. So do we.

Job was a successful and righteous businessman with huge holdings of livestock and real estate. One day God said to Satan, "Have you considered my servant Job?…He is blameless and upright, a man who fears God and shuns evil" (Job 1:8 NIV). Notice that God pointed Job out to Satan! God gave Satan permission to put Job through a trial of adversity. Job's herds were stolen, his servants were murdered, and all of Job's children were killed by a sudden tornado. He was even accused of sin by his closest friends.

Through his trial of adversity, he grew in strength, wisdom, and faith. His entire perspective on God was transformed by his suffering.

In order for the butterfly to fly, there must be a transformation process that is often developed through adversity.

## Question
Are you going through the process of transformation right now?

*Father, give me grace to embrace the transformation process.*

# To Know His Rest

*"This ignited my anger with that generation and I said about them, 'They wander in their hearts just like they do with their feet, and they refuse to learn my ways.' My heart grieved over them so I decreed: 'They will not enter into my rest!'"*
HEBREWS 3:10–11 TPT

Technology is supposed to make our ability to accomplish things easier and make us more productive. I love the technological gadgets available to us today. In twenty years, these will seem as old and archaic as the 8-track player. (See, some of you don't know what that is.)

Research reveals that the average person is working much longer hours today because we literally can work from anywhere. Our technology allows us to stay in constant contact with others, which means we are always on call. Unless we intentionally set boundaries, we will never rest from our work.

God got angry with the people of Israel because they did not know his ways. They chose to disregard his ways. This disobedience led to their inability to enter God's rest.

God's rest means that we can actually do our work and still be refreshed through his Spirit in our inner man. It means that the fruit of our work comes as a result of abiding in the vine of his grace and power. Jesus said you can do nothing (worthwhile) unless you are connected to the vine (see John 15:4).

In order to do this, you and I must do two things. We must understand his ways, and we must do his will. When we follow these two things, we will begin to experience his supernatural rest in all of our endeavors.

## Question
Are you experiencing God's rest even in the midst of your work?

*Father, help me to enter your rest.*

# Peace: Our Weapon against Fear

*God will never give you the spirit of fear,*
*but the Holy Spirit who gives you mighty power, love, and self-control.*
2 TIMOTHY 1:7 TPT

Fear is the enemy of faith. Fear is bondage. Satan wants us to live in bondage to the past and even the future, but God wants us to live in the freedom of his love and power in the present. As Paul wrote, "For you did not receive the spirit of bondage again to fear, but you received the Spirit of adoption by whom we cry out, 'Abba, Father'" (Romans 8:15 NKJV).

In order to be the leaders God calls us to be, we must conquer our fear and put it to death. We must replace our fear with the peace that surpasses understanding. As Jesus told his followers, "These things I have spoken to you, that in Me you may have peace. In the world you will have tribulation; but be of good cheer, I have overcome the world" (John 16:33 NKJV).

Paul told the Christians in Rome, "The God of peace will soon crush Satan under your feet" (Romans 16:20 NASB). The peace of God is our weapon against fear and Satan. Before going to the cross, Jesus told his disciples, "Peace I leave with you, My peace I give to you; not as the world gives do I give to you. Let not your heart be troubled, neither let it be afraid" (John 14:27 NKJV).

Doubts, fear, and shame are the weapons of Satan, but Jesus stands against Satan's fury and says with authority, "Peace, be still!" (Mark 4:39 NKJV). The peace of God shatters the weapons of Satan and sends our enemy fleeing.

## Question
### Are you using the peace of God?

*Father, I choose to walk in your peace.*

# Presuming the Future

*If you borrow money with interest,*
*you'll end up serving the interests of your creditors,*
*for the rich rule over the poor.*
PROVERBS 22:7 TPT

Do you think I should pay off my mortgage?" I said to the investment counselor.

"Oh, absolutely not; you can use that money to invest and make more than what you are paying in mortgage interest. Plus, you will get an interest deduction from your mortgage."

This was the counsel I got from a Christian investment counselor years ago when I had the chance to pay off all my debts—including my home mortgage. I chose to follow his advice and lived to regret it.

It was not long after that when I was thrust into a seven-year adversity that took all the financial assets I had available that could have paid that mortgage. Through a series of unusual circumstances, that money was gone.

The world's wisdom presumes upon the future. Debt is one of those instruments that has the ability to make one a servant to it. I don't believe the Bible speaks totally against debt, but it does give strong warnings that debt can be an evil taskmaster, and if you choose to use it, you need to know the consequences. After that experience, I decided to commit myself to becoming debt free.

Now, many years later. I can tell you I am a free man. I am no longer a servant to the lender. God is free to move in greater ways because of my lack of bondage to debt. And I am free to sow more into God's kingdom.

## Question
### Are you a slave to debt?

*Father, bring me into the promised land of debt-free living where I will find a peace that surpasses all understanding.*

# Little by Little

*If you work hard at what you do, great abundance will come to you.*
*But merely talking about getting rich while living to only pursue*
*your pleasures brings you face-to-face with poverty.*

PROVERBS 14:23 TPT

Is there something you would like to accomplish in life but simply cannot find the hours in the day to get started? Many of us suffer from procrastination. We justify putting our dreams aside because we don't believe we have the time or resources to accomplish the task.

Many times, people tell me they believe they are called to write a book. I tell them, "Great, if God has called you to write a book, begin to write it."

Sometimes the response is: "But I don't have a publisher."

"That has nothing to do with it," I say. "That is not your problem. If God calls you to write a book, you are to begin to write. You may not be writing to get published. You may be writing for other purposes."

If God has given you a vision to do something, begin by taking baby steps toward that project. Begin to focus on the vision and take action steps toward it. You will be amazed at what God can do with a little each day. Do not let procrastination prevent you from accomplishing what God may want to do through your life. Make plans today to take baby steps toward the vision that is in your heart.

## Question

What has God called you to do that you have been putting off?

*Father, I commit my works to you so that you might complete the work through me.*

# How Sharp Is Your Ax?

*If the ax is dull, and one does not sharpen the edge,
then he must use more strength; but wisdom brings success.*

ECCLESIASTES 10:10 NKJV

Manufacturing companies live and die by the ability of their designers, engineers, and staff to bring new products to market quickly. A team's capacity to turn promising ideas into new revenue is diminished because of fragmented business processes, a geographically dispersed workforce, and a lack of standards across the supply chain, according to an industry expert on innovation in technology.[49]

We live in an information age where the level of knowledge is increasing at warp speed. The way you did things two years ago may not be the same way you do it today. The knowledge you had two years ago may not be adequate to compete in the global marketplace today. Businesses have gone bankrupt because they were not willing to change with the times. Have you seen a Polaroid camera lately? Do you know someone over sixty years old who chose not to learn about computers? The world passes by such people because they are unwilling to "sharpen their ax."

God calls every workplace believer to model four key attributes: (1) excellence, (2) ethics and integrity, (3) extravagant love and service, and (4) signs and wonders.

The first quality of a Christian worker should be excellence. Excellence does not just mean the way we do our jobs, but it also means staying abreast of how we do our jobs. You will not compete in the marketplace today unless you make a commitment to stay abreast of innovation. This, too, is good stewardship.

## Question

What are the areas in your working life that need to be sharpened?

*Father, help me "sharpen my ax."*

# Knowing When to Quit

*When the donkey saw the Angel of the LORD, she lay down under Balaam;*
*so Balaam's anger was aroused, and he struck the donkey with his staff.*
NUMBERS 22:27 NKJV

Have you ever wanted something so badly that your perception of the situation became distorted? We can force situations so much that we lose perspective.

The Israelites were defeating all their enemies in the promised land. Balak, the king of Moab, feared that they would be defeated by the Israelites. Balaam was a prophet of the Lord whom Balak knew had the power to bless or curse a nation. So, he sent a delegation to get Balaam to curse the nation of Israel. Balaam wanted to do this for a nice fee that would come with his cooperation. However, God was not pleased (see v. 12).

Balaam was not being obedient to the Lord because he proceeded with his plan. God sent an angel to stop him, and were it not have been for his "talking donkey," he would have been killed by the angel.

In order to achieve godly success, we must be sensitive to those around us who can give input on the direction we may be taking. God will confirm his direction in our lives if we are willing to accept input from those around us. It can come through a spouse, a coworker, a boss, a secretary, or any other person. Be aware of situations that encourage you to press too hard for a particular outcome. Achieving goals should be a result of following the actions you believe God leads you to take.

## Question

Is there any situation right now that you are under pressure to get done?

*Father, help me to depend on you to make crooked places straight.*

# Actions Determine Your Position

*All children show what they're really like by how they act.*
*You can discern their character, whether they are pure or perverse.*
PROVERBS 20:11 TPT

In the marketplace, companies and products are known by their position in the industry they represent. Lexus, Mercedes, and Cadillac hold the top positions among luxury automobiles. They are known for their high quality. Nike is a sports merchandise company known for having excellent products, serving those who play sports, and holding the number one position in their industry. Coca-Cola is a soft drink company that currently has the number one position in the world among soft drinks. Companies spend millions trying to gain the number one position.

You also are called to achieve a certain position in what you do and how you do it. Your position is often a result of your actions taken over several years. Usually when your name is mentioned, your position is revealed. It is the most distinguishing attribute of your life and work, and people associate you with your perceived position.

In the workplace you are known more by what you do and what you achieve. Your reputation is often built either around productivity or the lack of it. Years of productivity in an industry can allow you to own the number one position in your industry.

## Question

Do your actions line up with the position God desires for your life? Are you modeling the fruits of the Holy Spirit in all aspects of your life?

*Father, I pray that I might have an excellent position for the benefit of the kingdom and your life.*

# Give Me Your Last Meal

*She said, "As the LORD your God lives, I do not have bread, only a handful of flour in a bin, and a little oil in a jar; and see, I am gathering a couple of sticks that I may go in and prepare it for myself and my son, that we may eat it, and die."*

### 1 KINGS 17:12 NKJV

God led Elijah to a poor widow who was on her last meal of flour. Why would God lead Elijah from one desperate situation into another? He wished to perform yet another miracle and show God's faithfulness to those who needed it most.

Elijah proceeded to tell the widow:

Elijah said to her, "Do not fear; go and do as you have said, but make me a small cake from it first, and bring it to me; and afterward make some for yourself and your son. For thus says the LORD God of Israel: 'The bin of flour shall not be used up, nor shall the jar of oil run dry, until the day the LORD sends rain on the earth.'" (vv. 13–14 NKJV)

Would you have questioned such logic in the face of a life-threatening situation? God multiplied her flour and her jug of oil. Provision followed obedience. "For the jar of flour was not used up and the jug of oil did not run dry, in keeping with the word of the LORD spoken by Elijah" (v. 16 NIV).

God often multiplies in a miraculous way what we already have in our hands when we yield it to him.

## Question

What resources has God placed in your hands that he can multiply?

*Father, reveal to me what I have in my hand that you can transform into a resource.*

# God versus Mammon

*"No one can serve two masters;*
*for either he will hate the one and love the other,*
*or else he will be loyal to the one and despise the other.*
*You cannot serve God and mammon."*

MATTHEW 6:24 NKJV

The New Testament contains 2,084 verses dealing with money and finance. Sixteen of Jesus' thirty-eight parables deal with money. Jesus spoke so much about money because he was revealing where a person's loyalty resided. "For where your treasure is, there your heart will be also" (Matthew 6:21 NKJV). He said a person could not serve two masters. Instead, he will love one but hate the other.

Mammon is an Aramaic demonic spirit that was worshiped as a false god by the Philistines. Mammon desires to be worshiped, have influence, and control of peoples' lives to require love and devotion through the use of money. Money is simply the instrument by which mammon seeks to have power.

The symptoms of being controlled by the spirit of mammon are revealed when we allow our activities to be governed by the amount of money we have instead of by God alone. It makes us believe one's provision is from his or her employer, spouse, investments, or other money sources. So, when we allow money to rule the choices in our lives, we have yielded to the spirit of mammon.

Paul writes to Timothy: "For the love of money is a root of all kinds of evil. Some people, eager for money, have wandered from the faith and pierced themselves with many griefs" (1 Timothy 6:10 NIV).

## Question
### Are you influenced by the spirit of mammon?

*Father, show me if I have been influenced by the spirit of mammon. If so, I renounce it and place my total trust in Christ as my source for all provision.*

# When Others Disappoint You

*Be diligent to come to me quickly;*
*for Demas has forsaken me, having loved this present world.*
2 TIMOTHY 4:9–10 NKJV

Adversity molded the apostle Paul into the greatest warrior for Christ the world has ever known. But there were times when adversity and disappointment took their toll on this rugged warrior. We can sense Paul's hurt and discouragement near the end of his second letter to Timothy:

> Do your best to come to me quickly, for Demas, because he loved this world, has deserted me and has gone to Thessalonica…At my first defense, no one came to my support, but everyone deserted me…Do your best to get here before winter. (2 Timothy 4:9–10, 16, 21 NIV)

However, in most of his letters, Paul seems to have an invincible spirit. He chose to look at life from a heavenly perspective. That's why he could write:

> We are hard-pressed on every side, yet not crushed; we are perplexed, but not in despair; persecuted, but not forsaken; struck down, but not destroyed—always carrying about in the body the dying of the Lord Jesus, that the life of Jesus also may be manifested in our body. (2 Corinthians 4:8–10 NKJV)

Paul had experienced a level of opposition and suffering that you and I can scarcely imagine. People said they would do things, but he refused to give in to despair when they disappointed him. His goal was to live in such a way that the life of Jesus would be revealed in his response to adversity.

## Question
Do you ever feel discouraged by the failure of others toward you?

*Father, give me the grace to overcome my disappointment in others.*

# How Solid Is Your Foundation?

*The king commanded them to quarry large stones,
costly stones, and hewn stones, to lay the foundation of the temple.*
1 KINGS 5:17 NKJV

Several years ago, I visited Jerusalem, the ancient city in Israel where Jesus walked. It was an incredible experience. Some of the most memorable things I saw were the actual stones used to build the foundation of the temple. These stones lay beneath the ground and can be accessed only by going into an underground tunnel.

The stones are massive, and they are perfectly rectangular in shape. The Bible says the stones were moved to the temple area in a quiet manner out of respect for the holy site. It says the foundation was of a "quality stone."

All these structures, from the outside to the great courtyard and from foundation to eaves, were made of blocks of high-grade stone cut to size and trimmed with a saw on their inner and outer faces. The great courtyard was surrounded by a wall of three courses of dressed stone and one course of trimmed cedar beams, as was the inner courtyard of the temple of the Lord with its portico.

In order to achieve anything worthwhile in life you must lay a quality foundation. Everything else is going to be impacted if that foundation is not laid with the best materials and the finest craftsmanship. The Bible says that Jesus must be the foundation from which we build everything in our lives (see 1 Corinthians 3:11). Anything else will result in a weak foundation.

## Question
Do you see the effort put into the type and quality of stone that would be used to build the temple of God?

*Father, help me build on a solid foundation that will last.*

# Making Judgments

*Jesus said, "Forsake the habit of criticizing and judging others,*
*and you will not be criticized and judged in return."*
LUKE 6:37 TPT

Have you ever made a judgment about a person or situation only to discover how wrong you were in your assessment? Such was the case in a story told by Os Guinness in his book *The Call*.

> Arthur F. Burns, the chairman of the United States Federal Reserve System and ambassador to West Germany, was a man of considerable gravity. He was economic counselor to a number of presidents from Dwight D. Eisenhower to Ronald Reagan. His opinions carried weight.
>
> Arthur Burns was Jewish, so when he began attending an informational White House group for prayer and fellowship in the 1970s, he was accorded special respect. In fact, no one knew quite how to involve him in the group and often passed him by during prayer—out of a mixture of respect and reticence.
>
> One week the group was led by a newcomer who did not know of Burns' status. The newcomer turned to Arthur Burns and asked him to close the time with a prayer. Some of the old-timers glanced at each other in surprise and wondered what would happen. But without missing a beat, Burns reached out, held hands with others in the circle, and prayed this prayer: "Lord, I pray that you would bring Jews to know Jesus Christ. I pray that you would bring Muslims to know Jesus Christ. Finally, Lord, I pray that you would bring Christians to know Jesus Christ. Amen." Burn's prayer has become legendary in Washington."[50]

## Question
Have you ever assessed a situation and were totally wrong?

*Father, help me view situations through your eyes.*

# Intimacy with the Upright

*For the devious are an abomination to the LORD;*
*but He is intimate with the upright.*
PROVERBS 3:32 NASB

It is human nature to want to be included in the inner circle. It means that you are qualified to hear things, experience things, and be privy to information the masses are not allowed to see.

Jesus had an inner circle of friends made up of Peter, James, and John. John had a very special relationship with Jesus. He was considered to be Jesus' best friend. It was John who recognized Jesus after the crucifixion when he came to them on the seashore. "Therefore that disciple whom Jesus loved said to Peter, 'It is the Lord!'" (John 21:7 NKJV).

The Bible tells us that John's friendship was such that he could even lay his head upon his shoulder at the last supper when he inquired about the betrayer: "So lying thus, close to the breast of Jesus, he said to him, 'Lord, who is it?'" (John 13:25 RSV). Almost forty years after the last supper, John wrote the final Gospel in AD 90. He was chosen by God to receive "the vision" and record it in the book of Revelation.

When it came time for Jesus to leave the earth for good, it was Peter, James, and John who had the privilege to see the transfiguration. "Now after six days Jesus took Peter, James, and John, and led them up on a high mountain apart by themselves; and He was transfigured before them" (Mark 9:2 NKJV).

## Question

Do you long to have an intimate relationship with your Creator?

*Father, help me to make my life upright and intimate with you.*

# Stephen: A Marketplace Minister

*Stephen, who was a man full of grace and supernatural power, performed many astonishing signs and wonders and mighty miracles among the people.*
ACTS 6:8 TPT

In the beginnings of the early church, the disciples found themselves preaching the Word of God all over the region. However, there became practical needs that arose among the people that the disciples were tending to. Since the apostles spent their time preaching, the physical needs of the people were not being met adequately. One of these needs involved food distribution to widows. There became an issue as to whether the needs of all the widows were being cared for. This brought pressure upon the disciples, who felt their primary focus must be to preach the gospel. They now realized they could not do both adequately. They appointed seven men to serve these needs.

The first man named to fill this responsibility was Stephen, described as a man full of faith and the Holy Ghost with a strong faith in Christ. He was full of courage, gifts, and graces. He was an extraordinary man and excelled in everything that was good; his name signified a crown.

One of the most interesting things one can notice when the disciples took this action is described in these passages. The word of God spread. The number of disciples in Jerusalem increased rapidly, and a large number of priests became obedient to the faith. It is as though the Lord took the cap off, and everything started happening. Even a large number of priests came into the faith.

## Question
Could your life be described as one full of faith and of the Holy Spirit, full of grace and power, and one that results in great wonders and miraculous things?

*Father, today help me to accomplish this in my life.*

# Our Staff as Our Protector

*Moses said to Joshua, "Choose us some men and go out, fight with Amalek. Tomorrow I will stand on the top of the hill with the rod of God in my hand."*
EXODUS 17:9 NKJV

Moses' staff represented his vocation as a shepherd. When God first met Moses in the desert at the burning bush, he told him that he was going to use his staff to perform miracles and bring a people out of slavery. God related to Moses through his vocation as a shepherd.

Moses later faced one of his enemies in the new land, the Amalekites. God told him to go to the top of the mountain and hold his staff up to heaven. As long as his staff was outstretched to heaven, Israel would win the battle. But if it was not uplifted, they would suffer defeat.

Isn't this an interesting picture? When we raise our "staffs" up to the Lord, he becomes our protector. He is our defender. As long we offer up our staffs before the Lord, he can work through it. He works on our behalf. When we lower them, we lose the blessing of God.

When God told Moses he was going to use his staff to bring a people out of bondage, Moses first had to lay his staff down on the ground. God changed it into a snake, and then God told Moses to pick it up by the tail. Moses took authority over the serpent in this prophetic act. When Moses picked up the staff, the Scripture tells us it was no longer Moses' staff, but it was now the staff of God.

## Question
Have you offered your "staff" up to the Lord?

*Father, may you use my work life to bring glory to your name.*

# Living under Authority

*Therefore submit yourselves to every ordinance of man for the Lord's sake, whether to the king as supreme, or to governors, as to those who are sent by him for the punishment of evildoers and for the praise of those who do good.*

1 PETER 2:13–14 NKJV

God used government authorities in the lives of many people in the Bible to accomplish his purposes in their lives. Scripture tells us that even the king's heart is in the hand of God (see Proverbs 21:1). God uses these authorities to continue the work that he has started in us and will continue to manifest his character in us through governmental authorities.

Moses, Joseph, Daniel, Esther, Jesus, and many others throughout the Bible became great men and women of God because they gave those in authority their rightful place.

If we find it difficult to live under the authorities in our life, we'll usually find it difficult to submit to the will of God in our lives too. Rebellion is reflected in our unwillingness to live under the authority placed over us. We may not have respect for the person who is the president of the United States, but we are still to honor and respect the position the presidency represents, and we are to recognize that God has placed that person in authority over us. As long as we are not asked to violate a biblical commandment, we must recognize those in authority as God-given and that God is going to work through them on our behalf.

## Question

Are you living under the authority God has placed over you?

*God, today I pray for those in authority over me.*

# Turning Tragedy into Triumph

*Death is at work in us, but life is at work in you.*
2 CORINTHIANS 4:12 NIV

On September 11, 2001, New York City firefighter Stephen Siller had just completed his shift when he heard on his truck's scanner that a plane had hit one of the World Trade Center towers. Siller quickly turned his truck around and joined his elite Squad One brothers. With seventy-five pounds of fire gear, he ran a mile and a half through the tunnel before an emergency vehicle picked him up and dropped him off at Tower Two.

Siller had been orphaned at the age of ten and raised by his much older brothers and sisters. Siller died that day, leaving behind a wife and five children.

His story became a legend in the newsrooms and firehouses of New York City. His six siblings—who, in many ways, viewed Siller as a son as well as a brother—found themselves grappling with a dilemma: should they allow the tragic circumstances of their brother's death to paralyze and embitter them, or should they use it as a catalyst to help others and preserve his memory?

The Siller family chose the latter.

Each year since 9/11, tens of thousands of runners have retraced the steps of a hero. As part of a fundraising event, 343 New York City firefighters, each representing a fallen comrade and holding an American flag, stand throughout the length of the tunnel. They are joined by firefighters from across the United States, each holding a poster-size picture of a firefighter who perished on 9/11.

More than $1 million has been donated to charities benefitting the families of those affected by the 9/11 attacks.

## Question

Is there a project you can support to keep someone's memory alive?

*Father, thank you for using the brave men and women who work as first responders across the country to save many lives.*

# Jesus and the Wedding

*Jesus said to her, "Woman, what does your concern have to do with Me?*
*My hour has not yet come."*
JOHN 2:4 NKJV

In Bible times, a Jewish wedding was a special celebration that could last seven days. It was a time of joy and celebration on behalf of the couple. Wine was an integral part of these weddings. Jesus, the disciples, and Mary, Jesus' mother, were invited guests to such a wedding. At some point during the celebration, there was no more wine. Mary became concerned and turned to Jesus to solve the problem. But Jesus had not yet performed any miracles. However, his mother must have known that he was capable of doing so.

When she proposed to Jesus that he solve this problem, he answered, "My time has not yet come."

You can almost hear that motherly Jewish tone…"Yes, it has, son. Please handle this emergency for me." She tells the servants to do whatever Jesus tells them to do, seeming to know that he was going to solve the problem but not really knowing how. Jesus proceeds to respond to his mother's request.

I can only imagine the next day's headline in Cana's Daily News: "Son of Mary Turns Water into Alcoholic Drink—180 Gallons!" What a way to begin a ministry! Thankfully, there was no negative press.

Imagine, 180 gallons of fine wine! The servants were an important part of the miracle as they did just what Jesus told them to do.

## Question

Have you ever asked Jesus to get involved in an unusual problem? No matter what problem you have, Jesus invites you to seek him as the solution to your problem.

*Father, thank you for knowing the solution to every problem I will ever have.*

# God Speaks through Circumstances

*As you do not know what is the way of the wind,*
*or how the bones grow in the womb of her who is with child,*
*so you do not know the works of God who makes everything.*
ECCLESIASTES 11:5 NKJV

God will often use circumstances in our lives to direct us in making and confirming decisions.

Years ago, I launched a magazine designed for Christians in the workplace, and I was having lunch with a Christian leader named Larry who headed a ministry that helps men and women apply biblical principles to managing money.

During our lunch, I explained to Larry that I had noticed that there were many grassroots workplace ministries cropping up all over the country. I asked Larry if he was familiar with some of the groups since he had taught a course and written a book on operating a business on biblical principles. But he said he was not. He then asked, "It would be nice to know what all these groups are doing so we don't duplicate efforts. Do you think you could invite some of these groups for a roundtable discussion?" I told him I would, and I proceeded to invite four main workplace ministries that I had worked with in the past.

Then something unexpected began to happen. I began to get requests from ministries all around the country asking if they could attend the roundtable. We had fifty-four people show up representing forty-five organizations from around the country! Then, at the last minute, a conflict arose for Larry, and he was not able to attend. He informed me that I would have to host the meeting myself. That was the birth of Marketplace Leaders!

## Question
Has God ever "tricked" you to move you in a particular direction?

*Father, I trust you to lead every aspect of my life.*

# Confirming Decisions

*Without counsel, plans go awry,*
*but in the multitude of counselors they are established.*
PROVERBS 15:22 NKJV

Confirming major decisions through the counsel of others is one way God protects us from poor decisions. This process is designed to confirm the direction for which we are seeking confirmation. Paul was sensitive not to get too heavy-handed in the confirmation process though. He offered advice to others but was not the enforcer of their decisions. "So here are my thoughts concerning this matter, and it's in your best interests. Since you made such a good start last year, both in the grace of giving and in your longing to give…" (2 Corinthians 8:10 TPT).

The requirement for efficient administration frequently requires single points of decision-making. Where there is willingness and trust to receive input, there is also humility, faith, and grace for God to work his pleasure in his servant. Where there is unwillingness, the opposite is true.

In some situations, I have felt strongly about a certain issue only to receive feedback from those close to me that revealed that I was not accurate in my assessment of the situation. I have learned to yield in such situations, trusting that God is working through those to whom I am accountable.

Peace of mind is another important confirmation requirement for making decisions. If you do not have peace about a decision, you should wait until God gives you peace. This does not mean your decision may not have some tension due to the faith aspect of it, but deep down, you should have peace that it is the right decision.

## Question
Do you need to make a major decision?

*Father, help me receive confirmation through others for all my decisions.*

# Miraculous Signs

*The apostles performed many signs and wonders among the people.*
*And all the believers used to meet together in Solomon's Colonnade.*

ACTS 5:12 NIV

When was the last time you saw a miracle in your workplace? Perhaps you prayed for a coworker, and he was instantly healed. Perhaps you prayed for a coworker's financial problem, and it was resolved. Perhaps you led a coworker to Christ. Or maybe God gave you an answer to a major problem at work that benefited your organization.

The disciples were working people. They turned the world upside down not because of their knowledge of Jesus but because of their outflow of the power of Jesus through them to others. And this was done in the public square, where all could see.

Workplace Bible and prayer groups are great, but you must transition to action if you want to change the spiritual climate in an organization. There is a risk—God might actually show up in a powerful way.

I taught a lunchtime Bible study in an insurance company for two years. God began to move powerfully in the meetings. People were coming to Christ. Some experienced healing. Word was getting out, and nonbelievers came to check us out.

When is the last time someone saw something happen through your life that could not be explained other than God working in your life?

## Question
When was the last time you saw a miracle at work?

*Father, make me a vessel of his power, not simply a vessel of words.*

# Seeing Thorns as Blessings

*The extraordinary level of the revelations I've received is no reason for anyone to exalt me. For this is why a thorn in my flesh was given to me.*
2 CORINTHIANS 12:7 TPT

Have you ever had something in your life you wish was not there? If God gave you one wish, perhaps it would be to change that one thing. Perhaps it is the source of pain or challenge in your life. You seek God continually for relief from it, but he seems strangely silent.

Paul also experienced an ongoing burden that he called a "thorn in his flesh." Bible scholars have speculated as to what this thorn might have been, but no one knows for sure. We do know Paul asked God on three different occasions to remove it from his life: "To keep me from becoming conceited, I was given a thorn in my flesh, a messenger of Satan, to torment me. Three times I pleaded with the Lord to take it away from me" (v. 7–8 NIV).

Paul acknowledged, "The extraordinary level of the revelations I've received is no reason for anyone to exalt me. For this is why a thorn in my flesh was given to me, the Adversary's messenger sent to harass me, keeping me from becoming arrogant" (v. 7 TPT).

The revelations and faith experiences that God gave Paul would have been too much for any man's humility. So, God, in order to ensure his investment in Paul's life, gave him a thorn in his flesh to help him maintain a humble, godly perspective.

## Question
Has God given you such a thorn designed to prompt you to place greater trust and reliance upon him?

*Father, reveal to me the blessing of the thorn you have placed in my life.*

# Vested Interests

*It so happened, when Sanballat heard that we were rebuilding the wall,
that he was furious and very indignant, and mocked the Jews.*
NEHEMIAH 4:1 NKJV

Leaders who attempt something greater than themselves will always get
attacked, and it often comes from those who have a vested interest in what
you are changing. Nehemiah was rebuilding the ancient wall of Jerusalem.
It was a major undertaking. Not everyone was pleased with this initiative.
Sanballat, another government worker, did not want this to happen.

When Jesus began confronting the Pharisees about religious traditions, he
was attacked by the religious establishment because they had a vested interest
that would be negatively impacted by his teaching. The apostle Paul confronted
a religious tradition that generated income for those in the trade. Opposition
arose because he was impacting a vested interest. You can read about this in
Acts 19:23–27. Paul's actions disrupted an entire industry in his city.

Whenever you introduce a new product into the market, expect
opposition from competitive products that have a vested interest. If God leads
you to initiate a cause greater than yourself, expect opposition from those who
may have a vested interest.

## Question
Are you aware of how your actions might disrupt the status quo?

*Father, give me the courage to be obedient to you, no matter the
consequences.*

# Stoplight Faith

*Their unbelief kept him from doing many mighty miracles in Nazareth.*
MATTHEW 13:58 TPT

You can learn a lot about people in traffic. For instance, I observe a lot when I see twenty cars in one line and only three cars in another. Those in the longer want to make sure they get to make their turn after the light. I want to get through the light first, then worry about making the next turn. This is a difference in risk-taking tolerance or faith; some might argue with me that I'm operating out of presumption versus real faith. The truth is that presumption is very close to faith. It requires us to believe something about the future based on our actions.

No matter which person you might be in this situation, both people's actions demonstrate faith, either faith to believe you will get through the light and into the correct lane or faith that you are satisfied to sit in the longer line because you are assured of being in the correct lane when you get through the light.

When the priests carried the ark into the Jordan River at flood stage, there was a risk they could lose the ark to the Jordan River. However, that is not what happened. The river parted when they put their feet in the water. God made it possible to walk across without the pressure of wading through the powerful water only when they took the first step.

When God leads us to take a risk, then he is there whether we succeed or fail. He is there in the success, and he is there in the failure. If he leads you to take a risk, it may not always succeed in the way you think. In fact, it could even fail.

The only true failure is when we fail to take the risk to exercise our faith when God is leading us to do so. Sometimes the fear of failure is the greater obstacle than the risk itself.

## Question
Has God called you to step out in an area that requires risk?

*Father, give me the courage to step out boldly in faith.*

# Pride That Leads to Arguments

*Reject a divisive man after the first and second admonition,*
*knowing that such a person is warped and sinning, being self-condemned.*
TITUS 3:10–11 NKJV

Have you ever had to deal with a person who just wanted to argue with you no matter which position they took? This person usually has a strong opinion and draws conclusions quickly, rarely giving credence to other's viewpoint.

The apostle Paul knew how to deal with such people. Once he saw this pattern, he confronted the person. If they continued, he cut off fellowship. However, if this person happens to be your boss, you will not be able to avoid the person.

The root stronghold of a person who is argumentative is pride and fear. Such people are not secure in who they are as a person. They mask their inadequacies through a need to always be right.

I had a business partner once who was deeply hurt by lawyers in a corporate take-over. Ever since that time, he was argumentative with every lawyer he had to deal with. One time, I had to confront him and tell him what was behind his behavior. Thankfully, he had the grace and humility to repent and renounce his stronghold of pride, insecurity, and fear. We proceeded to finish our project.

When you run into this in the workplace, pray for understanding. Negative behavior is like the warning light on your car dashboard. It's telling you there is something bad going on under the hood.

## Question
Is there any pride, insecurity, or fear operating in your life
or someone you know?

*Father, give me the grace to work with such a person and pray that God will deliver them and me if needed.*

# From Pain to Destiny

*My brethren, count it all joy when you fall into various trials, knowing that the testing of your faith produces patience. But let patience have its perfect work, that you may be perfect and complete, lacking nothing.*

JAMES 1:2–4 NKJV

God often allows pain to ignite destiny in our lives. Without motivation, many of us would never fulfill the purposes for which God created us. Oftentimes a measured assault invades our life and creates a depth of pain such that all we know to do is to press into God with all our being.

At first, our motivation is to alleviate the pain. After a season of extreme emotional and sometimes physical pain, a second phase begins. This phase moves us to discover a new and deeper relationship with God. We discover things about ourselves and about God that we would never have discovered without this motivation. Gradually, our heart changes our motivation from pain to loving obedience because there is a transition of the heart that takes place. No longer do we seek God for deliverance from the pain; we seek God because he is God. We seek his face and not his hand.

When we move to the second phase, we often find ourselves moving into a new destiny and calling for our lives because God often separates us from the old life in this process. No doubt Joseph and Peter felt the pain of their individual crises. However, later they could realize God's purposes in their crises. Like Joseph, we are able to say, "You meant it for evil, but God meant it for good."

## Question
Do you find that you are seeking God's hand or his face?

*Father, show me the secret things you have reserved for me as a result of the crisis I find myself in.*

# The Forty-Day Fast

*We fasted and entreated our God for this,*
*and He answered our prayer.*
EZRA 8:23 NKJV

I was in a difficult season in my life. I'd lost over half a million dollars and just lost another $50,000 on a recent project. I was angry at God and questioning my own calling. I needed answers. I decided I would begin a fast and keep fasting until God answered me.

I began my fast, and after three days, I had heard nothing. After six days I had heard nothing, then ten, then twenty, then thirty, and I still heard nothing. Finally, on the fortieth day, I was attending a marketplace conference in another city. On the opening night, a young man from South Africa came to the podium and read a prophecy for someone in the room. The prophecy described my life in detail.

I told the man that word was for me. It described me in detail, and even the Scriptures he quoted were Scriptures God had been speaking to me. We met for prayer the next day to pray about whether I should try to resurrect a project that had recently failed. We began our prayer, and within five minutes, he said, "God is not going to raise that up. But he is going to raise up something that seems insignificant in your eyes."

I would later realize the insignificant project was *TGIF: Today God Is First* devotional I had begun writing. It would later become the tip of the spear in my marketplace ministry.

Sometimes we must seek God more when we are in a desperate place. Consider fasting the next time you need a breakthrough.

## Question
Do you need a breakthrough in your life?

*Father, give me the grace to fast when a breakthrough is needed.*

# The Prayer Handkerchief

*For the "foolish" things of God have proven to be wiser than human wisdom.*
1 CORINTHIANS 1:25 TPT

Frank is a businessman who was flying overseas when the man next to him began to start up a conversation. Frank politely conversed with the man hoping it would be a brief conversation. However, as time went on, the man began to ask more and more questions. Finally, the conversation turned to family, and the subject of babies came up. Frank confided in the man that his daughter had been seeking to become pregnant for years without success.

"That's it!" said the man. "I knew there was something the Lord wanted me to press in on with you, but until you said that, I was searching and searching." Frank did not even realize the man was a believer until that moment. The man continued, "This may sound strange to you, but God has given me a strange kind of gift to help barren women become pregnant. Whenever I pray for women, they get pregnant. May I ask you to do something rather unusual? I would like us to pray over this handkerchief. When you get back to your daughter, I would like you to lay this handkerchief on your daughter's belly and pray over it."

Frank returned to the states and, a short time later, arranged a time for his daughter and her husband to come by the house. Frank felt very awkward because he knew his son-in-law would think this was foolishness. Nevertheless, Frank proceeded to explain what had happened, and they laid the handkerchief on his daughter's belly and prayed.

A few weeks passed, and Frank received a phone call from his daughter. "Dad, you will never guess what has happened. I am pregnant!" she exclaimed.

## Question

Has God ever asked you to do something that seemed strange, even foolish?

*Father, help me to always be open to your instructions.*

# Gideon's Success Test

*Gideon made it into an ephod and set it up in his city, Ophrah.*
*And all Israel played the harlot with it there.*
*It became a snare to Gideon and to his house.*

JUDGES 8:27 NKJV

Israel was at war with the Midianites and the Amalekites. So, God chose a humble young man, Gideon, to deliver Israel by cleansing the land of idols. After determining through a series of miracles it was God calling him, Gideon obeyed the Lord and destroyed the pagan idols in the region. Then he summoned a large army—over thirty thousand men—to fight the Midianites and Amalekites. God said the army was too large, so he first reduced Gideon's army to ten thousand men and then to a mere three hundred men. When God gave Israel the victory with an army of only three hundred men, all of Israel knew that it was the power of God, not the strength of his army.

If the story had ended there, all would have been well. But at the moment of Israel's triumph, Gideon stumbled. He told the people, "I do have one request, that each of you give me an earring from your share of the plunder" (v. 24 NIV). The Israelites took the gold from the bodies of the enemy dead, and Gideon made an idol.

This idol was an offense against God and a trap for the people. After Gideon's death, the Israelites again worshiped the pagan god Baal. They forgot the Lord God who rescued them from their enemies.

## Question

Have you ever failed the Success Test? If so, we must go back to God without fear. We can ask him to help us learn the lessons of our failure and to strengthen us for another effort.

*Father, help me to remain a humble leader and dependent upon your grace.*

# Tamar's Payback and Judah's Test

*"I made a covenant with my eyes not to look lustfully at a young woman."*
JOB 31:1 NIV

In Genesis 38, we read about Judah, one of Joseph's brothers.

Tamar, his daughter-in-law, was deprived by Judah of having children in memory of her husband, which was the custom of the day if a husband died. Under the law, Judah did a great injustice to Tamar. Although Tamar lived in Judah's house, Judah withheld his son from her.

So, Tamar devised a plan. Hearing that Judah planned to go to the town of Timnah, she disguised herself in a veil and posed as a Canaanite prostitute and waited for Judah to pass by. Soon, Judah propositioned her and promised a goat for payment.

Tamar asked for a pledge—*his personal seal and staff.* The staff was the symbol of Judah's position in the community. So, Judah gave her the staff and the seal with its cord. He slept with Tamar, and she became pregnant.

Time passed, and Judah discovered Tamar was pregnant. He knew that there was only one way this could have happened—she had prostituted herself! Enraged, Judah said, "Bring her out and have her burned to death!"

As the people brought Tamar out to be executed, she cried out, "I am pregnant by the man who owns these!" She held in her hands the seal and staff of Judah. Seeing them, Judah knew he stood convicted. He broke down and confessed, "She is more righteous than I am!"

Sexual sin can take everything away from a man or woman. Pray that God's grace keeps you pure.

## Question
Are there any areas in your life that are being compromised?

*Father, thank you for keeping me morally pure in my life.*

# When His Work Exceeds His Presence

*He said to Him, "If Your Presence does not go with us,*
*do not bring us up from here."*
EXODUS 33:15 NKJV

One of the great dangers in Christian service is when we move from experiencing God's presence in our daily work to operating purely on our natural skill. Once we become established in something, the daily maintenance can lead us into complacency until a crisis arises that forces us back to our knees to appeal to the Lord for his presence to return. If you are in management, you must know the condition of your team to know how long you can be away from hands-on leadership.

Things were going well for Moses as he led the people out of Egypt. God was calling him to Mount Horeb, the mountain of God, to receive the Ten Commandments. While he was there, the people fell away from the Lord by returning to the ways of Egypt by building and worshipping a golden calf under Aaron's watch.

When Moses came back and saw what had happened, he recognized the solution as well. Having God's presence return was the only way they could proceed and have success. "For how then will it be known that Your people and I have found grace in Your sight, except You go with us?" (Exodus 33:16 NKJV).

Moses also realized a weakness in his own ability to lead. He pleaded God to mentor him: "If you are pleased with me, teach me your ways so I may know you and continue to find favor with you" (v. 13 NIV).

## Question

Is the presence of God in your current activities? Are the people you lead mature enough in their faith that you can be off-site when you need to be?

*Father, help me live in your presence in my everyday work life.*

# A Great Number Two

*The Lord spoke to Moses face to face, as a man speaks to his friend. And he would return to the camp, but his servant Joshua the son of Nun, a young man, did not depart from the tabernacle.*

EXODUS 33:11 NKJV

An organization cannot grow without a trusted and skilled second-in-command or "number two" man or woman. Joshua was Moses' "number two" man. He could trust him implicitly in all matters. He came to Moses as a young man and demonstrated his devotion to Moses early. A situation arose in the camp in which Joshua felt others were seeking to usurp Moses' leadership.

> So Joshua the son of Nun, Moses' assistant, one of his choice men, answered and said, "Moses my lord, forbid them!"
> Then Moses said to him, "Are you zealous for my sake? Oh, that all the Lord's people were prophets and that the Lord would put His Spirit upon them!" And Moses returned to the camp, he and the elders of Israel. (Numbers 11:28–30)

His loyalty is an example of what is required of a "number two" man. Joshua never sought to elevate himself. He served Moses until the day came when God promoted him to be the leader. He was a model of servanthood. Once Moses' time ended, Joshua stepped into the role of leader. He had been trained well.

## Question
Do you need a "number two" man?

*Father, help me value and affirm those who support my vision. Help me be a support to others' visions.*

# Sharing Your Faith with Others

*I pray for you that the faith we share may effectively deepen your understanding of every good thing that belongs to you in Christ.*

PHILEMON 6 TPT

There is a strong correlation between those who publicly share their faith with others and an increase in spiritual growth for that individual. In my own journey, I've discovered that when I stop sharing my faith with nonbelievers, I begin to see a dryness in my walk with God.

Sometimes we justify our lack of verbal witness by saying we don't have the spiritual gift of evangelism. Or we conclude that because we have an introverted personality, we leave witnessing to others whom we deem as more qualified. As a well-qualified introvert myself, I've often wanted to use that excuse. Then, the Holy Spirit reminds me of a few instructions Jesus said to everyone: "Whoever denies Me before men, him I will also deny before My Father who is in heaven" (Matthew 10:33 NKJV). "He said to them, 'Go into all the world and preach the gospel to every creature'" (Mark 16:15 NKJV). There is not much confusion about what Jesus is saying in these verses. And it relates to all of us.

When we share Christ with others, God allows us to gain a deeper and greater understanding of every good thing in Christ.

## Question

Do you see the direct correlation between sharing your faith and your own spiritual growth? Paul says it's actually a prerequisite to spiritual growth.

*Father, help me be sensitive to your leading to pray for others I encounter on a daily basis.*

# Know Your Customer

*A shepherd should pay close attention to the faces of his flock
and hold close to his heart the condition of those he cares for.*
PROVERBS 27:23 TPT

Identifying and meeting the needs of customers is key to any successful marketing venture. Many years ago, Coca-Cola decided to introduce a new Coke. They conducted research among loyal customers to determine if Coke customers would embrace the new taste. The evidence proved that the new Coke would be successful. However, what Coke executives did not realize was the emotional attachment Coke drinkers had to their existing Coke product. It created a massive outpouring of negative publicity when Coke drinkers rebelled against the new Coke. Loyal Coke drinkers may have liked the taste of the new Coke, but they did not want it as a replacement for what they were accustomed to.

The man responsible for the new Coke campaign was fired. It became one of the most famous marketing blunders ever. However, the story does not end here. The company eventually turned a bad situation into a positive one. Coke ended up having two versions of Coke—new and old. The man responsible was rehired and went on to be successful in the company.

Jesus sought to meet the needs of his customers by ministering to their needs as his heavenly Father revealed them to him. Jesus did not meet their real need for salvation until he had met a physical need that allowed him to reveal the true need they had. Some of your "customers" have a perceived need for your product. But they also have a spiritual need they may not realize they have. God wants to use you to meet both needs.

## Question
Do you know your customer and his needs?

*Father, help me understand and meet the needs of my customers.*

# Giving and Receiving

*I mention this not because I'm requesting a gift,*
*but so that the fruit of your generosity may bring you an abundant reward.*
PHILIPPIANS 4:17 TPT

The apostle Paul had a tent-making business. However, over time, it was evident that more and more of his time was being given to vocational ministry activities. That required him to receive income from those in whom he invested his life. It became increasingly difficult to run a business, travel, and minister.

His letter to the Philippians gives us a perspective on giving. Although Paul appreciated the support financially, his real joy came in the fact that their gift was being credited to their heavenly account.

I now have all I need—more than enough—I'm abundantly satisfied! For I've received the gift you sent by Epaphroditus and viewed it as a sweet sacrifice, perfumed with the fragrance of your faithfulness, which is so pleasing to God! I am convinced that my God will fully satisfy every need you have, for I have seen the abundant riches of glory revealed to me through Jesus Christ! (Philippians 4:18–19)

Paul had confidence that God would always provide what he needed. Sometimes it came from his business. Sometimes it came through others. He was not overly concerned with where his provision would come from. His confidence was in God, his provider. So, his attitude was in affirming the benefit that came to the giver from a kingdom perspective.

Paul learned that it wasn't a church or a business that was his provider. It was God. These were merely tools God used to support him.

## Question
Who do you see as the provider of your needs?

*Father, thank you for being Jehovah-Jireh, my provider.*

# Confronting Your Industry Culture

*Upon entering Jerusalem Jesus went directly into the temple area and drove away all the merchants who were buying and selling their goods. He overturned the tables of the money changers and the stands of those selling doves. And he said to them, "My dwelling place will be known as a house of prayer, but you have made it into a hangout for thieves!"*

MATTHEW 21:12–13 TPT

Sometimes a corporate culture dictates the way business is conducted because it was established years before. We simply inherit whatever the accepted practice is. Some of these practices violate a biblical principle. For instance, in some governments, customs employees require a bribe in order to get your product into their country. One nation thinks nothing about its practice of software piracy because it has simply become a part of its culture. In other instances, large businesses know they can negotiate very low prices because of their influence in the marketplace, giving vendors very little margin to make a profit.

God never allows for situational ethics. There are absolutes in the kingdom of God. The Word of God does not change because of culture or accepted practice.

It was an "industry practice" to sell doves in the temple. But Jesus never accepted the practice because he knew it was turning a holy place of prayer into a commercial enterprise. It did not matter that it was an accepted practice.

God calls each of us to operate from a plumb line of righteousness in our work life, no matter the consequence.

## Question

Are your industry practices violating God's Word?

*Father, I pray that my plumb line is measured by your precepts.*

# Concealing a Matter

*If you cover up your sin you'll never do well.*
*But if you confess your sins and forsake them, you will be kissed by mercy.*
PROVERBS 28:13 TPT

David made a number of seemingly poor choices in his life that snowballed into an avalanche of suffering, shame, and tragedy. It started when he chose to stay at home in Jerusalem instead of going out to lead his troops into battle, as was his duty. David had too much time on his hands, which ultimately led to him committing adultery with Bathsheba and trying to cover up that sin with murder. So, God sent the prophet Nathan to tell King David a story:

> There were two men in one city, one rich and the other poor. The rich man had exceedingly many flocks and herds. But the poor man had nothing, except one little ewe lamb which he had bought and nourished; and it grew up together with him and with his children. It ate of his own food and drank from his own cup and lay in his bosom; and it was like a daughter to him. And a traveler came to the rich man, who refused to take from his own flock and from his own herd to prepare one for the wayfaring man who had come to him; but he took the poor man's lamb and prepared it for the man who had come to him. (2 Samuel 12:1–4 NKJV)

David responded:

> "As the Lord lives, the man who has done this shall surely die! And he shall restore fourfold for the lamb, because he did this thing and because he had no pity." Then Nathan said to David, "You are the man!" (vv. 5–7 NKJV)

David repented of his sin, and God restored him, though his son did die.

## Question
Have you ever tried to cover up a sin in your life?

*Father, help me be a person of integrity who takes responsibility for my failures.*

# Accepting My Design

*Are you denying the right of the potter to make out of clay whatever he wants? Doesn't the potter have the right to make from the same lump of clay an elegant vase or an ordinary pot?*

ROMANS 9:21 TPT

My wife and I like to go to movies. She often comments about the attractiveness of an actress.

Have you ever wished that God made you differently? Perhaps you wished you were more athletic or could have a totally different career. Or perhaps you wished you were handsomer or taller or even had a different nose.

God made every person differently and for different purposes. Not everyone is made to be in the public eye. Some are made to serve behind the scenes. It is important to know and be at peace with how and why God made you.

Paul tells us in Romans that we are all crafted out of the same clay. There is no one molded and shaped like you, and no one has the exact personality as you. Your DNA is one of a kind.

God uses the common to produce the uncommon. No matter how inferior you may feel you are in a particular area, God desires to use you for his purposes. Your unique qualities are made to fit with the way he plans to use you for his purposes. This is why we must accept our uniqueness. We want his power to be manifested in our uniqueness.

Thank God today for the way he made you.

## Question

What characteristic in your life do you need to thank God for?

*Father, thank you for making me uniquely me.*

# Beware of Mixture

*He received the gold from their hand,*
*and he fashioned it with an engraving tool, and made a molded calf.*
EXODUS 32:4 NKJV

Moses had gone up onto Mount Sinai to meet with God and receive the Ten Commandments. He left his brother Aaron in charge, whom Moses had mentored. However, we learn that Aaron still had vestiges of Egypt residing in him. He had not had a complete conversion from the ways of Egypt to the ways of God.

Today we see such mixture in the body of Christ. We promote guaranteed prosperity without the cross. We call adversity a sign of a lack of faith. We promote New Age philosophies mixed with the Scriptures and call it a new freedom in Christ. This is only mixture. It is an abomination to the Lord.

Aaron was not truthful to Moses when confronted with his actions.

Moses said to Aaron, "What did this people do to you that you have brought so great a sin upon them?" So Aaron said, "Do not let the anger of my lord become hot. You know the people, that they are set on evil. For they said to me, 'Make us gods that shall go before us; as for this Moses, the man who brought us out of the land of Egypt, we do not know what has become of him.'" (Exodus 32:21–23)

## Question
Have you ever replaced your faith with an excuse to follow the world's way of operating?

*Father, help me be faithful to the Word of God and not allow new philosophies to distort its ageless truths.*

# Are You Useful?

*"I appeal to you for my son Onesimus, whom I have begotten while in my chains, who once was unprofitable to you, but now is profitable to you and to me."*
PHILEMON 10–11 NKJV

Paul's letter to Philemon reveals something about a man named Onesimus. At one time, Paul viewed Onesimus as useless. But while Paul was in chains, he treated Onesimus as a son. Something changed in this man that made him useful instead of useless.

When Jesus met Peter, he saw an impetuous man who drew quick conclusions and was very opinionated. Most of us would have had his doubts about him for future leadership. However, Jesus saw something in Peter that was going to be useful once the rough edges were removed.

We all start out our spiritual journeys as babes. We often act and react to situations immaturely. The Bible calls this growth process sanctification. It is a lifelong process.

We are all going to err in our ways. The question is, once we know we have made a mistake before God, do we make the necessary adjustments that will allow him to intervene on our behalf? And will we avoid the same course of action in the future? God says that if we do, he will pour out his Spirit on us (see Proverbs 1:23).

When you work with people who have strong personalities but may be immature in their faith, you must discern if they are people who learn and grow from their mistakes. This will tell you whether to invest time and resources into their lives.

## Question
Are you working with someone who needs your mentorship?

*Father, help me be a mentor to someone who needs help to become God's man or woman.*

# The Perfectionist

*Moses said to the LORD, "O my Lord, I am not eloquent, neither before nor since You have spoken to Your servant; but I am slow of speech and slow of tongue."*

EXODUS 4:10 NKJV

One of the greatest affronts you can commit against God is to refuse the calling that he places upon you. Imagine arguing with your Creator and telling him you know better than him.

That is exactly what Moses did when God called him to be his spokesperson to Pharaoh. God and Moses got into an "I know best" competition.

The LORD said to him, "Who gave human beings their mouths? Who makes them deaf or mute? Who gives them sight or makes them blind? Is it not I, the LORD? Now go; I will help you speak and will teach you what to say."

But Moses said, "Pardon your servant, Lord. Please send someone else." (Exodus 4:11–13 NIV)

God actually relented in the argument. Can you imagine that? "Then the LORD's anger burned against Moses and he said, 'What about your brother, Aaron the Levite?'" (v. 14 NIV). God had to use Aaron as Moses' mouthpiece.

I battled these same demons when God led me into a writing and speaking ministry. "Lord, I am weak in grammar, and you know I'm an introvert." Then he reminded me his "power is made perfect in weakness" (2 Corinthians 12:9 NIV).

When God places his anointing on you, he uses whatever level of skill you have to fulfill his purposes in your life. This is why you need not fear moving into an unfamiliar area if he calls you there.

## Question

Have you ever not pursued something because it had to be perfect or because you felt unqualified?

*Father, help me embrace whatever calling you place on my life.*

# Called to the Ministry

*Usually a person should keep on with the work he was doing when God called him.*
1 CORINTHIANS 7:20 TLB

We've all heard stories of men and women in the workplace who left their jobs for the "ministry." Certainly, God does call people into vocational ministry. However, many times this move is more rooted in dissatisfaction with a career combined with a spiritual renewal or first-time commitment to the Lord. The idea of a "higher call" can also appeal to our sense of a greater and nobler destiny.

We have incorrectly elevated the role of the Christian worker who serves within "the church" or a traditional "ministry" role to be holier and more committed than the person who is serving in a secular environment. Yet the call to the secular workplace is as important as any other calling. God has to have his people in every sphere of life to meet the needs of his creation. Also, many would never come to know him because they would be separated from society.

I learned this lesson personally when I sought to go into "full-time" service as a pastor in my late twenties only to have God thrust me back into the workplace unwillingly. He knew I was more suited for the workplace.

We are all on missions. Some are called to foreign lands. Some are called to the jungles of the workplace. Wherever you are called, serve the Lord in that place. View your vocation as means to worship him.

Paul said it right: in most cases, God wants people to "remain in the situation they were in when God called them" (NIV).

## Question
Do you ever question the spiritual aspect of your work-life calling?

*Father, help me embrace my work life as a ministry and calling.*

# Creating Your Niche

*There's no one like her on earth, never has been, never will be.*
*She's a woman beyond compare.*
SONG OF SOLOMON 6:8–9 MSG

Every business must have a unique niche if you wish to separate yourself from others to compete in the marketplace. This is especially true if you are competing in an industry that is very crowded with competition and low price is a driving incentive for the customer.

It used to be that a cup of coffee was just a cup of coffee. Then a company came along and completely changed and violated every marketing rule. They overpriced their product. They changed the language—a small is actually a "tall." A medium is "grande." You get the idea.

This company is Starbucks, a specialty coffee retailer. Founded in 1971 by a Jewish man, Starbucks has grown from a single Seattle store to 8,941 company-operated and 6,387 licensed stores in the United States and 32,660 locations worldwide in 2020.[51] Many attribute the success of Starbucks to how it turned coffee from an everyday commodity into a high-quality customer experience, essentially changing how people drink coffee.

If you're thinking about starting a business or making an existing business better, ask yourself this question: "What's unique about my business or product? What problem does my product solve?"

God created each of us to be unique. Define this uniqueness in your work life and promote it with integrity, and you'll have a good chance for success.

## Question
What is unique about your product or service?

*Father, help me tap into your creativity to make a great product or service.*

# High Positions

*Let the lowly brother glory in his exaltation.*
JAMES 1:9 NKJV

Whenever God takes a saint to a very lowly state, the situation is designed to accomplish something only that process can do. Job learned that "He uncovers deep things out of darkness, and brings the shadow of death to light" (Job 12:22). Job's trials allowed him to learn things about God, himself, and his friends that we all need to know as well. He assumed things about God that he had to recant: "Therefore I have uttered what I did not understand, things too wonderful for me, which I did not know" (42:3).

God reveals things in the dark places of circumstances that He will use to reveal something he wants you and others to know. He has sent you ahead to learn these things so that you and others will benefit from your unique experience. God views this place where you receive these truths as a high position. The world views it as a place to be despised.

## Question

Do you find yourself in a lowly state? Realize your lowly state is considered a high position by God and that it is preparation soil for revealing deep things from the dark places that God desires you to learn.

*Father, help me to embrace my lowly state to bring glory to you.*

# Road Construction

*"The crooked places shall be made straight and the rough places smooth; the glory of the LORD shall be revealed, and all flesh shall see it together."*

ISAIAH 40:4–5 NKJV

I don't know about you, but I hate road construction. I live in a growing city, and it seems like there has been ongoing road construction for years. Everything is a mess, you can never plan your trips because of delays, and sometimes you get caught off guard when traffic signs are in unexpected places.

Recently, a sinkhole was discovered in the middle of one of our main local roads. The road was closed for more than a year. We had to take alternative routes that were inconvenient, and it took longer to get places.

Sometimes God takes us through our own life reconstruction project. Our lives get disrupted, we can no longer depend on the things we did before, and we don't have control over our circumstances or timetable. God is doing major construction.

However, even in the midst of the reconstruction, the glory of the Lord is revealed in that place. For some, it is the first time they've ever seen the hand of the Lord in their life to the degree that this process allows them to experience him.

Once the process is complete, things begin to flow better. Just as the new roads allow you to drive on a smooth, more spacious area, so, too, does God pave a way for you to move into an expanded place with him.

Be patient with God's reconstruction project. You will like the end result.

## Question
Is your life a reconstruction project right now?

*Father, give me grace to embrace the mess knowing the finished product will be great.*

# God's Timing

*As soon as He had spoken,*
*immediately the leprosy left him,*
*and he was cleansed.*
MARK 1:42 NKJV

Have you ever had a problem keeping a secret? Especially if that secret involves good news.

There is a timing that is ideal for releasing information or moving forward with a project. Jesus understood the importance of timing. When he performed his first healing miracle, he instructed the man he healed from leprosy not to tell anyone. Now that would be difficult—not to share being healed from leprosy with your friends who have known you and your condition. He could not keep the secret.

As a result, Jesus could no longer enter a town openly but stayed outside in lonely places. Yet the people still came to him from everywhere. Jesus desired to do more things in that city, but because the man could not keep quiet, he could not do so.

How often has Jesus been unable to move in your situation because you have failed to honor the right timing of the situation? Perhaps you have moved ahead when you were not supposed to move. In the Old Testament, David was fighting the Philistines. He won the first battle, but they were coming against him again. He inquired of God, and God said, "It shall be, when you hear the sound of marching in the tops of the mulberry trees, then you shall advance quickly" (2 Samuel 5:24). There was a strategic timing associated with his actions. "To everything there is a season, a time for every purpose under heaven" (Ecclesiastes 3:1).

## Question
Do you understand the timing of God in your life?

*Father, I pray for your perfect timing to be released on my projects.*

# The Wizard of Oz

*"I am the LORD, the God of Israel, who summons you by name."*
ISAIAH 45:3 NIV

During a workplace conference I met Ed, a small-business owner of a marketing communications company. I immediately felt a kindred spirit between us and appreciated his obvious talent. We began an exchange by email about providing services to our organization. Later Ed came up to me and shared a wonderful supernatural story of how God had led him to connect with me.

Driving to church one evening, a license plate on a car in front of me grabbed my attention. I don't recall the numbers on the plate, but the last three letters were OZZ. This kept coming to mind as I continued to drive to the service. A friend who had prophetic gifts came up to me at church and began to speak to me concerning things the Lord was doing in my work life. She said, "God had not given me the scarecrow, the tin man, or the lion, but he had given me OZ."

Several months later, after attending a LifeWorks conference at our church, I was writing an email to Os Hillman about some work I was doing for him. As I began to write the salutation, "Dear Os," I felt a rush that Os Hillman was the OZ of the prophecy and the OZZ from the license plate! My friend became so excited about the connection after I told her.

My connection to Os and Marketplace Leaders has proven to be an incredible blessing to me personally as well as professionally. While at the conference, the Lord continually affirmed my call in the workplace and fulfilled a significant dream I had nine years ago.

## Question
Are you watching for the activity of God in your life?

*Father, help me see the work of Spirit operating in my life.*

# Affirming New Leadership

*Moses said to him, "Are you zealous for my sake? Oh, that all the LORD's people were prophets and that the LORD would put His Spirit upon them!"*
NUMBERS 11:29 NKJV

One of the attributes of a kingdom leader is to recognize when God is raising new leadership and be a catalyst to affirm and encourage it. These leaders also model a level of humility that God blesses. Leaders who are insecure about their leadership will put down new leadership in order to maintain their own status.

The Bible says that Moses was the humblest man on the face of the earth. That is why God used him as a leader to bring an entire nation out of bondage.

Joshua was concerned that two young men prophesied in the camp and considered this an affront to Moses' leadership. Moses viewed the same situation very differently. He viewed it from the eye of a kingdom leader who modeled humility and a kingdom focus. Moses was secure in his own leadership, so he did not need to put down others whom he could construe as usurping his leadership.

The body of Christ is in great need of leaders who are secure in their leadership. If God has called you to be a leader, look for opportunities to encourage new leaders. As you do, God will ensure that you will fulfill the purpose for which he called you.

## Question
Are you supporting leadership that raises up others?

*Father, make me a leader that raises up other leaders.*

# Opposing God's Leadership

*The anger of the LORD was aroused against them, and He departed.*
NUMBERS 12:9 NKJV

Beware of trying to depose a leader that God has raised in your midst. Leaders are placed by God in business, government, churches—almost every place where leaders are required. When God places a person in a position of authority, it is a grievous sin to go against that leadership. God himself opposes those who come against his leadership.

God's leaders are not perfect. They make mistakes. That is why following a leader can require a faith that goes beyond faith in the leader. Our faith lies in the God who elevated the leader to his or her position.

Miriam and Aaron, the older brother and sister of Moses, had a family dispute about Moses' wife, who was an Ethiopian and Cushite. We do not know the nature of the dispute, but it was a typical family conflict.

However, the family conflict began to impact God's agenda for a nation. They were now meddling in God's business. And he did not like that in the least. God literally brought Aaron and Miriam into the switching house. He judged both Miriam and Aaron for their rebellion against his ordained leader. "Why then were you not afraid to speak against My servant Moses?" (Numbers 12:8).

Miriam was stricken with leprosy, and had it not been for Moses' appeal on her behalf, she would have been cast out for good. God gave her a second chance, but it required being cast away from the camp for seven days. Miriam and Aaron repented for their rebellion.

## Question
Do you struggle with a leader that God has over you?

*Father, help me give honor to those you have placed in leadership over me.*

# The Mercy Gift

*"Behold, I stand at the door and knock. If anyone hears My voice and opens the door, I will come in to him and dine with him, and he with Me."*
REVELATION 3:20 NKJV

Gerry was my neighbor. He was single and worked as an attorney from his home. He had an amazing gift of mercy, an incredible love for animals, and a malfunctioning front door. His door didn't shut properly, and the only way to keep the door closed was to lock it, which Gerry rarely did. One day while working at home, he heard his front door open. When he investigated the noise, he discovered that Buddy, one of the neighborhood dogs, had let himself in by simply pushing on the front door.

Gerry gave him a treat, and day after day, Buddy would visit. Each day it was the same routine. Buddy would push the door open, stand in the foyer, and patiently wait for Gerry to come to him and give him a treat. He never forced his way in or begged for food; he always waited for Gerry to come to him. And Gerry always came. A few weeks later, Buddy started bringing his friends—other dogs in the neighborhood—and soon the dogs started hanging out for days before they would go back home.

I laughed as I drove by Gerry's house and saw his front door wide open. And yet, I knew that inside he was enjoying the fellowship of the neighborhood dogs. We can have that same fellowship with Jesus when we open the doors of our hearts to him. He is standing at the door waiting for you to invite him in.

## Question
Do you have fellowship with Jesus every day?

*Father, thank you for desiring fellowship with me.*

# Completing the Work

*"I have glorified you on the earth by faithfully
doing everything you've told me to do."*
JOHN 17:4 TPT

The Lord has revealed to us that the number one thing we are to do is love the Lord our God with all our heart and to love our neighbor as ourselves. His desire is for us to know him and the power of his resurrection. The fruit of this relationship must then result in our glorifying him by completing the work he has given each of us to do. It will become a by-product of this relationship, not an end in itself.

What is the work God has called you to do? Jesus never did anything the Father had not instructed him to do. He lived in such communion with the Father that he knew when to turn left and when to turn to the right. Is it possible to have such a relationship with our heavenly Father? I think that if it weren't, he would not have given us such an example.

"Call to Me, and I will answer you, and show you great and mighty things, which you do not know" (Jeremiah 33:3 NKJV). What has he called you to do? Perhaps you are called to be the best lawyer, advertising executive, office worker, or assembly line person in your company. Whatever work he has called you to, he will use you as his instrument to accomplish something that he has uniquely prepared you to do.

When our life is complete, what a glorious day it will be if we can each say, "I have completed the work you gave me to do." This will have brought great glory to him.

## Question
What is the work God has called you to do?

*Father, may you be glorified in all the work of my hands.*

# Receiving Bad News

*Our adversaries said, "They will neither know nor see anything,*
*till we come into their midst and kill them and cause the work to cease."*
NEHEMIAH 4:11 NKJV

I opened the letter from the attorney and began to read the contents. The more I read, the sicker my stomach felt. I could not believe the words I was reading. Perhaps you've had a similar experience. Maybe you got the news that you've got cancer. Or someone has had an accident. Or you are being sued.

Nehemiah was rebuilding the wall in Jerusalem. The going was tough. As if things were not bad enough, he got a letter from another corrupt government official threatening to kill anyone involved in rebuilding the wall.

Now it happened, when Sanballat, Tobiah, the Arabs, the Ammonites, and the Ashdodites heard that the walls of Jerusalem were being restored and the gaps were beginning to be closed, that they became very angry, and all of them conspired together to come and attack Jerusalem and create confusion. Nevertheless we made our prayer to our God, and because of them we set a watch against them day and night. (Nehemiah 4:7–9)

There is but one response we should have to bad news. Pray to our God and take the necessary steps to defend ourselves against the threat. This was Nehemiah's response.

## Question
Have you received any bad news lately?

*Father, I submit all of my cares to you. You know what I am going through and will guide me through it.*

# Using Others

*"In everything you do, be careful to treat others in the same way you'd want them to treat you, for that is the essence of all the teachings of the Law and the Prophets."*
MATTHEW 7:12 TPT

Have you ever heard the phrase "Money talks"? This old cliché has some truth to it. How we handle money speaks very loudly about our values, especially among those in the marketplace.

One of the common business practices today is to extend payment on invoices due to use that time to extend a company's cash flow. The bigger companies can often insist upon even longer times for payment.

This delayed payment policy violates a basic biblical principle. "For because of this you also pay taxes, for they are God's ministers attending continually to this very thing. Render therefore to all their due: taxes to whom taxes are due, customs to whom customs, fear to whom fear, honor to whom honor" (Romans 13:6–7 NKJV).

One of your greatest opportunities to show you are different is in the practical matters of being faithful to your obligations. True servanthood is revealed when we have the best interest of others in mind. This means not always seeking to negotiate the lowest price for services but the price that is fair and still honors the vendor for his service or product. Use money to demonstrate your respect for others by paying others in a timely manner.

## Question
Do you ever withhold payment to someone
beyond your agreed-upon terms?

*Father, help me honor all my commitments.*

# Innovation

*In the beginning God created the heavens and the earth.*
GENESIS 1:1 NKJV

The concept is interesting and well-formed, but in order to earn better than a C, the idea must be feasible."[52]

Those were the words of a Yale University management professor in response to Fred Smith's paper proposing a reliable overnight delivery service. Smith went on to found Federal Express Corporation, now known as FedEx, which is the number one overnight delivery service in the world with 260,000 employees. Founder Fred Smith is synonymous with the word *innovator*.

God is the source of all creativity and innovation. He created the world in seven days. He has made you to create. If God has placed an idea in your heart to do, ask the Lord for his help in bringing it to reality. He desires to see his people create new things that can serve mankind and bring glory to God. Henry Ford is often credited with saying, "Whether you believe you can do a thing or not, you are right."[53]

Faith plays an important role when considering stepping out to launch a new endeavor. "Now faith is the substance of things hoped for, the evidence of things not seen. For by it the elders obtained a good testimony" (Hebrews 11:1–2).

Perhaps you've failed in the past, and you're afraid to step out again. Most successful entrepreneurs failed several times before they were successful. Don't let fear of failure keep you from success.

You were made to create. You were made to succeed.

## Question
Has God given you an idea you need to pursue?

*Father, thank you that you are the great Creator and innovator. I trust you to give me new ideas and inventions.*

# Modeling Christ to Your Employer

*Urge slaves to obey their masters and to try their best to satisfy them. They must not talk back, nor steal, but must show themselves to be entirely trustworthy. In this way they will make people want to believe in our Savior and God.*

TITUS 2:9–10 TLB

Sometimes I hear people say they don't see how they can have any significant impact on their workplace because they are low on the totem pole with little authority to make change. "I'm just a worker," they say. They fail to realize that the authority to impact any workplace comes from having authority with God, not man. And each person can have great authority in God.

The apostle Paul was instructing Titus on how common workers on the island of Crete could have an impact on their employers. These workers were often no more than slaves, working in deplorable conditions for masters who were likely involved in lawlessness, drunkenness, and idolatry. Not the nicest of working conditions.

Paul felt the way to win over one's employer was to follow several key principles: (1) don't talk back, (2) don't steal, and (3) be trustworthy.

There is a great example of a young girl who worked for the wife of an army commander named Naaman. He had leprosy. The godly servant girl from Israel told her employer how he could get healed through Elisha. What faith and boldness on the part of the servant girl! (See 2 Kings 5:1–3.)

Naaman followed the advice of the lowly servant girl. God healed him through Elisha. I can only imagine the conversations between the servant girl and her employers after this healing occurred.

## Question
How might God want to use you in your employer's life?

*Father, use me to build your kingdom in my workplace today.*

# Empowering Others

*"I tell you this timeless truth: The person who follows me in faith, believing in me, will do the same mighty miracles that I do—even greater miracles than these because I go to be with my Father!"*

JOHN 14:12 TPT

The CEO was excited that he'd found the right man to be general manager of his growing enterprise. He had all the training, the right skill set, and great people skills. The CEO gave him all authority to fulfill his role. However, after six months, the CEO had to fire him. It seems the general manager refused to use the empowerment given him to accomplish his tasks.

Great leaders, mentors, and managers must empower others to fulfill the mission of any organization. Jesus invested time and energy in developing leaders. Only at the point at which they could properly manage the resource did Jesus empower them. The teacher who offers empowerment too early sets up followers for failure. On the other hand, the leader who fails to empower capable people creates frustration.

Part two of good empowerment is engaging your followers to use the authority entrusted to them to fulfill their mission.

Jesus imparted to his followers a balance of both of these concepts. Peter was not ready for leadership before the crucifixion. He failed to use the empowerment given to him by Jesus. It required a failure in Peter's life before he matured in his leadership. However, once Peter began to acquire from Jesus what Jesus had imparted to him, Peter became a powerful and effective leader.

## Question

Do you need to empower others to allow them to become the leader you and God want?

*Father, help me empower others around me.*

# Staying the Course

*The angel of the LORD commanded Gad to say to David that David should go and erect an altar to the LORD on the threshing floor of Ornan the Jebusite. So David went up at the word of Gad, which he had spoken in the name of the LORD.*

1 CHRONICLES 21:18–19 NKJV

In 1857, an American businessman named Jeremiah Lanphier was sent out by his local church to begin a noonday prayer meeting on Fulton Street, right around the corner from Wall Street in New York City. A simple prayer, a willing heart, and an act of obedience resulted in city transformation throughout the United States. He began a businessmen's prayer meeting on September 23, 1857. However, at that very first meeting, no one showed up in the first thirty minutes. But Jeremiah waited. Gradually, six people wandered into the room for that first meeting. The meetings began slowly, but within a few months, many noonday meetings were convening daily throughout the city.

Six months later, ten thousand people were meeting for prayer throughout New York City. This led to one of the greatest spiritual renewals in United States' history. It is estimated over two million came to Christ around the world from this one man's act.[54]

What would have happened if Lanphier had decided to abandon the idea after thirty minutes? Simple obedience can lead to things you cannot imagine.

## Question
### Are you willing to be used by God?

*Father, use me to bring revival to my workplace, city, and even nation.*

# The Church

*"Five of you shall chase a hundred,*
*and a hundred of you shall put ten thousand to flight;*
*your enemies shall fall by the sword before you."*
LEVITICUS 26:8 NKJV

The church is called to impact the world. The biblical definition of *church* is not an institution or building, but rather it is made up of individuals. Jesus said, "Where two or three gather together as my followers, I am there among them" (Matthew 18:20 NLT). The biblical word translated as "church" is *ekklesia*, which is the original Greek meaning "the people of God."

The New Testament used this word in two different ways. Sometimes it refers to people of God gathered together in congregations. That is our traditional idea of the local church. But other times it means believers in general, wherever they might find themselves.

God calls the church to be transformers of society through their collective influence. Jesus prayed that his church would be unified in order for the world to respond to him. "They may be brought to complete unity. Then the world will know that you sent me and have loved them even as you have loved me" (John 17:23 NIV). The enemy of the church is secularism, a religion that says there is no God. Conversely, when the body of Christ—the church—puts its collective resources together to solve societal issues, our enemies (crime, poverty, sexual perversion, etc.) will fall by the sword of a unified church.

God is birthing city coalitions of his church among congregations in the city in order to fulfill John 17:23.

## Question

Are you willing to be a catalyst in your community to see his church take back your city?

*Father, use me to be a catalyst to bring together the body of Christ in my city.*

# God Is the God of Success

*"Now it shall come to pass, if you diligently obey the voice of the LORD your God, to observe carefully all His commandments which I command you today, that the LORD your God will set you high above all nations of the earth."*

DEUTERONOMY 28:1 NKJV

Our God is a God of success. You are created to be a success. Success is rooted in our relationship with God, not in our abilities. When our abilities are separated from our relationship with God, success is short lived.

> All these blessings will come on you and accompany you if you obey the LORD your God…The LORD will send a blessing on your barns and on everything you put your hand to. The LORD your God will bless you in the land he is giving you. (Deuteronomy 28:2, 8 NIV)

Sometimes God allows you to fail in order for you to succeed. Each of us must first experience our own death and resurrection from our old nature. This is for you to learn who the source of true success is. You will be amazed how easy success will come when your life is in proper alignment with the purposes of God. God delights in giving to his sons and daughters.

## Question
Are you committed to following his ways in all that you do?

*Father, thank you for the promise of your blessing as I follow you wholeheartedly.*

# Adversity: Catalyst to a Call

*Saul stood to his feet, and even though his eyes were open he could see nothing—*
*he was blind. So the men had to take him by the hand and lead him into*
*Damascus. For three days he didn't eat or drink and couldn't see a thing.*

ACTS 9:8–9 TPT

The entry door to the larger story of your life is often a crisis. Such was the case for John Wesley.

John Wesley (1703–1791) was a small man, just over five feet tall and skeletally thin. In his early years, he suffered greatly from feelings of guilt, inadequacy, and a morbid fear of death. Though he didn't understand the Christian gospel, he devoted himself to doing good works for the poor in an effort to earn his way to heaven. While in his early thirties, he sailed to America to do missionary work among the American Indians.

While crossing the Atlantic, Wesley's ship passed through a violent storm that broke the main mast off its base and nearly sank the ship. He survived the storm but was wrought with fear. He continued to struggle in his relationship with God for several more years.

Finally, back in London, he attended a meeting on Aldersgate Street, where he heard a preacher say that salvation comes by faith in Christ alone. He said, "I felt my heart strangely warmed." Soon after, Wesley began preaching the gospel. His fifty-two-year preaching ministry became the foundation of the modern evangelical movement. But it never would have happened if John Wesley had not been tossed on the stormy seas of adversity.[55]

Adversity is often God's manure for spiritual callings.

## Question
Is God taking you through a depth of soul experience?

*Father, help me to receive all you desire for me through my adversities.*

# You Have an Anointing

*The wonderful anointing you have received from God is so much greater than their deception and now lives in you.*

1 JOHN 2:27 TPT

Do you know your anointing? An anointing is a gift that functions easily when it is operating in you to benefit others and the kingdom of God. If one has to "work it up," one has probably gone outside one's anointing.

One area in which I have a God-given anointing is networking. I have never sought to develop such an anointing. But I know a lot of people. Despite my being an introvert by nature, God has connected me with people all around the world. Many times people call me about something, and my natural response is, "Oh, you need to contact so and so. He can help you with that." A mentor once said to me, "Your inheritance is in relationships." What he was saying is that my anointing is in relationships and networking.

My wife has an anointing in the area of disarming people. She can be someone's best friend in five minutes because he disarms people faster than anyone I know. There is no way you can be a shy person around my wife. I have seen people open up to Angie where they would not open up to anyone else. It is her anointing.

## Question

Where do you move naturally in your life? What do you do that you don't have to work at it? Chances are, that is your anointing. God wants you to walk in the anointing he has given to you.

*Father, thank you for anointing me with the gifts I have to build your kingdom.*

# Self-Deliverance

*Trust in the Lord completely, and do not rely on your own opinions. With all your heart rely on him to guide you, and he will lead you in every decision you make.*

PROVERBS 3:5 TPT

Oswald Chambers advises, "Whenever God gives a vision to a saint, he puts the saint in the shadow of his hand, as it were, and the saint's duty is to be still and listen…When God gives a vision and darkness follows, waiting on God will bring you into accordance with the vision he has given if you await his timing. Otherwise, you try to do away with the supernatural in God's undertakings. Never try to help God fulfill His word."[56]

Solomon warns us not to rely on our own fallible wisdom while trying to do God's perfect will. God wants us to wait for his deliverance. His means of bringing us to spiritual maturity requires us to wait on his deliverance through adversity so that we will be able to discern the difference between our own self-deliverance and God's authentic deliverance in our lives.

It's a paradox, but it's true: God often calls us to a ministry—then he deliberately thwarts our efforts to achieve our goals! We see it in the life of Moses. Again and again, Moses returned and demanded freedom for his people. Again and again, Pharaoh refused.

But God was teaching Moses and the people of Israel to persevere, to obey, and to wait upon the Lord with patient trust for God's perfect time for deliverance.

## Question
Are you waiting for a vision to be fulfilled?

*Father, help me to trust in your timetable to fulfill my vision.*

# Deliverance from the Black Hole

*"I will not leave you nor forsake you."*
JOSHUA 1:5 NKJV

A black hole is a place of total nothingness. It's a time in our life when God removes the resources and supports that we normally rely on to feel secure— our careers, finances, friends, family, health, and so forth. It is preparation time.

When you find yourself in a black hole experience, don't just sit and brood. Take stock of your life. Take a look at your relationship with God.

First, ask God if there are any sins, habits, or attitudes that he might be judging in your life. It's important to discern whether the trial we face is the result of God's discipline.

Second, when you enter a black hole, don't trust your feelings. Trust God. Your feelings will tell you, "God has rejected you." He has not.

Third, remember that your black hole experience is not only intended to refine and define you; it's also intended to influence and change the lives of hundreds or even thousands of other people you will touch.

Fourth, don't try to hurry the black hole process along. Remember, when Joseph was in the depths of the pit, there was nothing he could do about it.

Fifth, lean on God. Even when you don't want to pray, pray. Even when you don't want to read his Word, read. Listen for his still, quiet voice.

Sixth, be alert to new truths and new perspectives. During a black hole experience, God often leads us to amazing new discoveries.

## Question
Do you find yourself in a black hole today?

*Father, thank you that you know every adversity I am experiencing and promise to see me through. I trust you to guide me.*

# Studying to Give or to Know

*When He had said this, He breathed on them, and said to them,*
*"Receive the Holy Spirit."*
JOHN 20:22 NKJV

Sometimes you would think the Trinity is Father, Son, and Holy Scriptures instead of the Holy Spirit. There can be a tendency in Christianity to give so much focus to the Holy Scriptures that we fail to acknowledge the role of the Holy Spirit in our daily activity.

There is also a second danger. We must be careful in studying the Scriptures for the sake of giving to others instead of desiring more of God for ourselves. This is particularly dangerous for the professional Christian worker who is under continued pressure to feed and teach his people. If we are not careful, this process becomes a religious exercise of production instead of a time of seeking, learning, and experiencing his presence.

Jesus told his disciples that when he left, he would be leaving the Holy Spirit, which would help them live victoriously for him. "All this I have spoken while still with you. But the Advocate, the Holy Spirit, whom the Father will send in my name, will teach you all things and will remind you of everything I have said to you" (John 14:25–26 NIV).

It is the Holy Spirit that draws us into intimacy with the Father. He prompts us with a Scripture verse to share with a friend or coworker. He endues us with the power to live for him and not in our own strength.

## Question
Is the Holy Spirit leading and guiding you in all you do?

*Father, I ask the Holy Spirit to baptize me and guide me into all truth and empower me to live a victorious life.*

# When Others Fail You

*Again Jesus said, "Peace be with you!*
*As the Father has sent me, I am sending you."*
JOHN 20:21 NIV

Have you ever entrusted someone to carry on a project only to have them fail miserably? What was your response? Many times leaders shame others in order to help them realize the gravity of their failure.

Bill ran a manufacturing company. His executive management team sought the company in a hostile corporate takeover. After it was unsuccessful, Bill was left to manage the same team that betrayed him.

When Jesus was crucified, many of the disciples fled. Peter denied Jesus three times. He was a leader without followers. Jesus had now come back to life. How would Jesus handle this reunion among those who had totally abandoned him and the mission?

What an incredible greeting after all they had experienced. No shame. No harsh words. Just a reaffirmation of the mission and his commitment to them. Jesus used grace and total acceptance as motivation for his followers to carry on the mission.

He didn't need to remind them of their failure. They already felt bad enough. It was time to recast the vision with new life. When there is failure in the organization, it is more important to revitalize the team, not focus on the past.

## Question
Do you need to rally your team around a mission
that has stalled, failed, or gotten offtrack?

*Father, help me forgive those who betray me.*

# Making Adjustments

*"Cast the net on the right side of the boat, and you will find some."*
JOHN 21:6 NKJV

A former client of mine was the marketing director of a large food-brokerage company and told me a story about a client grocery store located in the upper Midwest. The managers of the store could not understand why sales plummeted at a certain time every winter. They studied their product line and interviewed customers. They did everything possible to uncover the mystery. Finally, someone made a remarkable discovery that changed everything.

It seemed that whenever it was really cold outside, the manager raised the temperature in the store. When customers came into the store, they removed their coats and placed them in their shopping carts. This meant less room for food and resulted in reduced sales overall. They lowered the temperature of the store, and as a result, the sales climbed back to the levels they were accustomed to.

Jesus stood on the shoreline and watched Peter and a few of the disciples fish. Jesus yelled from the shoreline, asking if they had caught anything. They had not. He then suggested they cast their line on the other side of the boat. Without knowing the person who was addressing them, they took his advice. They began catching so many fish they could not bring them in.

Adjusting our lives to God is the first thing that has to happen in order to begin experiencing him in our daily lives. For some, it is simply following the advice of those above us. For others, it may require a major change in our job situation or relationships. Whatever the case, you can be sure that until we adjust our lives to God, we will not receive his full blessing.

## Question
Has God brought you into a place in your life where you need to make some adjustments?

*Father, help me to adjust my life so that it aligns with where you are calling me.*

# The Valley of Baca

*"Blessed is the man whose strength is in You, whose heart is set on pilgrimage. As they pass through the Valley of Baca, they make it a spring."*
PSALM 84:5–6 NKJV

There is a spiritual law in the kingdom of God. Every great leader in the kingdom will pass through the Valley of Baca. *Baca* means "to weep."

However, Baca is also a place of springs. There is nothing better on a hot day when you're thirsty and weary than to drink water from a mountain spring. It refreshes. It renews. It gives you a second wind to continue your journey. Those who commit themselves to a pilgrimage with God will experience the Valley of Baca. But in the midst of Baca they will discover that in this valley, they will also drink from a very special spring that refreshes with a different kind of living water.

It becomes the source of "hidden things in secret places" described by the prophet Isaiah (Isaiah 45:3) reserved only for those willing to journey on the great pilgrimage with God. Once you drink from this spring, you will be energized in your spiritual man from strength to strength. Each Valley of Baca will result in a new spiritual spring from which you will drink. Know this will be used to provide a refreshing drink for others you will encounter who are also on their pilgrimage.

Ultimately, Baca leads to the presence of God. There is something about being in a place with God that results in our weeping and crying out to him.

## Question

Do you find yourself in this place with God today? If so, know that his springs are also available to you.

*Father, I choose today to drink from your spring available in the Valley of Baca.*

# Destroying High Places

*Now it came to pass the same night that the Lord said to him, "Take your father's young bull, the second bull of seven years old, and tear down the altar of Baal."*
JUDGES 6:25 NKJV

I first met Bishop Julius Oyet, who was from Uganda, in Argentina in November 2005. Bishop Oyet believes God is able to do exceedingly, abundantly above all that he can ask or think because of the power that works within us.

Just as God led Gideon to tear down demonic altars, God led Julius to do the same in his nation of Uganda. These altars were the source of strongholds over the nation for the rebels. For seventeen years, Joseph Kony and the Lord's Resistance Army destroyed thousands of innocent lives, wrecked the economy, and left thousands of homesteads burned and ruined in northern Uganda. Julius proclaimed, "You cannot fight spiritual strongholds with bullets!" Julius met the president of his nation, which allowed him to share what he believed God was saying about the war.

Julius led an "Operation Gideon" team of twenty-two people to the first of several sites to conduct onsite prayer vigils with pastors and leaders to tear down sacred altars they believed had spiritual powers for the rebel army. These actions required the protection of the nation's army to go into these dangerous areas. His story is documented in a video entitled *The Unconventional War*.

A great turning point in the war took place, with many rebel leaders surrendering and giving their lives to Jesus Christ. God gave Julius gained great favor in his nation, and God is doing great work in central and northern Uganda.

## Question
Has God called you to tear down some sacred altars?

*Father, give me courage to stand against unrighteousness in my culture.*

# Jesus Wept for the City

*When Jesus caught sight of the city,*
*he burst into tears with uncontrollable weeping over Jerusalem.*
LUKE 19:41 TPT

Jesus was making his triumphal entry into the city of Jerusalem. The Pharisees were complaining about the exuberance of his disciples as he made his way into the city. They were celebrating a life that had blessed them and countless others:

> Then, as He was now drawing near the descent of the Mount of Olives, the whole multitude of the disciples began to rejoice and praise God with a loud voice for all the mighty works they had seen, saying:
> "Blessed is the King who comes in the name of the LORD!"
> Peace in heaven and glory in the highest! (Luke 19:37–38 NKJV)

Jesus was saddened by the response of the Pharisees. He knew what he could do for the city. His presence could bring peace if they embraced who he was as the author of peace. Now his presence would be hidden from their eyes because of unbelief.

Every city can be blessed by the presence of Jesus in its midst. However, it requires city leaders to invite the presence of Jesus into their city in order for that city to experience peace. Jesus comes to bring peace in any situation. However, he also realizes he will divide city leaders because of unbelief and political correctness.

## Question

Does your city need the presence of Jesus?
Do you desire to see peace in your city?

*Father, I pray for the peace of Jerusalem and my city.*

# Is There Hierarchy in Calling?

*Now you are the body of Christ, and each one of you is a part of it.*
1 CORINTHIANS 12:27 NIV

All legitimate work matters to God. God himself was a worker. In fact, human occupations find their origin in his work to create the world. Work is a gift from him to meet the needs of people and the creation.

However, there is often an unspoken hierarchy that positions clergy (as well as missionaries, evangelists, and pastors) at the top, occupations of the "helping professions" (such as doctors and nurses, teachers and educators, social workers) next, and "secular" workers (including business executives, salespeople, factory laborers, and farmers) at the bottom.

So, what determines the spiritual value of a job? How does God assign significance? The hierarchy assumes sacred and secular distinctions and assigns priority to the sacred. But does God view vocations that way? No, he does not.

God creates people to carry out specific kinds of work in order to meet human needs. God uniquely designs each of us, fitting us for certain kinds of tasks. That work includes "spiritual" tasks but also extends to health, education, agriculture, business, law, communication, the arts, and so on.

Paul was a tentmaker by occupation, along with Aquila and Priscilla. Other church leaders practiced a wide variety of professions. There's no indication that God looks at vocations in the form of spiritual hierarchy.

The next time you consider your vocation a second-class spiritual calling, consider what God says. Your work matters to God and is valued by God equally to other forms of calling.

## Question

Have you ever felt like you were a second-class citizen because you have a secular job?

*Father, thank you that my work is a holy calling ordained by you.*

# You're Different Now

*My brethren, count it all joy when you fall into various trials,*
*knowing that the testing of your faith produces patience.*

JAMES 1:2–3 NKJV

I was in Switzerland visiting an acquaintance I had met briefly almost ten years earlier at a Christian conference on the island of Cyprus. I was sitting in the kitchen talking with my friend when I said, "You are different. There is a different spirit about you than when I met you ten years ago. I have to admit, I thought you were a bit aloof."

"Hmm, you know, Os," he said, "I thought the same about you." We both chuckled at our observations.

There was a difference in both of us because something dramatic had happened in both of our lives. My friend was a very successful businessman in Switzerland and was running a family business when things went very wrong. He lost millions as a result. Although his fortune was not totally wiped out, it impacted him greatly. It brought humility and a newfound trust in God that had not been there before.

I had a similar story. I had gone through a seven-year "pit experience" in which I had major losses in family, business, and personal income. Now we were both on the other sides of our "pits." We could recognize something in each of us that had resulted from our experiences. There was a level of humility that was not there before. Sometimes God creates circumstances in our lives to create humility and greater dependence upon him.

I often tell others, "You can get humility voluntarily or involuntarily. It is much easier if you get it voluntarily."

## Question
Would others say you are a humble man?

*Father, make me a humble man.*

# The Power of Influence

*I want you to know, brethren, that the things which happened to me have actually turned out for the furtherance of the gospel.*

PHILIPPIANS 1:12 NKJV

Have you ever heard these statements: "Money talks"? Or how about this: "He who has the gold makes the rules"? Both of these statements have truth in them.

When Jesus was crucified, there was a question as to where Jesus would be buried. Those who hurried him to the cross felt he should make his grave with the wicked, but God decided he would make it with the rich (see Isaiah 53:9), and so he did.

In order for Jesus to be buried with honor, a man of influence was permitted to take the body of Jesus. His name was Joseph of Arimathea. It seems this man had a personal relationship with Pilate. He was a man of influence and owned a burial cave that was reserved for the rich.

Joseph of Arimathea was called an honorable counselor and a person of character and distinction. He held an office of public trust and was one of Pilate's privy council. He also had a role in the church as one member of the Jewish Sanhedrim, the high priest's council.[57]

The Bible says that God desires his people to be the head, not the tail. If we are to influence the culture, there must be men and women of influence whom God uses to impact the culture. Consider Paul's words: "What has happened to me has actually served to advance the gospel" (NIV).

## Question

Are you using your influence and life to advance the gospel?

*Father, use my influence to build your kingdom on earth.*

# "Go to Christ Church"

*The Lord said to him, "Arise and go to the street called Straight, and inquire at the house of Judas for one called Saul of Tarsus, for behold, he is praying."*
ACTS 9:11 NKJV

We stepped into the cab to take our first drive to downtown Jerusalem. It was an exciting time for us!

Moses, a cab driver, offered to drive us throughout the city. We were rookies, not sure what we were getting ourselves into. It was a dangerous time to roam through Jerusalem. Our cab driver began to talk openly with us when he discovered we were believers in Jesus. He was a born-again Jew. He used to work on the family farm for his rabbi father-in-law. He had been excommunicated from his family for his belief that Jesus is the Savior. The Jewish–Palestinian conflict had cut tourism by 90 percent, so as a cab driver, Moses had plenty of time on his hands.

He began to share his story with us. "I'd been questioning my purpose in life. I began thinking there had to be more. My Jewish laws didn't satisfy something in me. I became very depressed. Then one day a remarkable thing happened. I was in my bedroom. Suddenly, I heard a voice in my room that said, 'Go to Christ Church!' I thought I was imagining things. Then, I heard it a second time!

"I looked in the yellow pages and discovered that Christ Church was located downtown in the 'Old City.' The people there explained to me what happened. Jesus was calling me to know him. I have known him ever since."

## Question
Do you have a faith that makes you willing to be rejected and ostracized by those close to you?

*Father, help me be a faithful follower of Jesus no matter the cost.*

# Truth in the Inward Parts

*Behold, You desire truth in the inward parts,*
*and in the hidden part You will make me to know wisdom.*
PSALM 51:6 NKJV

History reveals that Sir Arthur Conan Doyle, the author of the popular mystery stories about Sherlock Holmes, once played a practical joke on twelve respected and well-known men he knew. He sent out twelve telegrams with the same message on each: "Flee! All has been discovered." Within twenty-four hours, they had all left the country![58] History is replete with leaders who had a secret life that resulted in dire consequences or ended poorly due to some type of tragic situation.

Around 1923, the most powerful men of the day included Charles Schwab, Samuel Insull, Howard Hopson, Richard Whitney, Albert Fall, Jesse Livermore, Ivan Kruger, and Leon Fraser.

These men were "movers and shakers," the kind many people envy and wish to be like. Despite their influential roles in business, finance, and politics, something went terribly wrong with these men's lives. Look where they were twenty-seven years later:

Charles Schwab left behind an insolvent estate with debts and obligations totaling $1.7 million. Samuel Insull died of a heart attack in a Paris subway station with twenty cents in his pocket. Howard Hopson died in a sanitarium. Richard Whitney had just been released from Sing-Sing prison. Albert Fall died at home, broke. Jesse Livermore committed suicide a week after Thanksgiving in 1940. Ivan Krueger committed suicide. Leon Fraser committed suicide.[59]

## Question

Are you the same person behind closed doors as you are in public?

*Father, help me live a life of integrity and honesty before you.*

# Pray for Those in Authority

*Most of all, I'm writing to encourage you to pray with gratitude to God. Pray for all men with all forms of prayers and requests as you intercede with intense passion.*
### 1 TIMOTHY 2:1 TPT

Paul exhorts his young protégé to make the first work of the church prayer and intercession for those in authority.

Whereas we once thought of those in politics, military, religion, and economics as controlling the earth, today we recognize the enormous influence wielded by those in the workplace. Our mindsets are changing; those in the workplace, including business leaders, we now include as those in authority. They, too, are among those Paul exhorted Timothy to cover in prayer.

God is transferring his anointing to be placed upon all saints to get the job done. This requires the local church to give more focus on equipping men to live out their faith in the workplace. If we are going to see a major harvest in the last days, it will have to come through the largest segment of the body of Christ—those who are Christ's representatives in government, business, and education.

The book of Acts records Lydia, a businesswoman, as God's instrument to introduce the gospel to Europe. The Ethiopian eunuch who was in charge of the treasury of Candace, "Queen of the Ethiopians," introduced the gospel to Africa. Peter launched the gospel into the gentile world through Cornelius, a Roman centurion. And three "workplace ministers" reached Europe, Africa, and the gentiles. These examples indicate the importance of the workplace influence and why intercession is so important for leaders in places of authority.

## Question

Do you understand the important role you play in furthering the gospel as a workplace minister?

*Father, I pray for leaders in government, business, and education that you will restore the biblical foundations in these areas.*

# Serving Kings

*If you are uniquely gifted in your work, you will rise and be promoted.*
*You won't be held back—you'll stand before kings!*
PROVERBS 22:29 TPT

I was sitting in a room of four hundred businesspeople from seventy-five different nations to begin an international conference. After a time of worship, a man stood up and exhorted Christians in the United States to pray for their president. It was a difficult time in our nation because President Bill Clinton was in the midst of a scandal.

The man who challenged us to pray was pastor Romain Zannou from the small African nation of Benin. Many years ago, God had given him a burden to pray for his Marxist dictator president, Mathieu Kerekou. For ten years, he prayed for two hours a day for Kerekou's salvation and for God to give Kerekou wisdom to lead the nation. One day Romain felt he had a word for the president. Twenty-four hours later, he was standing in a room with Kerekou.

Though he and Romain had agreed to meet after their first free elections for a time of Bible study, the former president refused to meet with Romain after only a few meetings. Romain went to Kerekou's home only to be told that Kerekou did not wish to see him. "I will wait," and he stood outside the wall for hours. And he kept coming back to wait many times in the rain and heat in hopes that Kerekou would let him in.

A year and a half later the former president finally received him and greeted him with the words, "Pastor Zannou, you are a very persistent man." They began an in-depth study of the Bible which led to the former president receiving Christ.

## Question
Who are the people of influence God has called you to impact?

*Father, use me to influence leaders of leaders.*

# The Poor and the Marketplace

*"'When you reap the harvest of your land, you shall not wholly reap the corners of your field, nor shall you gather the gleanings of your harvest. And you shall not glean your vineyard, nor shall you gather every grape of your vineyard; you shall leave them for the poor and the stranger: I am the Lord your God.'"*

LEVITICUS 19:9–10 NKJV

God has a special place in his heart for the poor. In the book of Isaiah, we read these words:

> Is this not the fast that I have chosen:
> to loose the bonds of wickedness,
> to undo the heavy burdens,
> to let the oppressed go free,
> and that you break every yoke?
> Is it not to share your bread with the hungry,
> and that you bring to your house the poor who are cast out;
> when you see the naked, that you cover him,
> and not hide yourself from your own flesh? (Isaiah 58:6–7)

So how does God want us to care for the poor? God gives us his answer in the Old Testament story of Boaz, Ruth, and Naomi. It was God's law for farmers to not glean their entire fields in order to leave some of the crop for the poor to glean. This allowed the poor to work to receive their provision.

Notice that God created a partnership between the marketplace and the poor. By providing an opportunity to glean something from our businesses through an opportunity to work, we provide provision and dignity to the poor.

## Question
How can you serve the poor through the gleanings in your business?

*Father, help me be sensitive to the plight of the poor.*

# Work to Acquire, Work to Play

*"I have glorified You on the earth.
I have finished the work which You have given Me to do."*
JOHN 17:4 NKJV

A popular TV commercial comes on the screen, and a voice raises the question of why the viewer works long hours, all while the screen shows beautiful pictures of a luxurious car. The message is clear. We work in order to acquire.

There are many motivations for work. Some might say it is simply to put food on the table. George Barna, the American researcher on religious habits, found disturbing results from his study on the motivations of many Christians in American society.

> We are not a society that simply enjoys its time off. We are driven by our leisure appetites. It is increasingly common to hear of people turning down job offers because the hours or other responsibilities would interfere with their hobbies, fitness regimens and other free time activities. Even our spending habits show that playing has become a major priority. The average household spends more money on entertainment than it does clothing, health care, furniture or gasoline.[60]

His study also found that many people define success in surprisingly non-Christian terms: He found that 66 percent of Americans define success in life as the acquisition of sufficient money, education, material possessions, or career prestige; only 7 percent related success to their faith condition and its influence upon their life.[61]

## Question
Why do you work? What are your primary motivations?

*Father, help me glorify you in my work.*

# Transforming a Workplace

*Do not be conformed to this world, but be transformed by the renewing of your mind, that you may prove what is that good and acceptable and perfect will of God.*
ROMANS 12:2 NKJV

A cab driver in the Philippines became radically saved. He was taught that he now had the power of God in his life to transform his community. He took a literal approach to believing what the Bible says about prayer and miracles.

He decided that the best mission field for him was the local bar in his neighborhood. So he began to visit this bar to find the most qualified sinner he could find in order to minister to him. The local bartender was a great prospect because he was also a drug addict and a pimp to thirty-five prostitutes. The cab driver got to know the bartender while drinking his "usual" Coke. The Lord used the cab driver to bring this man to Christ.

God moved greatly in the bartender, and he was delivered from his lifestyle. He began to change his life and share Jesus with the prostitutes. All thirty-five of them became Christians, and they began meeting in the bar for Bible study.

Soon, the owner of the bar was saved. The bar became a church, and the group started ten cell group churches in the neighborhood.[62]

God desires a moment-by-moment relationship with us, and he wants to demonstrate his loving power to others through us. We can approach God about any situation, for there is nothing that is too small or too great for him.

## Question
How does God want to transform others through you?

*Father, help me be a transformer in my workplace and city.*

# Seeing Backward

*I remember boasting, "I've got it made! Nothing can stop me now!
I'm God's favored one; he's made me steady as a mountain!"
But then suddenly, you hid your face from me.*

PSALM 30:6–7 TPT

It is often difficult to recognize the hand of God when we are in the midst of adversity. We often feel God has hidden his face from us. When the Lord takes us through deep valleys, there will be fruit from the deep valley that we cannot see.

God uses the deep valley to frame our lives to create a change in our nature, not just a change in habits. The depth and width of our valley are often indicators of the level of calling and influence we will have on others in the future. Our adversity is not just for us but also for others who will be on our future path of influence. This is not very comforting when you are in the middle of the valley but know this is a truth in the kingdom.

Life is often lived forward but understood backward. It is not until we stand on the mountain looking back through the valley that we can appreciate the terrain God has allowed us to scale and the spiritual deposits he has made in our life. "He reveals the deep things of darkness and brings utter darkness into the light" (Job 12:22 NIV). When you begin to realize this, you sit back and breathe a sigh of relief because you know that God was in control all along. It didn't seem like it at the time, but he was.

## Question

Do you find yourself in the valley? Now is the time to fully trust him to guide you to higher ground.

*Father, give me the grace to walk through my valleys successfully.*

# Jehovah-Jireh

*Abraham called the name of the place, The-Lord-Will-Provide;
as it is said to this day, "In the Mount of the Lord it shall be provided."*
GENESIS 22:14 NKJV

I got onto the bus with the other delegates attending a workplace conference in South Africa. It was a season in my life in which I had experienced many losses, both financially and relationally. God was stripping away the old wineskin and creating a new one. One of the things he was teaching me was that he—not my skills, not my work—was my provider of financial needs during this season of training.

God provided me the means to attend the conference. One day before the registration deadline, a man came to my office and gave me $2,500 and told me I was to go. During that same trip, a different man I had just met when sitting on a bus in another country placed an envelope in my hand. "Here, God says I'm to give this to you." Inside were ten crisp American $100 bills—$1000! The man was from Kuwait.

Every believer needs to come to know Christ as their provider. *Jehovah-Jireh* means "God is my provider." When God called the Israelites from their place of slavery, they had to walk through the desert. There is no way to earn a living in the desert. So, God provided manna each day for them. Sometimes he even brought water from rocks. They had to experience a new way of gaining provision that was not rooted in sweat and toil. God had to demonstrate his faithfulness as Jehovah-Jireh to his people.

## Question
Do you know God as your provider? Do you have a need?

*Father, thank you for your faithfulness as my Jehovah-Jireh.*

# Coming Signs of Persecution

*They have said, "Come, and let us cut them off from being a nation,*
*that the name of Israel may be remembered no more."*
PSALM 83:4 NKJV

God calls us to know the signs of the times. The Bible is clear that Jesus will return to the physical place of Jerusalem to collect his bride, represented as all those who believe and trust in Jesus, the Messiah. "Let us rejoice and be glad and give him glory! For the wedding of the Lamb has come, and his bride has made herself ready" (Revelation 19:7 NIV).

Israel will always be a place of conflict in the world because Satan knows that this is the place Jesus must come back to in order to collect his bride. And when Jesus does that, it will be the end of Satan's influence on the earth through anti-Christian nations. But until Jesus returns, the land of Jerusalem will be in a tug-of-war among the nations.

A growing trend of anti-Semitism and persecution will emerge against Jews and committed Christians. Christians will be called to stand with our brothers and sisters in Israel. When this happens, it will be one of the reasons Jews will believe in the Messiah.

There is a season of persecution to come. "Yet if anyone suffers as a Christian, let him not be ashamed, but let him glorify God in this [matter. For the time has come for judgment to begin at the house of God; and if it begins with us first, what will be the end of those who do not obey the gospel of God?" (1 Peter 4:16–17 NKJV).

## Question
Are you seeing the signs of the times and how you must respond?

*Father, I pray that I will be faithful.*

# Reflecting the Light

*"He was the burning and shining lamp,*
*and you were willing for a time to rejoice in his light."*
JOHN 5:35 NKJV

The moon is lovely on a clear night only because it reflects the light of the sun. It has no qualities by itself to reflect its beauty. Without the sun shining onto its surface, you and I would never see the moon. It would simply be a dark object in the sky.

A diamond is designed to reflect the light to reveal its true value. The cut of a diamond determines its brilliance. There is no single measurement of a diamond that defines its cut but rather a collection of measurements and observations that determine the relationship between a diamond's light performance, dimensions, and finish.

Jesus came to bring the light of his love and grace to each of us. However, we are born into a world dulled by the sin created by Adam and Eve that makes our lives dark until we meet Jesus. "For all have sinned and fall short of the glory of God" (Romans 3:23 NIV).

Jesus contrasted in many parables that those who allow his life to live in them will live in the light amidst darkness. When you invite Jesus Christ to live in your heart, it is as though a light is shining upon your life in order to reflect the glory of God's Son through you.

Jesus calls you to be a vessel to reflect the brilliant light of his love to others. The workplace is a great place to reflect his glory.

## Question
Is your life a reflection of God's glory?

*Father, make me a reflection of your love and grace and glory.*

# We All Need Our Purahs

*"If you are afraid to go down, go down to the camp with Purah your servant, and you shall hear what they say; and afterward your hands shall be strengthened to go down against the camp."*

JUDGES 7:10–11 NKJV

The Israelites did evil in the eyes of the LORD, and for seven years he gave them into the hands of the Midianites. Because the power of Midian was so oppressive, the Israelites prepared shelters for themselves in mountain clefts, caves and strongholds" (Judges 6:1–2 NIV). God called Midian to be Israel's deliverer, but he was not sure he was the man for God.

Gideon was very insecure about this assignment from God, so God told him to go into the camp during the night to eavesdrop on their soldiers. God told Gideon that what he would hear would encourage him. Gideon was terrified by the whole idea. So, God took another step in order to use Gideon for his purposes. He sent a trusted friend and soldier named Purah with him.

God knew that Purah was the person Gideon could confide in, probably one of the ten who had helped him to break down the altar of Baal. God told Gideon that he must take Purah and no one else with him. Purah would be a witness to what Gideon would hear from the Midianites.

We all need "Purahs" in our lives. We need people who are willing to take risks and who can be used by God to bring our faith up to a level.

## Question

Has God called you to a daunting assignment? Perhaps he has also placed a "Purah" in your life to encourage you.

*Father, bring faithful friends into my life whom I can confide in.*

# The Coming Wealth Transfer

*A good man leaves an inheritance to his children's children,*
*but the wealth of the sinner is stored up for the righteous.*
PROVERBS 13:22 NKJV

In the last days, there will be a transfer of wealth into the hands of the righteous for the purpose of funding a great harvest of souls and for believers to have a greater influence on society. This will happen in at least four ways.

1. Supernatural Transfer: Like the Israelites leaving Egypt, Christians and nonprofit organizations will receive major gifts from individuals or foundations to carry out their Christian mission. In 2004, the Salvation Army received one of the largest gifts ever for Christian ministry via the founder's wife of McDonald's, Joan Kroc, in the amount of $1.5 billion.[63]
2. Power to Make Wealth: God is going to give witty inventions to believers throughout the world that will generate wealth.
3. Social Entrepreneurship: Just as Joseph was entrusted with the resources of Egypt to solve a societal problem resulting from a famine in the land, God is going to transfer money to believers who are solving societal problems.
4. Wealthy Individual "Conversions": Finally, many nonbelievers who are wealthy will become Christians in these last days and will begin to use their wealth for kingdom purposes.

The transfer of wealth is designed to accelerate God's activity on the earth, not to simply make believers wealthy.

## Question
Is God making you a channel for his last days transfer of wealth?

*Father, use my work-life call to accelerate your kingdom on earth.*

# Regaining the Art of Community

*If we walk in the light as He is in the light, we have fellowship with one another, and the blood of Jesus Christ His Son cleanses us from all sin.*

1 JOHN 1:7 NKJV

I have a friend who spent three months living in Israel with Jewish believers. During one of their conversations, the Jewish man noticed how often my friend came to visit him only to discuss a project. He turned to my friend during dinner and admonished him: "You Western Christians! You always seem to need a program or an event to get together. Why can't you fellowship with one another just because you love each other?"

My friend was convicted by his assessment. They began to talk about how Jesus modeled love for the disciples and how they simply hung out together because of their love for one another. "A new commandment I give to you, that you love one another; as I have loved you, that you also love one another. By this all will know that you are My disciples, if you have love for one another" (John 13:34–35).

Jesus often spent unhurried times of fellowship with the disciples. They shared countless meals together. It is often during such times we get to know others at a deeper level.

Love for one another is one of the greatest signs of faith in Christ. However, the pace of life often contributes to a life being lived for the next event instead of for a relationship rooted in the love of Christ.

## Question

How many relationships do you have in your life that would allow you to fellowship simply because you cared for one another?

*Father, help me to be a friend to others without a motive for any personal gain.*

# The Tipping Point

*He Himself gave some to be apostles, some prophets,*
*some evangelists, and some pastors and teachers.*
EPHESIANS 4:11 NKJV

Malcolm Gladwell authored a secular marketing book entitled *The Tipping Point*. The tipping point is the moment when an idea, product, or movement becomes accepted by the masses. It is the best way to understand the emergence of fashion trends, crime waves, or unknown books becoming bestsellers. Gladwell says, "Ideas and products and messages and behaviors spread just like viruses do,"[64] but he has discovered there are usually three types of people involved: connectors, mavens, and salesmen.[65]

Connectors are "people with a special gift for bringing the world together." They know lots of people who have the ability to make an impact.[66]

Mavens are people who accumulate knowledge about a particular area. They are "information brokers" who like to get information and share it with others to help solve their problems.[67]

Salesmen have an ability "to persuade when we are unconvinced of what we are hearing." They are critical to the tipping point for word-of-mouth epidemics.[68]

I believe these three people correlate to the apostle (connectors), often defined as "one who is sent"; the prophet (mavens), defined as "one who proclaims truth"; and the evangelist (salesmen), "one who wins the lost"—all described in Ephesians 4:11.

Mavens, connectors, and salesmen make an idea contagious by working together to spread the message. Consider bringing these three types of people together to see real success on your next project.

## Question

Are you a connector, maven, or salesman?

*Father, use my unique gifting to build your kingdom.*

# His Vision, His Way, His Timing

*God said, "Take your son, your only son, whom you love—Isaac—and go to the region of Moriah. Sacrifice him there as a burnt offering on a mountain I will show you."*
GENESIS 22:2 NIV

Have you ever wanted something so badly that you would do almost anything to get it? Have you ever gotten so close to fulfilling a dream only to have it disappear right before your eyes? Such was the case for Abraham.

God promised Abraham that he would be the father of many nations. He would have a son. However, Abraham panicked when Sarah aged beyond childbearing years and tried to help God by birthing Ishmael, who was not the promised son, through Sarah's servant. Eventually, Isaac was born, who was the promised son.

However, God told Abraham to sacrifice his only son on an altar to demonstrate his obedience to God. Truly, this was one of the hardest instructions given to one of God's people in all of Scripture. It compares only to the heavenly Father sacrificing his own Son. God intervenes and allows a ram to get caught in the bushes nearby, symbolizing the Lamb of God as a prophetic sign of what is to take place in the future.

God often births a vision in our lives only to allow it to die first before the purest version of the vision is manifested.

When God's vision is finally birthed, nothing will stop it. Our job is to allow God to birth his vision through us his way and in his timing.

## Question
Has God birthed a vision that had to die first before it was fulfilled?

*Father, I entrust my vision to you to fulfill in your timing.*

# Being a Workplace Minister

*Let every activity of your lives and every word that comes from your lips be drenched with the beauty of our Lord Jesus, the Anointed One.*

COLOSSIANS 3:17 TPT

Over 70 percent of our waking hours are spent in the workplace, yet our training and teaching in local churches focus on areas where we spend much less time. The workplace is the greatest mission field of our day and represents the greatest opportunity for societal transformation, yet we do not train workplace believers on how to effectively integrate their faith life into their work life. The wall between Sunday and Monday still exists, and most workplace believers do not understand that all of life is spiritual, not just life on Sunday.

Alarmingly, the majority of Christians do not feel they've been adequately trained to apply biblical faith in their work life. We have focused on the fringes rather than the center, where most people spend most of their time.

God is removing the wall of separation by speaking to pastors and workplace believers all over the world. A pastor recently shared how his church ordains their workplace believers for their calling to the workplace. Another pastor described their church's commitment to integrating training for their workplace believers on the theology of work. We are changing the 80/20 rule in the nine-to-five window from 20 percent of the people doing ministry to 80 percent.

## Question
Are you one of the men God is raising up for this task?

*Father, I pray you will help local church leaders understand and affirm this calling and that they will respond by training their people for their own ministry in their workplaces.*

# Retirement or a New Assignment?

*A man may do his work with wisdom, knowledge, and skill.*
ECCLESIASTES 2:21 NET

He was sixty-nine years old and had already had a successful Hollywood movie career when he decided to try his hand at politics. He would become known as one of the United States' greatest statesmen. He was also known for the extraordinary love he had for his wife.

His name was Ronald Reagan, and he did not begin his greatest work until he was sixty-nine years old. By this age, most are thinking of retirement. Ronald Reagan decided to run for President of the United States and successfully served two terms as our fortieth president.

It was Reagan's faith that led him to see the Soviet Union as an "evil empire." He'll be remembered as the president who brought down communism in the Soviet Union. And it was his Christian faith that gave him quiet confidence and earned him the title "the great communicator."

Where did he get his spiritual values? First and foremost was his mother, Nelle Reagan. I'm confident that had Nelle Reagan died in the winter of 1918–1919—a near-victim of the devastating influenza epidemic that killed millions of healthy, middle-aged mothers around the world—Ronald Reagan very likely would not have become president. It was Nelle who insisted her boy go to church—a request he happily obliged—and it was in church where Reagan picked up not only those core beliefs and values but also the intangibles so vital to his success: his confidence, his eternal optimism (which he called a "God-given optimism"), and even his ability to communicate his message.[69]

## Question
Could your greatest work yet be ahead of you?

*Father, use me in whatever way and at whatever age you want to use me.*

# Worship and Work

*One person esteems one day above another;*
*another esteems every day alike.*
*Let each be fully convinced in his own mind.*
ROMANS 14:5 NKJV

Avodah is a Hebrew noun used in the Bible that has two distinct yet intertwined meanings: worship and work. It is also derived from the Hebrew verb *L'Avod*, which also has two meanings: to work and to worship. The dual meaning offers powerful wisdom for modern times for how we are to view our work lives.

Work, if done with integrity and unto God, is a form of worship in the biblical Hebrew context. There has never been a concept of segmenting our work from our faith life in the Bible. It is in the realm of the sacred to bring God into our everyday life. Hebrews did not set aside a "day of worship," such as Saturday or Sunday, but every day was a place and time of worship. They did set aside a Sabbath day of rest.

It is a western idea to segment our faith life from our work life. In the Middle East and Asia, their cultures would never separate their faith from their work life, even though their faith foundations might clearly contradict Christian beliefs.

God calls us to do our work as an act of worship to him. Our work is not to be a place of sweat and toil but an expression of our love, faith, and adoration of Jesus Christ. Today, before you work, ask God to help you see your work in a new way as worship to him.

## Question
Do you seek your work as worship?

*Father, help me to see my daily work as worship unto you.*

# Relating to Those Different from Us

*The woman of Samaria said to Him, "How is it that You, being a Jew, ask a drink from me, a Samaritan woman?" For Jews have no dealings with Samaritans.*
JOHN 4:9 NKJV

Do you find it difficult to relate to others who are different from you? Do you shy away from interacting with those who may have a different belief?

Jesus interacted with his culture and especially those who thought differently. When Jesus met the Samaritan woman at the well, it was much like a Christian speaking to a Muslim or a Jew speaking to a Palestinian. Jesus built a relationship with the woman instead of taking an adversarial position.

In order to influence our culture, it is vital believers engage with those unlike us. We often assume others who come from other cultures do not want to engage with us. This is a deception from Satan.

Every person is looking for a genuine relationship with God. Jesus operated based on that assumption when he spoke into the life of the Samaritan woman.

Once Jesus established a rapport with the woman, he began to engage with her. He spoke supernaturally into her life, which broke through the religious spirit that prevented a theological debate. This led to faith in Christ and even the city being impacted.

## Question
Do you seek out relationships with someone different from yourself?

*Father, help me build relationships with those I may find different from me.*

# The Queen of Heaven

*The children gather wood, the fathers kindle the fire, and the women knead dough, to make cakes for the queen of heaven; and they pour out drink offerings to other gods, that they may provoke Me to anger.*

JEREMIAH 7:18 NKJV

If you want to change the spiritual climate of your city, you must address the principalities that rule that city. Such was the case for the apostle Paul when he went to the city of Ephesus. There was a territorial principality that was worshiped by the people of Ephesus named Diana of the Ephesians. The people gave money to this false god, and it strongly influenced the economy because of this. The city was also the center for magic and the occult.

Her temple in Ephesus was listed as one of the Seven Wonders of the Ancient World—the most outstanding and opulent example of architecture in the whole city. Her followers called her "magnificent," "great goddess," "savior," and "Queen of Heaven."

Paul preached in Asia for two years with great success in confronting this territorial principality. By the gospel, Paul began to neutralize Diana's power so much that the common people began to notice. The silversmiths who were manufacturing idols were going out of business, so they staged a public riot.

Many who were converted burned all of the idols and magic books. "When they calculated the value of the scrolls, the total came to fifty thousand drachmas [$4 million in modern American value]. In this way the word of the Lord spread widely and grew in power" (Acts 19:19–20 NIV).[70]

## Question
Are you aware of the spiritual forces over your city?

*Father, give me discernment about the spiritual forces impacting my community.*

# God Is Not about Your Success

*Most assuredly, I say to you, unless a grain of wheat falls into the ground and dies, it remains alone; but if it dies, it produces much grain. He who loves his life will lose it, and he who hates his life in this world will keep it for eternal life.*
JOHN 12:24–25 NKJV

God is all about your death so that *his* success can be realized through you! This is why the church is having such little impact—there are too many believers who have not yet died to their old nature so that Christ can live fully through them. When believers come to the end of themselves, they will lose their lives to him and live through the power of the Holy Spirit and begin to see the reality of a living gospel that impacts lives, workplaces, cities, and nations.

"Much of our modern Christian enterprise is 'Ishmael,' i.e., it is born not of God, but of an inordinate desire to do God's will in our own way—the one thing Our Lord never did," said Oswald Chambers.[71]

How does one die so that Christ can be our all and all? It usually takes a crisis of significant proportions for most people to relinquish the control of their lives. It means we come to the end of ourselves and our striving to control the events in our lives, and we finally come to the place where we can say, "Lord, I surrender. Please take full control of my life."

## Question
Have you come to this place with God in your life?

*Father, I lay my life before you as my source for all success in life.*

# You Think That?

*Who is wise and understanding among you? Let him show by good conduct that his works are done in the meekness of wisdom. But if you have bitter envy and self-seeking in your hearts, do not boast and lie against the truth.*

JAMES 3:13–14 NKJV

I can't believe you think I said that!" I complained to my wife. "I was simply trying to explain that I don't have the same feelings about that issue as you do." Her response left little empathy for my position because of the tone in which I responded to her. We resigned ourselves to agree to disagree.

We all see things through our own set of glasses at times. Men view things differently than women. Bosses see things differently than employees. One ethnic group will see a situation totally different than another. Our life experiences, our past treatment of circumstances, and our personalities all contribute to how we view situations in daily life.

Whenever conflict arises, there is really only one way to resolve the difference. Usually, the other person is offended more by our tone than the position taken. If the other person is offended, or first response should be: "I'm sorry. Will you forgive me for my tone?"

Humbling ourselves is the only way to resolve the relational breach. This does not mean you must agree with the other person's position; it simply means you acknowledge his right to his position, and you apologize for the manner in which you responded to his statements. This will usually allow most conflicts to avoid a breach in the relationship.

## Question

Is there someone you need to seek forgiveness from for taking an adversarial tone and attitude?

*Father, help me affirm others even when I disagree with their position.*

# Using Business for Ministry

*Our Father in heaven, hallowed be Your name. Your kingdom come.*
*Your will be done on earth as it is in heaven.*
MATTHEW 6:9–10 NKJV

Near Santa Barbara, California, Al Merrick began a surfboard manufacturing business. Although his business started small, Al always dedicated his work to God by praying over the boards as he worked and writing Bible verses on them. His high-quality work made him one of the best surfboard shapers. Some of the best surfers in the world bought boards from him. Al's devotion to God never wavered. He often opened his Bible and talked about Jesus with his customers. Through a Jesus People coffeehouse and an at-home Bible study, Al and his wife found more ways to minister to the surfer community. Al's company, Merrick's Channel Island Surfboard, became the largest surfboard manufacturing company in the world.

Today, this company's devotion to workplace ministry has continued through the next generation. The day their son, Brett, rededicated his life to Christ, he invited surfers from a local beach to join a Bible study. Many of these people accepted Jesus. Not only has he expanded the company with his own line of surfboards, but he has also transformed many lives by leveraging his family's reputation in the industry to share the gospel. He and his family have brought heaven and earth in their business.[72]

## Question

What might God want you to do to bring transformation to your workplace?

*Father, make me an instrument to bring heaven on earth.*

# Simply Obey

*Naaman became furious, and went away and said, "Indeed, I said to myself, 'He will surely come out to me, and stand and call on the name of the LORD his God, and wave his hand over the place, and heal the leprosy.'"*

2 KINGS 5:11 NKJV

Naaman was an army general who needed healing from leprosy. A young servant girl of the king's house suggested that the prophet Elisha could heal him. He followed her advice, and Elisha sent a message to him to do the following: "Go, wash yourself seven times in the Jordan, and your flesh will be restored and you will be cleansed" (v. 10 NIV). However, when Naaman heard the instruction for what he was to do, it seemed ridiculous to him.

Like many of us, Naaman expected God to perform his miracle through Elisha in a dramatic and "religious" way. Sometimes we fail to recognize that God can work through a simple act of obedience that seems unrelated to the problem. God told Joshua to walk around Jericho seven times to win the battle. He told a man to wash mud from his eyes to be healed. He told Peter to catch a fish to get a coin to pay his taxes.

There are other times God calls us to use the natural to receive a breakthrough. Sometimes we simply need to change our diet or go see a doctor to see a breakthrough in our health. Sometimes we need to change the way we are doing our work to get a breakthrough in our careers.

## Question
Do you have a problem for which you need a solution?

*Father, what steps am I to take for my breakthrough? Please lead me in the way I should go.*

# I'm Not Ready

*Blessed is the man who endures temptation; for when he has been approved, he will receive the crown of life which the Lord has promised to those who love Him.*
JAMES 1:12 NKJV

God will seldom call you into service when you *think* you are ready. This is intentional on God's part.

You can be sure that when God calls you, you will have similar responses as Saul did when he was called to be the first king, Gideon when he was called to take down the idols in his nation, or Moses when he was called to deliver his people from Egypt.

Saul answered and said, "Am I not a Benjamite, of the smallest of the tribes of Israel, and my family the least of all the families of the tribe of Benjamin? Why then do you speak like this to me?" (1 Samuel 9:21)

So [Gideon] said to Him, "O my Lord, how can I save Israel? Indeed my clan is the weakest in Manasseh, and I am the least in my father's house." (Judges 6:15)

Moses said to God, "Who am I that I should go to Pharaoh, and that I should bring the children of Israel out of Egypt?" (Exodus 3:11)

When God calls, you will most likely be in the most unlikely circumstances to receive that call. God does this because he wants you to know your call is based only on his ability, not yours.

## Question

Has God called you to something you have failed to do because you felt you were not ready?

*Father, give me grace to respond to your call no matter how difficult I perceive the assignment.*

# Playing to One Conductor

*It would be wrong for the eye to say to the hand, "I don't need you,"*
*and equally wrong if the head said to the foot, "I don't need you."*
1 CORINTHIANS 12:21 TPT

I watched as the conductor looked over to the violin section, then the percussion, then there was a seemingly insignificant lady standing way back in the corner waiting to play her one or two notes on a chime-looking instrument. *Who would even notice if she didn't play her instrument?* I wondered to myself. *The conductor would*, said the still voice in my spirit.

An orchestra is a great picture of the way the body of Christ should operate. I am sure the lady who only plays a few notes in the back of the room must think she doesn't measure up to the great violinist who sits right up close to the conductor.

However, imagine if you slowly removed each member of the orchestra, one at a time. At first you may not notice any difference without a trained ear. But as you remove each member of the orchestra, you will begin to miss the powerful and melodic sound of many instruments playing together. Finally, when all but a few of the instruments are removed, you will notice a big difference in the sound and the void left by key instruments.

Every member of the body of Christ matters. Your contribution matters to God and has no hierarchy of importance.

## Question
What instrument has God called you to play?

*Father, thank you for reminding me my gifts are important to fulfilling your purposes.*

# Picking Fruit

*Because of you, I know the path of life, as I taste the fullness of joy in your presence.*
*At your right side I experience divine pleasures forevermore!*
PSALM 16:11 TPT

Golf has been a part of my life since I was eleven years old. I used to live on the golf course. The game has taught me many life lessons. I went to college on a golf scholarship and later turned professional for three years.

I would often walk on the golf course at sundown for exercise and use this time to pray. It is a quiet and beautiful place to walk. When I walk, I usually find one or two golf balls along the way. But one time was different.

On this particular walk, I began to find golf balls everywhere I looked. When I had collected five, I began to notice how strange this was. Then, it became eight, then ten, and finally, my pockets were literally stuffed with thirteen golf balls!

When something unusual happens in our daily life, it is a time to tune in to your spiritual antennae. God is often at work. So, I prayed, "Lord, what are you saying through this?"

The answer came quickly: "I have called you to walk a specific path. I will bring the fruit to you. All you will have to do is pick it up and stay on my path for you. That is what it means to abide in Me."

## Question
Are you walking the path God has for you?

*Father, thank you that you will cause the fruit of my calling.*

# Obedience versus Skill and Ability

*"When you hear a sound of marching in the tops of the mulberry trees, then you shall go out to battle."*

1 CHRONICLES 14:15 NKJV

The Philistines were attacking, and God revealed to David that he was to attack the Philistines straightaway. David followed God's instruction and gained victory. Shortly after, the Philistines mounted another attack. "David inquired again of God, and God said to him, 'You shall not go up after them; circle around them, and come upon them in front of the mulberry trees'" (v. 14).

David was a well-trained warrior and strategist. Yet, we find that David's dependence on God to direct his efforts was great. In fact, after he won the first battle, he went right back to inquire again. This is the most important lesson we can learn from this story. God told David when to attack the second time.

How many times have we done something the same way over and over just because it was the way we did it before? "So David inquired of God…" We are to learn from these important words.

## Question

Are you stuck trying to solve a problem because you're approaching it the same way you have before?

*Father, thank you for having the solution to every problem I encounter. I trust you to give me the wisdom to solve my problem.*

# Grace Abounds

*God is able to make all grace abound toward you, that you, always having all sufficiency in all things, may have an abundance for every good work.*
2 CORINTHIANS 9:8 NKJV

A few years ago, God was allowing my business to dry up. It happened in order to lead me to an entirely new calling. Lack of provision is one way God leads us to a new place. This was a scary proposition because I had many outstanding obligations to banks and others, and I had to have some significant cash flow to make these payments.

I was ending a consulting contract with a client and saw no prospects for replacing it. Days before the contract expired, I received a call from a new ministry that was consistent with the calling I sensed God was leading me to. They asked me to consult with them for the next year. At the end of that year, I learned that God spoke to the ministry's founder to pay my entire salary out of his own pocket in order to meet the needs I had at that time. This was no insignificant amount either.

At the conclusion of my contract with them, I was wondering where my income was going to come from for the next year. The day before I was informed that their commitment would decrease by 50 percent, I received a call from the administrator of our foundation. They informed me that a supporter had just given $20,000 to our ministry. God encouraged me through this gift to know that he was my provider.

## Question
Is there a lack of resources for you right now?

*Father, I trust you to bring me what I need in your perfect timing.*

# The Value of Age and Wisdom

*He rejected the advice which the elders had given him, and consulted the young men who had grown up with him, who stood before him.*

2 CHRONICLES 10:8 NKJV

Age and wisdom do not always equate to one another, but they often do. Rehoboam was the son of Solomon. It appears that Solomon had become heavy-handed in his employment practices by placing an overbearing burden on the workers. This was causing a problem with the northern tribes. It was the equivalent of a threat of a labor strike. Jeroboam was like the head of the labor union. In fact, he had fled from Solomon because of the abuse he perceived was happening. When Rehoboam was selected as the new king, Jeroboam came and appealed to Rehoboam about the plight of the people.

So, Rehoboam asked for advice from the older men who had served Solomon, and then he asked for advice from his younger contemporaries. The elders advised Rehoboam to give these people a favorable answer, being kind and pleasing them. They told him that if he did, they would be loyal workers the rest of their days. He chose not to take this advice. The younger advisors told him to tighten the reigns more. This turned out to be bad advice. As a result, the northern tribes rebelled, and the kingdom was permanently divided.

Today there is a tendency to discount input from older people. However, God has placed wisdom in older people that the young can learn from.

## Question
Are there older men you know whom you can learn from?

*Father, help me value the older men who have wisdom I can learn from.*

# Being Led into the Desert

*The devil took Him up into the holy city, set Him on the pinnacle of the temple, and said to Him, "If You are the Son of God, throw Yourself down. For it is written: 'He shall give His angels charge over you,' and, 'In their hands they shall bear you up, lest you dash your foot against a stone.'"*

MATTHEW 4:5–6 NKJV

After Jesus was baptized by John the Baptist, he was led by the Holy Spirit into the desert to be tempted by the devil. Satan wanted him to give in to temptation, abuse his power, and sin. It was the first real test of Jesus' human nature.

While some may wonder if Jesus could really be tempted if he's God, we must not forget Jesus became a human and dwelt among us. He was fully God and fully man. Scripture tells us Jesus "was in all points tempted as we are, yet without sin," which is how he, as our High Priest, can sympathize with our weaknesses (Hebrews 4:15). Jesus experienced desert times just like we do. He wept when Lazarus died (see John 11:35). He experienced great sorrow at Gethsemane (see Matthew 26:38). These times of trial mean Jesus experienced what it was like to be human.

God led the people of Israel into the desert to learn something about themselves. "And you shall remember that the LORD your God led you all the way these forty years in the wilderness, to humble you and test you, to know what was in your heart, whether you would keep his commandments or not" (Deuteronomy 8:2).

When God leads you into the desert, he is allowing you to learn something about yourself. As we press into God during these times, the roots of our faith are forced deeper and deeper into the soil of his grace.

## Question
### Has God taken you into the desert?

*Father, help me withstand Satan's temptations so I can be faithful to my calling.*

# Marketplace Forgiveness

*…looking carefully lest anyone fall short of the grace of God; lest any root of bitterness springing up cause trouble, and by this many become defiled.*
HEBREWS 12:15 NKJV

Bill had a partner in business who took advantage of their relationship and embezzled money from his firm. He was caught and arrested. However, Bill decided to drop the charges if he agreed to repay the money. This allowed both men to gain freedom from a wrong committed.

In business and life, the opportunity to harbor bitterness for a wrong suffered is great. We are given plenty of opportunities to grow bitter from relationships that bring hurt and pain. The writer of the Hebrews passage above admonishes us not to miss the grace of God so that we won't take up bitterness as a response to life's pain. He cautions us against this because he knows that a bitter root grows and grows until it eventually defiles many others. If bitterness is allowed to take root, we become imprisoned by it. God's grace will no longer have as great an effect on our lives. We become ineffective, insensitive, and spiritually dead. We can even become physically ill from it. God does not live in bitterness. He lives in grace. He has provided grace for every person to walk in.

This is the real place where Christ's power is most revealed. We cannot live without his supernatural grace.

## Question
Are you in need of grace today?

*Father, help me to extend grace and forgiveness where it is needed.*

# Preparation in Arabia

*I had no desire to run to Jerusalem and try to impress those who had become apostles before me. Instead, I withdrew into the Arabian Desert. Then I returned to Damascus, where I had first encountered Jesus.*

GALATIANS 1:17 TPT

The apostle Paul clearly understood the call Jesus placed on his life at his conversion. He did not have to consult other men about this calling. But before he was released to begin his own mission, he went to Arabia for three years. Why did Paul have to go to Arabia for three years before he ever met another disciple of Jesus Christ?

The Scripture does not tell us plainly why Paul spent three years in Arabia. However, based upon many examples of God placing special callings on people's lives, we know it often requires a time of separation between the old life and the new life. No doubt, Paul had plenty of time to consider what had taken place in his life and time to develop an intimate knowledge and relationship with the newfound Savior. His life was about to change dramatically.

So often when God places a call on one of his sons, it requires a separation between the old life and the new life. There is a time of being away from the old in order to prepare the heart for what is coming. It can be a painful and difficult separation. Joseph was separated from his family. Jacob was sent to live with his uncle Laban. Moses was sent to the desert.

## Question
Has God placed you in your own desert period?

*Father, help me embrace your desert process in my life to prepare me for my life calling.*

# I Needed Power

*"How much more will the perfect heavenly Father give the Holy Spirit's fullness when his children ask him."*

LUKE 11:13 TPT

Oswald Chambers struggled to understand the role of the Holy Spirit in his life.

I was in Dunoon College as a tutor in philosophy when Dr. F. B. Meyer came and spoke about the Holy Spirit. I determined to have all that was going, and went to my room and asked God simply and definitely for the baptism of the Holy Spirit, whatever that meant. I had no conscious communion with him despite winning many souls. The Bible was the dullest, most uninteresting book in existence, and the vileness and bad-motiveness of my nature was terrific.

A well-known lady led our meeting and set us to prayer. Oswald thought, "Either Christianity is a downright fraud, or I have not got hold of the right end of the stick." Then and there I claimed the gift of the Holy Spirit in dogged commitment to Luke 11:13.

Then like a flash something happened inside of me, and I saw that I had been wanting power in my own hand, so to speak, that I might say, "Look what I have by putting my all on the altar."

If the four previous years had been hell on earth, these five years have truly been heaven on earth. The last aching abyss of my heart is filled to overflowing with the love of God. Love is the beginning, love is the middle and love is the end. After He comes in, all you see is "Jesus only, Jesus ever."[73]

## Question

Have you had a personal encounter with the Holy Spirit?

*Father, I invite you to baptize me with your Holy Spirit.*

# Come out of the Stronghold

*"Do not stay in the stronghold; depart, and go to the land of Judah."*
*So David departed and went into the forest of Hereth.*

1 SAMUEL 22:5 NKJV

David and his fighting men had been hiding in the cave of Adullam. He was fleeing Saul. Many of life's down-and-out men had come and joined David's army. David was content to stay in the stronghold of safety. Then, God's prophet came to David and told him that he must leave the stronghold and go into the land of Judah. *Judah* means "praise."

I recall when I went through a very difficult time. It seemed to drag on and on with no change until, finally, I wanted to retreat to a cave and forget pressing on. It was a great time of discouragement. A godly man came to me and said, "You must keep moving! There are too many who are depending on you in the kingdom."

I didn't totally understand what he meant at the time. Now I know he was saying that God is preparing each of us to be the vessel he wants to use in the life of another person, but we will never be that vessel if we give up and hide in our cave of discouragement. Not only must we keep moving, but we must also move into a new realm. Our attitude must move from discouragement to praise.

It is only when we move past discouragement to praise that we begin living above our problems. Make a decision today to go into the land of Judah.

## Question
Have you been in a place of captivity?

*Father, I praise you for being my deliverer.*

# Made for Heights

*The LORD God is my strength;*
*He will make my feet like deer's feet,*
*and He will make me walk on my high hills.*
HABAKKUK 3:19 NKJV

The book of Habakkuk inspired Martin Luther's reformation and the book *Hinds' Feet on High Places* by Hannah Hunnard. Habakkuk encourages us to question what God is doing in our lives. When we are thrown into suffering for a period of time, or our enemies are prospering while we are just barely getting by, we wonder about the equity of God and life. Habakkuk affirms that God is God, and we are made to scale the mountains of adversity. We just need to be still and know he is at work. He is who he says he is and does keep his promises.

God equips his people to scale the heights even in the midst of great challenges. He enables us to go to the higher places with him where we are set apart from the world.

When Jesus told the disciples he was going to send the Holy Spirit to them, it was in order for them to scale the mountain before them with a new form of power they had not experienced. "But you shall receive power when the Holy Spirit has come upon you; and you shall be witnesses to Me in Jerusalem, and in all Judea and Samaria, and to the end of the earth" (Acts 1:8).

## Question

Do you find yourself in a place of doubting God and his plan for your life? Know that this is a normal aspect of your journey in God.

*Holy Spirit, enable me to achieve the heights for which I was created.*

# Two Pillars

*He set up the pillars before the temple, one on the right hand and the other on the left; he called the name of the one on the right hand Jachin, and the name of the one on the left Boaz.*

2 CHRONICLES 3:17 NKJV

In 2003, I took my first trip to Israel. I visited the Western Wall, the only part left of the original temple built by David's son Solomon. I took an underground tour of the temple foundation, which allowed us to see the incredibly huge square boulders that were used to lay the foundation. History states that these boulders were cut off-site and transported to the temple location to avoid loud noises in the temple area. Pillars are designed to provide the foundation for a structure.

What's remarkable are the names of the two pillars that stood in front of the temple: *Jakin*, which means "it establishes," and *Boaz*, which means "in it is strength." Jakin was a priest, and Boaz was a businessman also known as a "king" in the Scriptures. It is a picture of two people God would use to represent the entrance into God's presence and the forming of the foundation of Christ's church. The Bible says we are both kings and priests, but we also have two separate, distinct roles to play in his body.

Kings and priests are joining together to bring the presence of God into the place that has been forbidden territory—the workplace. It is only when this partnership cooperates in unity, mutual respect, and affirmation that we see God's power released.

## Question
Can you see God's prophetic statement for how the church will be established through both the kings and priests?

*Father, make me a godly king and priest.*

# Check Your Armor

*Neither will I be with you anymore,*
*unless you destroy the accursed from among you.*
JOSHUA 7:12 NKJV

Battle commanders want to know the vulnerabilities of their enemies. Companies want to know the vulnerabilities of their competition. We also need to know our spiritual vulnerability.

This is the message God told Joshua when he attempted to go against a small army at Ai, which was the Israelites' second battle in the promised land. Sometimes we try to figure out why we are not successful in an endeavor from the natural only. We look at all aspects of our performance to see what went wrong. Perhaps our strategy was flawed, our timing was off, or our pricing was wrong. For the people of Israel, it was not easily seen on the surface. Everything seemed just as it should be from Joshua's vantage point, so when his army was soundly defeated, he cried out to God, "Alas, Sovereign LORD, why did you ever bring this people across the Jordan to deliver us into the hands of the Amorites to destroy us?" (Joshua 7:7 NIV).

The people had been defeated because God could not bless them. One person had violated the covenant with God. They were not to take any possessions from the first battle, but one person failed to be obedient, and the whole army suffered.

Sin makes our armor vulnerable to attack from Satan, who then gains permission from God to attack us in the area where we have failed to uphold righteousness.

## Question

Is your armor secure? Make sure you are not susceptible to attack.

*Father, help me remain pure in my walk with you to keep me from being vulnerable to attack.*

# Discerning Roadblocks

*You need the strength of endurance to reveal the poetry of God's will and then you receive the promise in full.*
HEBREWS 10:36 TPT

How do you know when God has placed obstacles in your path to protect you or that Satan is hindering God's purposes in your affairs?

I was in California traveling four hours to a speaking engagement when terrible fires broke out in Southern California and many of the highways were being shut down. I was questioning whether I should turn around and go back. I stopped at a convenience store. A woman pumping gas next to me said the interstate was closed down ahead, and if I was going north, I would never get there, and even if I did get there, I'd have difficulty getting back.

Suddenly, the prospect of being stranded in a strange place struck me with fear. I quietly prayed, asking the Lord whether this was a warning for me to turn back or Satan's hindrance. I went into the convenience store to inquire about a map. A man walked up to me and said, "Where are you trying to go?" I told him, and he explained that the interstate was open just north of where we were and that he had to go to this exact spot and would be glad to guide me there. He took me through all sorts of side roads in very unfamiliar areas. I would never have gotten there by myself, nor would I have made the attempt.

I arrived at the luncheon on time and ministered to the businessmen.

## Question

Do you have a situation in which it is difficult to discern whether God is protecting you or Satan is hindering you?

*Father, thank you for giving me wisdom as you promise to give it liberally.*

# Recognizing the Source of Success

*"Now therefore, thus shall you say to My servant David, 'Thus says the Lord of hosts: "I took you from the sheepfold, from following the sheep, to be ruler over My people, over Israel."'"*
2 SAMUEL 7:8 NKJV

David was nearing the end of his life. The prophet Nathan was responding to David's idea to build a temple where the ark of the covenant would stay. God reminded David through the prophet of his roots and where he had brought him. God took David from the fields of pasturing sheep to pastoring a nation. God reminded David that he cut off all of David's enemies for his sake and the sake of his nation. David never lost a battle.

Have you ever felt tempted to look at your accomplishments with pride as if you were the reason for your success? Have you ever thought your prosperity was due to your ingenuity? Has your material success been a testimony to others that God is the ruler of all aspects of your life, even the material side?

The greatest temptation some of us will ever face is pride of ownership. If we think our success is a result of our own effort, we affront God and open the door to pride. "A man's pride will bring him low, but the humble in spirit will retain honor" (Proverbs 29:23).

## Question

Do you have a proper understanding of who you are? Do you understand that it is God who has given you the ability to work and achieve?

*Father, teach me to be a humble marketplace leader.*

# Complete the Work

*Say to Archippus, "Take heed to the ministry which you have received in the Lord, that you may fulfill it."*

COLOSSIANS 4:17 NKJV

Have you ever driven by a construction project that was half finished but was now abandoned? It is a lasting testimony of something that had a vision, often with significant money invested, but something happened that killed the project.

Why do projects fail to be completed? There could be a number of reasons. There could have been a failure to raise adequate funds to complete it. There could have been a fall-out among management. The project could have been simply ill-conceived.

Good planning is key to estimating what it will take to complete a project. "Write the vision and make it plain on tablets, that he may run who reads it" (Habakkuk 2:2).

We must conceive the project and clearly write out the vision with detailed specifications that identify what will be needed to complete it. Some entrepreneurs have a tendency to conceive projects without estimating the financial and manpower requirements to complete the projects. Many a project has died because of this trait in entrepreneurs.

Great entrepreneurs understand their need to have detail people around them who can take their ideas and make sure all the details are included in the project. These are wise entrepreneurs who have learned to complement their weaknesses with those who can help them achieve their vision.

## Question

Do you have a vision for a work God has called you to do?
Identify what you will need to achieve success.

*Father, help me consider all the costs before I begin my next venture.*

# For Only $19.95

*His divine power has given to us all things*
*that pertain to life and godliness.*
2 PETER 1:3 NKJV

During my career in advertising, I worked with many well-known companies, such as American Express and Steinway & Sons. We also created direct response TV commercials for products or services via a free call. We learned that the "magic" price point for a product was $19.95. Anything over this would significantly reduce response.

Another key to success was that the product had to be able to demonstrate an ability to solve a perceived need by the viewer. Household items that could solve a problem that most people experienced were the most successful.

Advertising is designed to appeal to people's wants versus their needs. What we perceive as a need is often simply a want. Peter tells us that the gospel provides every believer divine power to receive what we need for life and godliness. One way we access this power is through our knowledge of God.

The Bible says the "truth shall make you free" (John 8:32). When we know what Christ has provided to us, we are able to tap into it. We are able to access what he has provided to meet a need or access a solution to a problem. However, if you do not study the Scriptures daily, you will never know what is available to you. This would be like receiving a check for a million dollars but never cashing it because you didn't know you had to. Knowing what to do would allow you to access the money.

## Question

What do you need your Father to provide for you today?

*Father, thank you for being the great problem solver.*

# Going beyond Your Paradigm

*He went there to Naioth in Ramah. Then the Spirit of God was upon him also,*
*and he went on and prophesied until he came to Naioth in Ramah.*

1 SAMUEL 19:23 NKJV

Whenever God calls you into a new thing, you can expect to do things you've never done. Saul had just been anointed to be the first king of Israel. He was being launched into a whole new calling. He was hanging out with the spiritual leaders of the nation.

When he began to prophesy, the prophets wondered if he, too, was a prophet. He was not a prophet, but God was doing a new thing through Saul—activating something in him that had been dormant until then.

When God calls you into a new endeavor, you will find that God will anoint you in areas you considered your weakest traits. God turns shepherds like Moses into leaders of nations. He turns farmers like Gideon into reformers. He turns impetuous and unstable personalities like Peter into leaders who can transform a culture and lead a movement.

This is the way of God.

When God looks at an individual, he looks at his future, not his past. God is always looking at the person he has created you to become, not the person you are now. When Samuel anointed the young shepherd boy, David, to be the next king of Israel, it would be years before this would happen. However, God already knew who he was to become.

## Question
How does God view your life?
What is the destiny he has chosen you to fulfill?

*Father, I pray I can experience miracles as evidence of your activity in my life.*

# Being Chosen

*He said to them, "Follow Me, and I will make you fishers of men."*
*They immediately left their nets and followed Him.*
MATTHEW 4:19–20 NKJV

Do you recall how good it felt when you were chosen to be on a team? It makes one feel special to be preferred over another.

During the time of Jesus, rabbis were well-known in their community. Each rabbi had a following of students. Jesus was a "superstar" rabbi. He was unlike the others. He often confronted the accepted thinking of other rabbis and Pharisees. The younger men had great respect for Jesus, the rabbi. To be selected by Jesus would be a great honor because most rabbis would usually select only the cream of the crop in the community as their disciples. By these standards, Peter and the other disciples would not have qualified. But Jesus had a purpose in mind for Peter and the disciples.

Jesus called you into relationship with himself because his desire is for you to be a faithful priest in your work life, family, and city. "I will raise up for myself a faithful priest, who will do according to what is in my heart and mind" (1 Samuel 2:35 NIV). He desires that you be a willing participant in his agenda. He has not called you for your purposes but his.

Sometimes we think it's all about us. It has to be all about him in order for us to fulfill what is in his heart and mind for his overall plan for his kingdom. He doesn't need us, but he has chosen to use us.

## Question
Are you willing to be his faithful priest and king to do what is in Jesus' heart and mind?

*Father, thank you for choosing me.*

# The Power of Serving Others

*Every believer has received grace gifts, so use them to serve one another as faithful stewards of the many-colored tapestry of God's grace.*

1 PETER 4:10 TPT

There is a kingdom principle I find few others really understand. The principle is this: when you focus on serving others, your need is often met through God's supernatural law of serving.

I've seen this happen so many times. The law of sowing and reaping comes into play in this kingdom principle. "Sow for yourselves righteousness; reap in mercy; break up your fallow ground, for it is time to seek the LORD, till He comes and rains righteousness on you" (Hosea 10:12 NKJV). Second Corinthians 9 communicates a similar message:

> But this I say: He who sows sparingly will also reap sparingly, and he who sows bountifully will also reap bountifully. So let each one give as he purposes in his heart, not grudgingly or of necessity; for God loves a cheerful giver. And God is able to make all grace abound toward you, that you, always having all sufficiency in all things, may have an abundance for every good work. (vv. 6–8 NKJV)

Whenever God calls me to serve another person with my time and resources, I notice how God measures resources back to me from unrelated sources. Sometimes it comes through an unexpected donation to our ministry or a speaking engagement or a new opportunity. It is uncanny how this happens consistently when I serve others.

We don't serve others to get. However, when we do serve others, this kingdom principle works on your behalf, producing the fruit of your service.

## Question
### Is there someone you need to serve today?

*Father, teach me to walk in this kingdom principle.*

# Building a Mighty Team

*These are the names of the mighty men…*
2 SAMUEL 23:8 NKJV

David and Jesus pulled together two teams that were the most unlikely groups to accomplish what they achieved. David's small army of men became known as "David's Mighty Men" because of their extraordinary exploits. However, they were the rejects of society.

Jesus' team was made up of common men who would never have been chosen by other rabbis. They would have been men who would not have qualified for mentorship by most rabbis of their day. Yet, they were chosen by the superstar of up-and-coming rabbis—Jesus.

We can learn three key things about David and how he related to his Mighty Men. First, David's men came to him as a result of battle. They had fought together and learned firsthand from one another's capabilities. And they trusted each other.

Second, David modeled servant leadership with his men. When three of his mighty men risked their lives to obtain drinking water for him during a battle, David refused to drink it, choosing instead to pour it out onto the ground. This, no doubt, made a big impression on his men and only drew greater devotion to him because of his own sacrifice.

Finally, David and his men experienced God-size victories when they were the underdogs. They fought bigger and more resourceful enemies than themselves. They saw God's hand in their victories.

Keep these things in mind as you build your own team. Learn from the management styles of David and Jesus by modeling their servant leadership.

## Question
Would others say you are a servant leader?

*Father, make me a servant leader among those I lead.*

# A Prophet without Honor

*"Is this not the carpenter, the Son of Mary, and brother of James, Joses, Judas, and Simon? And are not His sisters here with us?" So they were offended at Him.*
MARK 6:3 NKJV

Have you ever noticed how difficult it can be to spiritually impact your immediate circle of relationships and family? Jesus warned us of this phenomenon. We often relate to family and friends differently because they have a history with us that no one else has. Family members most likely have not had the privilege to witness the spiritual transformation that you have experienced and is evidenced by others in your life.

The spiritual authority that others may recognize in you is not there with your own family and friends. *After all, you're just my sister or brother, with whom I fought, played with, and lived everyday life* is what is thought. Imagine growing up with Jesus. It would have been difficult to see Jesus as the son of God without direct revelation from God, especially in his own family and community's eyes. It was too difficult to change old perceptions of someone they knew so well. So, too, it is for your family members.

The sad result of this mindset is that we often do not experience the same fruit of ministry in our family's lives that we do outside this circle. It is an unfortunate truth. "Jesus still healed a few sick people," meaning there is still a remnant of faith that can be received from you and me.

Many did not receive Jesus. Therefore, many will not receive you. Nevertheless, allow God to touch the few in your circle he chooses to touch through you.

## Question

Do you find it difficult to minister to your family and friends?

*Father, give me wisdom to know how to share Christ with my family and friends.*

# Adorned by God's Doctrine

*Exhort bondservants to be obedient to their own masters, to be well pleasing in all things, not answering back, not pilfering, but showing all good fidelity, that they may adorn the doctrine of God our Savior in all things.*

TITUS 2:9–10 NKJV

The island of Crete was known for its corruption and many false gods. It was also the center of the jewelry trade. Thus, the use of the word *adorn* in the above passage may have been intentional by Paul due to this fact. The greater the corruption, the greater your light can shine. It is not a time to flee, but it is a time to shine brighter. Crete was a difficult place to live as a Christian.

Paul addressed five unique things believers could do: (1) Be obedient to their masters and submit to their authority structures. (2) Be well pleasing in all things. This meant doing their work with excellence. (3) Don't answer back to negative people. They were to handle conflict with wisdom and courtesy. (4) Don't pilfer. They were not to steal but to model integrity. (5) Show all good fidelity. This meant demonstrating loyalty and dependability.

I once heard a talk about an industry survey that revealed the average person will encounter hundreds of people over the course of a year through their work. What better opportunity to let your life be adorned by the doctrine of God! We should all be a living message of the gospel through our life, whether in word or deed.

## Question

Do you find your environment difficult to work in? The answer is to live to glorify the Lord in the midst of your culture.

*Father, I pray that my life demonstrates the love and power of Christ today to others.*

# The Signs of the Times

*"Where is He who has been born King of the Jews?*
*For we have seen His star in the East and have come to worship Him."*
MATTHEW 2:2 NKJV

God is looking for leaders who recognize the signs of their times. Such was the case of the wise men who were so in tune with their times that they were able to pinpoint when the long-awaited Messiah was born. They recognized God had come in their midst.

These men were philosophers, priests, or astronomers devoted to astronomy, religion, and medicine. They lived in Persia and Arabia. They were marketplace ministers of the Eastern nations and held in high esteem by the Persian court, which allowed them to be counselors even following the camps in war. They came from the professional ranks in society and were sought out by the kings of the nation. They would be the authorities in their field of expertise. This is why they were able to meet with King Herod.[74]

They were likely aware of the prophecy of Balaam, "There shall come a Star out of Jacob" (Numbers 24:17 KJV). They came and gave three distinct gifts—each represented a prophetic significance.

Like the men of Issachar, who "understood the times and knew what Israel should do" (1 Chronicles 12:32 NIV), the three wise men knew what they were to do because they were aware of God's activities in their times.

## Question
Are you recognizing God's activity in your times?

*Father, make me a man who understands the time in which we live.*

# Insecure Leadership

*When Herod realized that he had been tricked by the wise men, he was infuriated. So he sent soldiers with orders to slaughter every baby boy two years old and younger in Bethlehem.*
MATTHEW 2:16 TPT

Any leader who is not secure in God will be insecure in their leadership actions. King Herod was such a leader. He feared the loss of power and had to control every aspect of the people he was ruling. When Herod heard about Jesus' coming birth, his insecurity became out of control and led to making life-threatening decisions for those in Jerusalem and Bethlehem.

Such a leader has deep-seated control issues rooted in the fear of loss of power, money, and prestige. This also led to lying to protect his kingdom. When the wise men told Herod about the coming Messiah, Herod told them he wanted to know when he was born in order to worship him. He had no such plans. He wanted to kill him.

Herod told the wise men to report back to him when the child was born. The wise men were divinely warned not to return to Jerusalem and report back to Herod. When Herod discovered this, he became furious and issued the edict to kill every child under two years old in Bethlehem and the surrounding districts.

Whenever a leader has deep-seated control issues rooted in fear, their actions surface repeatedly when placed under stress. Arguments, manipulation of others, and confrontation with subordinates usually follow.

A secure leader realizes God is the source of his power and leadership, and he does not need to fear others who may demonstrate leadership qualities.

## Question
Are you secure in your leadership?

*Father, I pray you make me a leader who is secure in the position you have given me.*

# Avoid the Escape Mentality

*Blessed be the LORD my Rock, who trains my hands for war,
and my fingers for battle.*
PSALM 144:1 NKJV

One of the best-selling American books of all time is a fiction series that focuses on the end-time called *Left Behind*. It deals with the rapture of Christians from the earth before the final end-times crisis takes place and the Antichrist rules.

If we are not careful, we will fall into a mindset that we are simply buying time until Jesus calls us home. No matter what the end-times Scripture teaches, it is clear that believers should model behavior that is more like a soldier in battle desiring to take the land rather than a person waiting for an airlift.

When God placed man on earth, he desired man to rule the earth. "God blessed them, and God said to them, 'Be fruitful and multiply; fill the earth and subdue it; have dominion over the fish of the sea, over the birds of the air, and over every living thing that moves on the earth'" (Genesis 1:28).

Today, we often have a cruise ship mentality in the church of Jesus Christ instead of a battleship mentality designed to engage the enemy of our souls. Our army is often ill-equipped to know how to take the land that God has provided through his Son. This is why believers in the workplace must see their work and calling as an assignment from God to demonstrate his power in all of society in order to restore his rule upon the earth. Jesus died on the cross to restore that which was lost (see Luke 19:10).

## Question
### Are you engaged in the battle?

*Father, I pray that all believers can be instruments of bringing heaven on earth in every area of society.*

# The Marketplace Psalm

*LORD, who may abide in Your tabernacle?*
*Who may dwell in Your holy hill?*

PSALM 15:1 NKJV

If Psalm 15 were the core value of every business plan and purpose statement and reviewed with every employee before hiring, the workplace would be a very different place. What type of person can live in the presence of God? The psalmist tells us:

> He who walks uprightly,
> and works righteousness,
> and speaks the truth in his heart;
> he who does not backbite with his tongue,
> nor does evil to his neighbor,
> nor does he take up a reproach against his friend;
> in whose eyes a vile person is despised, but he honors those who fear the LORD;
> he who swears to his own hurt and does not change;
> he who does not put out his money at usury, nor does he take a bribe against the innocent.
> He who does these things shall never be moved. (vv. 2–5)

## Question

Are you blameless in your approach to your work life? Are you truthful in all your dealings? Do you treat customers, vendors, and fellow employees as your neighbor? Do you say what you do truthfully and do what you say? Do you follow through even if the outcome may not be positive? Will you lend money without usury to a friend and refuse a bribe? If you can say yes to these questions, then you are a Psalm 15 man, and you can dwell on God's holy hill.

*Father, make this psalm a part of my life and show me how to live like this.*

# Learn from God's Creation

*In reality, the truth of God is known instinctively,
for God has embedded this knowledge inside every human heart.*
ROMANS 1:19 TPT

Have you ever had someone say, "I don't see any evidence of God. How can a person believe in someone you can't see or see any evidence even exists?"

The Bible tells us that God is revealed in his creation every day. Look at the human body and consider how unlikely it is that thousands of body parts could randomly work together. Someone created it to work this well. If it were a manufactured product, it would be in the repair shop all the time because of all the moving parts required to make it work.

Consider the wonderful order and balance of nature and how the seas know their boundaries, the beauty of the mountains, and the balance of rain and oxygen needed to sustain the ecosystems. Consider God's signature, the rainbow.

The twelfth-century Scottish Christian mystic Richard of St. Victor said, "The whole of this sensible world is like a book written by the finger of God."[75] Look at nature and wonder at the creative design of the hundreds of thousands of species of animals like the tiger, the elephant, the great whales, and the millions of species of birds, just to name a few.

Yes, God has revealed himself in his creation.

## Question
Have you looked at God's creation with awe to build your faith?

*Father, thank you for your creativity and evidence of your activity and creation.*

# Labor Alone Will Not Satisfy

*All the labor of man is for his mouth,*
*and yet the soul is not satisfied.*
ECCLESIASTES 6:7 NKJV

How would you feel about yourself if your job were removed from you tomorrow? Let's imagine that your income wouldn't change, just what you did every day.

One of the schemes that Satan uses in the life of the Christian worker is to get him to view his value solely based on the type of work he does and how well he does it. We call this performance-based acceptance. It says, "As long as I have a good job and I do it well, I have self-esteem."

This is a "slippery slope" and can be used by Satan to keep our focus on our performance versus Christ. We are never to find our value in what we do. Instead, our value is solely based on who we are in Christ. The apostle Paul wrestled with this after he came to faith in Christ. He had grown to the top of his field as a Jewish leader.

> If anyone else thinks he may have confidence in the flesh, I more so: circumcised the eighth day, of the stock of Israel, of the tribe of Benjamin, a Hebrew of the Hebrews; concerning the law, a Pharisee; concerning zeal, persecuting the church; concerning the righteousness which is in the law, blameless. But what things were gain to me, these I have counted loss for Christ. (Philippians 3:4–7)

You'll never really know the degree to which your self-esteem is rooted in your work until your work is removed. Unemployment, illness, or a financial crisis can lead to job loss.

## Question
Does your value in life depend on your work?

*Father, thank you that my identity is in knowing you and you only.*

# Perseverance for Success

*Even in times of trouble we have a joyful confidence, knowing that our pressures will develop in us patient endurance. And patient endurance will refine our character, and proven character leads us back to hope.*
ROMANS 5:3–4 TPT

Perseverance is the key to every great accomplishment because nothing of lasting value has ever been achieved without it. Industrialist Henry Ford is one of the great success stories of American history, but he failed in business five times before he succeeded. A Ford Motor Company employee once asked his boss the secret of success, and Henry Ford is often credited with replying, "When you start a thing, don't quit until you finish it."

The path ahead of you is strewn with obstacles. People will oppose you. There will be financial setbacks, time pressures, illnesses, and misfortunes. Some of the biggest obstacles will be inside of you: self-doubt, insecurity, procrastination, and worry. You must give yourself permission to succeed.

When we persevere through adversity, we win the approval of our Lord Jesus Christ, who told the suffering church at Ephesus, "You have persevered and have patience, and have labored for My name's sake and have not become weary" (Revelation 2:3 NKJV).

Life is a marathon, not a sprint. The race doesn't go to the swiftest but to those who don't give up. We need endurance in order to deal with the stress of adversity. When going through adversity, watch out for pessimists, blamers, and toxic personalities. Beware of people who try to talk you out of your dreams and goals. Spend time with optimists and encouragers. Seek out people of faith. Persevere to the end.

## Question
Do you need to persevere right now?

*Father, thank you for the grace to persevere through every trial.*

# Endnotes

1   "Omar," The Bump, accessed January 6, 2022, https://www.thebump.com/b/omar-baby-name.

2   John Woodbridge, ed., *More Than Conquerors* (Chicago: Moody Press, 1992), 348–49.

3   Os Guinness, *The Call* (Nashville, TN: W Publishing, 1998), 242.

4   Woodbridge, *More Than Conquerors*, 140.

5   *Field of Dreams*, directed by Phil Alden Robinson (Universal City, CA: Universal Pictures, 1989), film, 107 min.

6   Andrew Murray, *The Two Covenants and the Second Blessing* (London: J. Nisbet, 1899), 176.

7   Woodbridge, *More Than Conquerors*, 342.

8   Otto Koning, "Session 1: The Pineapple Story" (sermon), 1987, Embassy Media, video, 56:13, https://embassymedia.com/speaker/otto-koning.

9   A. W. Tozer, *The Root of the Righteous* (Chicago: Moody Press, 2015), 165, Kindle.

10  F. B. Meyer, *From the Pit to the Throne* (London: Elliot Stock, 1886), 23–24.

11  Diane Severance, "Melanchthon, the Number Two," Christianity.com, May 3, 2010, https://www.christianity.com/church/church-history/timeline/1201-1500/melanchthon-the-number-two-11629903.html.

12  Bill Johnson, *When Heaven Invades Earth* (Shippensburg, PA: Treasure House, 2003), 29.

13  Barbara Glanz, "Johnny the Bagger," KarmaTube, video, 3:16, accessed January 14, 2022, https://www.karmatube.org/videos.php?id=108.

14  *Chariots of Fire*, directed by Hugh Hudson (Los Angeles: 20th Century Fox, 1981), film, 124 min.

15  Watchman Nee, "The Latent Power of the Soul (3)," in *The Collected Works of Watchman Nee: Vol. 10, Present Testimony (3)* (Anaheim, CA: Living Stream Ministry, 1992), 515.

16  "The Johari Window Model," Communication Theory (website), accessed January 14, 2022, https://www.communicationtheory.org/the-johari-window-model/.

17  Oswald Chambers, "Not Knowing Wither," in *The Complete Works of Oswald Chambers* (Grand Rapids, MI: Discovery House Publishers, 2000), 905.

18  A. B. Simpson, "April 28," in *Streams in the Desert*, ed. Mrs. Charles E. Cowman (Los Angeles: The Oriental Missionary Society, 1925), 131.

19  *The Leadership Bible* (Grand Rapids, MI: Zondervan, 1998), 1378.

20  Billy Graham, *The Holy Spirit: Activating God's Power in Your Life* (Nashville, TN: Thomas Nelson, 1988), 122.

21  Guy Yocom, "My Shot: Tom Watson," *Golf Digest*, July 1, 2013, https://www.golfdigest.com/story/myshot_gd0407.

22  Yocom, "My Shot."

23  Stanley Tam, quoted in *The Complete Christian Businessman*, ed. Robert J. Tamasy (Brentwood, TN: Wolgemuth & Hyatt Publishers, 1991), 52.

24  Ed Silvoso, *Anointed for Business* (Ventura, CA: Regal Books, 2002), 123.

25  Henry Blackaby, Richard Blackaby, and Claude King, *Experiencing God: Knowing and Doing the Will of God*, rev. ed. (Nashville, TN: Lifeway Press, 2007), 28.

26  "Who We Are," Chick-fil-A (website), accessed on January 14, 2022, https://www.chick-fil-a.com/about/who-we-are.

27    Kate Taylor, "Chick-fil-A Is the Third-Largest Fast-Food Chain in America, and That Should Terrify Wendy's and Burger King," *Business Insider*, May 14, 2020, https://www.businessinsider.com/chick-fil-a-third-largest-fast-food-chain-us-sales-2020-5.

28    "Who We Are."

29    Michael Novak, *Business as a Calling: Work and the Examined Life* (New York: The Free Press, 1996), 123.

30    Pat Williams and Jay Strack, *The Three Success Secrets of Shamgar* (Deerfield Beach, FL: Health Communications, 2004), 103.

31    George Washington, "General Orders, 2 May 1778," *Founders Online*, National Archives, https://founders.archives.gov/documents/Washington/03-15-02-0016. [Original source: *The Papers of George Washington*, Revolutionary War Series, vol. 15, May–June 1778, ed. Edward G. Lengel (Charlottesville: University of Virginia Press, 2006), 13.]

32    Mark Markiewicz, personal article to author, 2004.

33    Woodbridge, *More Than Conquerors*, 308–12.

34    Mike and Sue Dowgiewicz, *Demolishing Strongholds: God's Way to Mental Freedom* (Nashville, TN: Restoration Ministries International, 2005), 8, PDF, https://walkworthy.org/pdf/demolishing-strongholds.pdf.

35    Elmer Towns, *Understanding the Deeper Life: A Guide to Christian Experience* (Grand Rapids, MI: Zondervan, 1984), 224–25.

36    Brother Lawrence, *The Practice of the Presence of God*, ed. Harold J. Chadwick (Alachua, FL: Bridge-Logos, 1999), 26.

37    Billy Graham, *Answers to Life's Problems* (Dallas, TX: Word Publishing, 1988), 251–52.

38    Marvin Wilson, *Our Father Abraham: Jewish Roots of the Christian Faith* (Grand Rapids, MI: Eerdmans, 1990), 150.

39   Wilson, *Our Father Abraham*, 150.

40   Wilson, *Our Father Abraham*, 150.

41   Jason Miles, "'Justice Was Served': Enron Whistleblower Reflects on 20th Anniversary of Company's Collapse," KHOU 11, December 2, 2021, https://www.khou.com/article/money/business/enron-whistleblower-20th-anniversary/285-f0c3ad1a-3c31-4511-bfc6-5372b1196f24.

42   Michael Tummillo, "Faith in the Workplace," FaithWriters, March 10, 2006, https://www.faithwriters.com/article-details.php?id=40903.

43   J. Oswald Sanders, "Lessons I've Learned," *Discipleship Journal* 15 (1983): 14.

44   Robert J. Morgan, *Nelson's Complete Book of Stories, Illustrations, and Quotes* (Nashville, TN: Thomas Nelson Publishers, 2000), 369.

45   Peter Drucker, *The Effective Executive* (New York: HarperCollins, 2017), 38, Kindle.

46   Drucker, *The Effective Executive*, 40.

47   Drucker, *The Effective Executive*, 41.

48   "I Asked God for Strength, That I Might Achieve," quoted in James Robertson Jr., "An Unknown Confederate Soldier," Radio IQ, December 15, 2019, https://www.wvtf.org/civil-war-series/2019-12-15/an-unknown-confederate-soldier.

49   Jacques Bughin et al., "Artificial Intelligence: The Next Digital Frontier?" McKinsey Global Institute, June 2017, https://www.mckinsey.com/~/media/mckinsey/industries/advanced%20electronics/our%20insights/how%20artificial%20intelligence%20can%20deliver%20real%20value%20to%20companies/mgi-artificial-intelligence-discussion-paper.ashx.

50   Guinness, *The Call*, 101.

51 "Number of Starbucks Worldwide 2022/2023: Facts, Statistics, and Trends," FinancesOnline, accessed January 17, 2022, https://financesonline.com/number-of-starbucks-worldwide/.

52 Vincent Chan, "How Fred Smith Saved Fedex at the Blackjack Table," Startup War Story, February 28, 2016, https://blog.warstory.co/how-fred-smith-saved-fedex-at-the-blackjack-table-902e2e412e67.

53 "Henry Ford Quote," *The Reader's Digest* 51 (September 1947): 64.

54 Alvin L. Reid, *Join the Movement: God Is Calling You to Change the World* (Grand Rapids, MI: Kregel, 2007), 94–98.

55 "John Wesley's Big Impact on America," Christianity.com, May 3, 2010, https://www.christianity.com/church/church-history/timeline/1701-1800/john-wesleys-big-impact-on-america-11630220.html.

56 Oswald Chambers, *My Utmost for His Highest: An Updated Edition in Today's Language* (Grand Rapids, MI: Discovery House Publishers, 1992), entry for January 19.

57 Matthew Henry, "Mark 15 Bible Commentary," Christianity.com, accessed January 17, 2022, https://www.christianity.com/bible/commentary/matthew-henry-complete/mark/15.

58 Rick Koole, "'Flee! All Has Been Discovered!'" Village News, last updated October 8, 2018, https://www.villagenews.com/story/2018/10/04/news/flee-all-has-been-discovered/54158.html.

59 David Mikkelson, "How Did These Famous and Powerful Men of 1923 Fare?" Snopes, September 8, 2003, https://www.snopes.com/fact-check/fortunate-sons/.

60 George Barna and Mark Hatch, *Boiling Point* (Ventura, CA: Regal Books, 2001), 223.

61 Barna and Hatch, *Boiling Point*, 223.

62   Silvoso, *Anointed for Business*, 118–19.

63   Jacqueline L. Salmon, "Kroc Leaves $1.5 Billion to Salvation Army," *The Washington Post*, January 21, 2004, https://www.washingtonpost. com/archive/politics/2004/01/21/kroc-leaves-15-billion-to-salvation- army/062b7ff7-c1bf-450d-bab0-041c4637dc4a/.

64   Malcom Gladwell, *The Tipping Point: How Little Things Can Make a Big Difference* (New York: Little, Brown, 2006), 7, Kindle.

65   Gladwell, *The Tipping Point*, 13.

66   Gladwell, *The Tipping Point*, 38.

67   Gladwell, *The Tipping Point*, 69.

68   Gladwell, *The Tipping Point*, 70.

69   Wikipedia, s.v. "Nelle Wilson Reagan," last modified on January 2, 2022, https://en.wikipedia.org/wiki/Nelle_Wilson_Reagan.

70   C. Peter Wagner, *Confronting the Queen of Heaven* (Colorado Springs: Wagner Books, 2001), 14–17.

71   Chambers, "Not Knowing Wither," 913.

72   Silvoso, *Anointed for Business*, 189.

73   V. Raymond Edman, *They Found the Secret* (Grand Rapids, MI: Zondervan, 1984), 33–34.

74   Albert Barnes, "Barnes' Notes on the Whole Bible: Matthew 2," Truth according to Scripture, accessed January 18, 2022, https://www. truthaccordingtoscripture.com/commentaries/bnb/matthew-2.php.

75   Henri de Lubac, *Medieval Exegesis: The Four Senses of Scripture, Vol. 3* (Grand Rapids, MI: Eerdmans, 1998), 78.

# About the Author

Os Hillman is an internationally recognized speaker, author, and consultant on the subject of faith at work.

He is the founder and president of Marketplace Leaders Ministries, an organization whose purpose is to train men and women to fulfill their calling in and through their work life and to view their work as ministry.

Os formerly owned and operated an ad agency in Atlanta for twelve years. He has written over two dozen books on faith and work-related subjects and a daily workplace email devotional entitled *TGIF: Today God Is First*, which is read by hundreds of thousands of people daily in 105 countries. He has been featured on TBN, CNBC, NBC, *The Los Angeles Times*, *The New York Times*, *The Associated Press*, *Newsmax*, *The Christian Post*, *Charisma News*, *Crosswalk*, and many other national media outlets as a spokesperson on faith at work. Os has spoken in twenty-six countries.

Os attended the University of South Carolina and Calvary Chapel Bible School, a ministry of Calvary Chapel of Costa Mesa, California. Os is married to his incredible wife, Pamela, and they live in north Atlanta with their four dogs. Os has one daughter, Charis, and son-in-law, Justin.

# Additional Resources from Os Hillman

## Books by Os Hillman

*31 Decrees of Blessing for Your Work Life*

*Overcoming Hindrances to Fulfill Your Destiny*

*Listening to the Father's Heart*

*Experiencing the Father's Love*

*The Upside of Adversity: From the Pit to Greatness*

*Change Agent: Engaging Your Passion to Be the One Who Makes a Difference*

*The 9 to 5 Window: How Faith Can Transform the Workplace*

*The Purposes of Money*

*Faith & Work: Do They Mix?*

*Faith@Work Movement: What Every Pastor and Church Leader Should Know*

*How to Discover Why God Made Me* (Booklet)

*TGIF: 270 Four-Minute Meditations Arranged by Topic* (Paperback)

*TGIF* (Pocket Version)

*TGIF: Volume 2* (Hardcover)

*TGIF: Small Group Bible Study*

*TGIF for Women*

*TGIF for Men*

*Birdies, Bogeys, and Life Lessons from the Game of Golf*

*The Joseph Calling: 6 Stages to Discover, Navigate, and Fulfill Your Purpose*

*The Joseph Calling: 12-Week Bible Study*

*Proven Strategies for Business Success*

*So You Want to Write a Book?*

*Are You a Biblical Worker? Self-Assessment*

To order: TGIFBookstore.com
678.455.6262 x103
info@marketplaceleaders.org

# Websites and Electronic Resources

TodayGodIsFirst.com
CAMasterMentor.com
MarketplaceLeaders.org
TGIFBookstore.com

Subscribe free to *TGIF: Today God Is First* at TodayGodIsFirst.com.
Download our free app TGIF Os Hillman via Google Play or iTunes app store.

# To Contact Os Hillman

os@marketplaceleaders.org
678-455-6262 x103
Marketplace Leaders, P.O. Box 69, Cumming, GA 30028

Want to be mentored by Os Hillman? Check out the *Change Agent MasterMentor* program at CAMasterMentor.com.